Izabe

Gran

Walking on a Miniature Continent

72 selected walks along the coasts
and in the central mountains

Preface

Sun, sand, and the sea – this is what comes to mind when we think of Gran Canaria. However, only few people know that the island's true gems lie beyond the beach resorts in the south. Once you have left the dunes behind, you will walk past palm tree oases that have an African touch, sparse pine forests and reservoirs glittering in the sun. In the north, the scenery is completely different. Sheep graze on lush meadows, oranges and bananas are cultivated on terrace fields and with its almost 2000m, the mighty Pico de las Nieves – the "Snowy Summit" – towers above this truly enchanting landscape. Its diverse scenery has earned Gran Canaria the nickname "miniature continent".

The best hiking can be found in the island's centre, which is like a "fossilised storm of fire and lava". Rock towers rise up into the sky like gigantic exclamation marks, and the rugged mountain ridges and craggy gorges have been formed by millions of years of volcanism. In 2019, the sacred mountains of Gran Canaria were awarded the status of a UNESCO world heritage site.

Another great advantage for hikers is the abundance of ancient trails meandering across the island which were developed after the Spanish conquest to connect the mountain villages with the coast. The trails, which are known as "Royal Trails" or *Caminos Reales* due to being financed by royal funds, were paved and are wide enough for farmers to get through with their mules. This guide covers many of these restored trails, and – wherever possible – I have designed circular walks that don't require you to hike back the same way. The starting point of most walks can be reached by bus. The trails lead to cave villages situated in spectacular settings and to remote beaches or follow ridgelines high above the clouds and to breathtakingly beautiful viewpoints.

I have recently walked all the trails to provide the latest information on their condition. However, as landscapes constantly change due to human interference or natural events, please inform the publisher if you have a correction to make or anything to add.

I hope you will enjoy the walks as much as I did.

Autumn 2021

Dr. Izabella Gawin

The devastating wildfires from 2019 are almost forgotten and the only walks that still show traces of the fires are 9–22, 27, 52 and 55. Heavy downpours and the strict lockdowns in 2020 and 2021 allowed the island's nature to recover as it was undisturbed for many months.

Contents

Preface 3

Overview map 8
General information 10
    Symbols. 11
    GPS tracks and coordinates for the starting points. 12
    The best walks on Gran Canaria 15
Walking on Gran Canaria. 18
    Recreational activities 23
Information and addresses 24
    Climate table. 26
    Accommodation 28
    Timetables of the most useful bus routes. 30

The Central Island 34
TOP 1   2.00 hrs   Circling Roque Nublo 35
2   3.30 hrs   From Aserrador to Roque Nublo 37
3   2.00 hrs   From Ayacata to La Goleta 40
TOP 4   4.00 hrs   Picturesque circular walk from La Goleta 42
TOP 5   4.15 hrs   From Ayacata to the Cruz Grande pass 45
6   1.50 hrs   Via the Montañón to Degollada de los Hornos . . . 48
7   6.00 hrs   From Cruz Grande to Pico de las Nieves 50
8   2.40 hrs   From Llanos de la Pez to Pico de las Nieves. 53
TOP 9   2.50 hrs   From Cruz de Tejeda to the Cuevas del Caballero . . 56
10   2.45 hrs   From Cruz de Tejeda to Artenara. 59
11   3.00 hrs   From Artenara to Cruz de Acusa 62
12   2.30 hrs   Circular walk around Acusa 64
13   4.30 hrs   From Artenara to Tamadaba forest 67
14   2.00 hrs   Above Coruña and Las Hoyas 70
TOP 15   3.30 hrs   On the Altavista 72
16   2.00 hrs   Grand Tamadaba circular walk 74
17   2.00 hrs   Risco Faneque. 76
18   1.15 hrs   Circling the Pico de Bandera. 78
19   1.30 hrs   Mirador El Reventón 80
20   5.00 hrs   Grand circular walk on the northern flank of the Cumbre 82
21   3.45 hrs   Pinos de Gáldar volcanic crater 86
TOP 22   4.30 hrs   From Cruz de Tejeda to Teror. 89
23   2.50 hrs   Barranco de la Mina 92
24   2.30 hrs   Becerra circular walk for bon vivants 95

JP 25	5.30 hrs	Grand circular route from the Cruz de Tejeda 98
26	1.30 hrs	Via La Isa to Tejeda 102
27	1.30 hrs	Via the Vuelta del Rincón to Tejeda 104
JP 28	3.30 hrs	From Tejeda to La Culata 106
29	1.45 hrs	The sacred summit Roque Bentayga 108
30	3.45 hrs	Circling around the Bentayga 110
31	4.00 hrs	In the Pajonales nature reserve 112
JP 32	4.15 hrs	From Aserrador to Cruz de la Huesita 114
33	2.20 hrs	From the Presa Cueva de las Niñas to Cruz de la Huesita. . . 116
34	2.15 hrs	The Cueva de las Niñas reservoir 118
35	2.00 hrs	High above the Soria lake 122
36	2.00 hrs	Circling the Chira lake 124

The Southern Island 126

JP 37	4.00 hrs	Circular walk around San Bartolomé 127
38	5.00 hrs	From Fataga to Santa Lucía 130
JP 39	4.15 hrs	La Fortaleza and La Sorrueda: Grand route from Santa Lucía 134
40	2.00 hrs	From Santa Lucía to Cruz del Siglo 138
41	1.30 hrs	Santa Lucía's mill route 140
42	3.30 hrs	From Santa Lucía onto the Altos de Pajonales 142
43	1.00 hrs	The necropolis at Arteara 145
44	3.00 hrs	Gran Canaria's "Sahara" 148
45	6.00 hrs	Above Ayagaures 151
46	3.30 hrs	Palmitos circular walk 155
47	2.00 hrs	Ascent to Tauro 158
48	3.10 hrs	From Tasarte to Mogán 160
49	6.00 hrs	To the beach at Güi Güí 164
50	2.00 hrs	Playa Chica in the Barranco del Perchel 167

The Northern Island 170

51	2.45 hrs	A short circular walk in the Agaete valley 171
JP 52	7.15 hrs	Grand circuit route Agaete valley and Tamadaba 173
53	2.15 hrs	To the beach at Guayedra 178
54	1.50 hrs	From Agaete to El Juncal and La Caleta 180
55	5.30 hrs	From Mirador Pinos de Gáldar to Guía 183
56	2.40 hrs	From Fontanales to Moya 186
57	1.00 hrs	Laurel forest Los Tilos 189
JP 58	4.40 hrs	Barranco de la Virgen 191
59	4.00 hrs	From Corvo to Teror 194
60	5.00 hrs	From Firgas into the Barranco de Azuaje 198
61	2.00 hrs	Circular walk around the Bahía del Confital 202
62	1.00 hrs	Jardín Canario 205
JP 63	1.50 hrs	Bandama volcanic crater 208

64	1.20 hrs	At the upper rim of the Bandama crater	210
65	2.40 hrs	Atalaya circular walk	212
66	2.00 hrs	Ruta del Vino	215
67	1.30 hrs	Ruta del Agua	218
68	0.50 hrs	Cuatro Puertas	221
69	2.20 hrs	Barranco de los Cernícalos	223
TOP 70	6.45 hrs	Circular walk through the Barranco de Guayadeque	226
71	1.30 hrs	Ascent from Cuevas Bermejas to the mountain ridge	230
72	2 days	Camino de Santiago	232

Index 236
Geographical Glossary Spanish – English 239

Sometimes barrancos become simply streams – Valle de Agaete (Walk 51).

GRAN CANARIA

0   2 km   4 km

General information

Grade
Most of the walks lead along distinct trails and can be recommended for the even less experienced walker. Many of the routes, however, may include a considerable difference in altitude to negotiate, so that they require good physical fitness and often sure-footedness. In order to assess the individual demands of the walk, the walk numbers have been colour-coded as follows:

Easy   These trails are usually broad, only moderately steep in ascent or descent, and can be walked during inclement weather without any danger.

Moderate   These trails are mostly sufficiently broad and easy to walk, but because of the differences in height that must be negotiated, can sometimes be strenuous. Some short stretches can be somewhat precipitous and some spots demand a certain degree of route-finding ability.

Difficult   These alpine paths are narrow for long stretches and are often very steep. They are sometimes precipitous and there is a danger of slipping while traversing slopes, so these trails should only be undertaken by sure-footed and physically fit walkers who possess a high degree of route-finding ability.

Getting there
All of the walks can be reached by a hired car and/or bus service provided by the Global bus company (refer to the timetables for the main bus routes on pp. 30/31). Further information concerning the approach can be found in the individual tour descriptions in this guide.

Coastline near Puerto de las Nieves.

Symbols

Symbol	Description	Symbol	Description
🚌	approach possible by bus	⊼	picnic area
✕	refreshment available en route	Δ	campsite
👫	suitable for children	)(	bridge, dam
▲	settlement with bar/restaurant	∩	cave
▲	staffed hut, inn	✿	mill
⌂	forester's house, private hut	▲	museum
🚌	bus stop	∴	archaeological site
P	established car park	♠ ♦	church/chapel, cemetery
†	peak, wayside cross	⅂ Γ	turn-off, fork
)(	pass, saddle, col	⠀	waterfall
🔺	viewpoint	▨	beach, bathing possibility

Walking times and height differences

The times listed in the walk heading and in the height profile refer to actual walking times and do not include rest stops, refreshment stops or other longer interruptions of the walk. The specified differences in height are calculated as the sum of the total differences, including intermediate ascents and descents.

Equipment

Sturdy shoes with non-slip soles, durable trousers, sunscreen with a higher SPF, protection from rain, wind and cold, as well as provisions for along the way (plenty of liquids!), are demanded for most of the walks. Light, comfortable headgear is recommended for stretches lacking shade, and for walks following more rugged, mountainous stretches, possibly a pair of telescopic trekking poles.

Dangers

By the sudden building of cloud bank, visibility can be restricted within a few minutes and can plague the walker with serious orientation problems. Storms and heavy downpours are rare on Gran Canaria, but can occur unexpectedly in the winter months. Unsecured paths can be transformed into threateningly slippery water courses, and rock fall is not uncommon on such days. On the mountain ridges, a strong, gusty wind, quite like the stormy *Föhn* wind of the Alps, may develop.

When approaching hamlets or isolated farmsteads, the walker might get a fright from barking dogs. Most animals are leashed. You shouldn't confront barking, feral dogs eye to eye, but instead, brandishing a stick or a stone will usually scare them away (refer to "Hunting season" on p. 26).

Best times of the year

Gran Canaria is a year-round destination for walkers, but from November to March, the weather is not quite as stable as it is in the summer. For two or three days, precipitation can even cause snowfall, but only at altitudes above about 1400 metres. The centre of the island is spectacular at the end of January when the almond trees are in blossom; the rest of the flora "explodes" from March to April. In summer time, it is recommended not to hike in the midday sun (13–17.00)!

Refreshment and accommodation

Aside from the tourist resorts situated on the south side of the island, there are a large number of other accommodations (refer to p. 28) and refreshments elsewhere. In the keynoted preface to the individual walk descriptions, you can find information about where to find accommodation and refreshment en route. Particularly tailored to walkers are the accommodations in San Bartolomé de Tirajana, in Tejeda and Cruz de Tejeda, in La Aldea de San Nicolás, Agaete and Fontanales, and due to good bus connections, in the capital of Las Palmas as well. Very popular for young people are the hostels located in the capital, but also, for example, in Artenara (www.hostelworld.com).

Maps and guides

The walking maps provided with the routes drawn in (with a scale of 1:50,000, some of them 1:100,000, 1:75,000 or 1:25,000) are an essential element of the guide. For anyone who would like to purchase an additional map, we would recommend the road and leisure map "Gran Canaria" with a scale of 1:50,000 from Freytag & Berndt. Among the travel guides, our recommendation would be the comprehensive Marco Polo Travel Handbook "Gran Canaria".

Books and maps are also available from the Rental Bike Station Las Palmas 24 (Calle 29 de Abril, 63, tel. +34 928 93 54 11).

Waymarking and trail network

It is possible, when walking a trail which leads over more than one municipality, that the initially well-marked trail may suddenly "vanish into thin air" because the neighbouring municipality has no interest in walking tourism. Numerous times we found that the waymarkers had been removed or even replaced with new and anomalous (as well as often incorrect) markings, which is the reason that signage is so seldom referred to in this walking guide. An often better aid to route-finding are the low drystone walls or the cairns, built by the more supportive walking fans, or the arrows painted on the ground, all created to point the walker in the right direction when the route is no longer clear. These are usually very helpful, but not always! When in doubt, please rely on the directions given in the guide (and on the GPS track).

Well-signed: en route at the Cruz de Timagada pass (Walk 28).

On Altavista, with a fantastic view towards the west coast (Walk 15).

Nature and protecting the environment
Please respect the flora and fauna, adhere to the usual dos and don'ts of walking, and be sure to respect the private property of the local inhabitants. Do not leave your rubbish behind (remember to bring along a rubbish bag for later disposal) and do not carelessly toss your cigarette stubs away (fire hazard!).

Tips for linear and long-distance walking
Some walks are designed as linear routes where the destination lies far away from the starting point. Normally, these will have a bus connection. Only for some of the alternative routes can it happen that a taxi must be availed upon. Long-distance walkers will find excellent combinations possibilities on Gran Canaria; for these walkers, we recommend carrying along a sleeping bag.

The best walks on Gran Canaria

The Central Island

Circling the Roque Nublo

The most popular walk onto the "Cloudy Crag" (Walk 1, 2.00 hrs).

Grand Caldera Circular Walk

Panoramic walk along the plunging rock face of the crater basin (Walk 4 from La Goleta, 4.00 hrs; with Walk 3 when starting from Ayacata, 6.00 hrs; Walk 25 from Cruz de Tejeda, 5.30 hrs).

From Ayacata to the Cruz Grande Pass

Camino de la Cumbre – *Camino Real* in the central mountains (Walk 5, 4.15 hrs).

To the "Lord's Caves"

Delightful pass route along the north/south meteorological divide with a magnificent view into the grand Caldera de Tejeda (Walk 9, 2.50 hrs).

On Altavista

Splendid walk along a mountain ridge (Walk 15, 3.30 hrs).

From Cruz de Tejeda to Teror

Historical pilgrimage route to the town of the wooden balconies (Walk 22, 4.30 hrs).

From Tejeda to La Culata

Descent through groves of almond trees to a valley floor (Walk 28, 3.30 hrs).

From Aserrador to Cruz de la Huesita

Vast views from a long ridge, rocky fortresses and remoteness (Walk 32, 4.15 hrs).

The Southern Island

Circling San Bartolomé

Pleasant walk taking in caves and a valley (Walk 37, 4.00 hrs).

Circular Route from Santa Lucía

Gigantic rock face fortress and an idyllic lake (Walk 39, 4.15 hrs).

The Northern Island

Agaete valley and Tamadaba

An adventurous pilgrimage route, pine forest and a dramatic *barranco* (Walk 52, 7.15 hrs).

Barranco de la Virgen

In the charming "Valley of the Virgin": the rural side of Gran Canaria (Walk 58, 4.40 hrs).

Bandama volcanic crater

Ascent over lava ash to the most beautiful crater on the island (Walk 63, 1.50 hrs).

Through the Barranco de Guayadeque

Spectacular gorges, a crater and a craggy peak (Walk 70, 6.45 hrs).

Here are some suggestions, which are covered in detail in this walking guide through the described walks and alternative routes:

■ Ayacata – Cruz de Tejeda – Artenara – Tal von Agaete (2 days), Cruz Grande – Cruz de Tejeda – Teror (2 days), Cruz de Tejeda – Aserrador – Soria – San Bartolomé – Los Palmitos (3 days).

■ Counting as a stretch of the pilgrimage route Camino de Santiago, is the leg San Bartolomé – Cruz de Tejeda – Santa María de Guía/Gáldar (2 days, see also Walk 72). The first section of this pilgrimage route, which starts off from the Playa del Inglés and heads northwards, is not recommended due to its lack of appeal.

The stone cross at the Cruz de Tejeda, Gran Canaria's geographical centre.

Major starting points for walks

- **Agaete valley**: this valley, over 10km long, cutting into the island's centre starting from the north-west coast, is one of the island's most fertile and most beautiful (bus lines 101–103). From San Pedro, ascend into the valley and pass cave-dwellers' villages and reservoirs – or climb up to the Tamadaba pine forest and take an adventurous pilgrimage route to return to the valley. Hotels, apartments and private rooms in Agaete and Puerto de las Nieves.
- **Fontanales**, 1010m: a typical settlement in the "middle altitudes of the northern island": a tidy and somewhat sleepy village, surrounded by chestnut and fruit trees. Fontanales (bus line 127, connections to Las Palmas 116/117) can be incorporated into a number of circular routes – leading to the volcanic crater Pinos de Gáldar and into the Barranco de la Virgen. Accommodation in *fincas* creates a holiday with a rural touch; in the village centre, you can stay in comfortable houses made of wood.
- **Artenara**, 1220m: Gran Canaria's highest-lying mountain village (bus line 220) is an ideal starting point for the interior of the island. From here, walks begin for the Tamadaba massif, which is accessible via shady and well-marked forest trails. The tourist office will help you find accommodation.
- **Cruz de Tejeda**, 1509m: the geographic centre of Gran Canaria, and at the same time, a pivot point for major trails and island roads (bus line 305). Many attractive walks begin here and fan out in all directions, for example, towards Teror, Tejeda and Artenara. Day trippers' inns are set up to greet excursionists; you can enjoy the best view from the Hotel Parador's terrace café. The Parador provides a comfy sojourn; in the village of Tejeda, 10km away, there is also less expensive accommodation.

- **Tejeda**, 1049m: this mountain village (bus lines 18 and 305) perches on the rim of the caldera of the same name, crowned by the craggy monoliths of the Roque Nublo and the Roque Bentayga. Thanks to numerous accommodations here, this makes a good base for exploring the central highlands. A spectacular panoramic trail leads south-westwards to circle the caldera; on the valley floor, the hamlet of La Culata is hidden away, where even more Royal Trails intersect. One of them provides a return route to Tejeda, others lead to Roque Nublo, or pass it by on the way to Ayacata or to Degollada del Aserrador.

- **Mountain road GC-60**: The road (GC-60) that runs southwards from Tejeda to San Bartolomé winds through a rugged, bizarre mountain landscape. Along this route (bus line 18, numerous times daily), lie Tejeda and Ayacata. Starting points for walks can also be found at the cluster of houses situated at the turn-off, Cruce del Bentayga (km6.3), at the crests of the passes of Aserrador (km11.4), of Hoya de la Vieja (km12) and of Cruz Grande (km19.5).

- **Ayacata**, 1290m: from Ayacata (bus line 18), a hamlet at the foot of rugged, furrowed mountains, you can reach La Goleta in about an hour, and from there, you can pick up the walk to Roque Nublo, as well as into the erosion crater, Caldera de Tejeda. The walk heading southwards towards Cruz Grande is spectacular.

- **Cruz Grande**, 1249m: the crest of Cruz Grande pass on the GC-60 Ayacata – San Bartolomé at km19.5 (bus line 18) is a pivot point for major *Caminos Reales*. The ascent, starting here to the Pico de las Nieves, is a popular one. A *Camino Real* approaching from the centre of the island ends here, and you can continue on along it, e.g., to San Bartolomé.

Almond trees in flower near Ayacata.

- **San Bartolomé de Tirajana**, 887m: bus line 18 also services this settlement from the touristic southern island. A marvellous walker's hotel is located here, as well as some restaurants. Trails head towards Ayagaures and Cruz Grande; in the neighbouring village of Santa Lucía, some beautiful trails set off as well.

Walking on Gran Canaria

The island – a miniature continent

Gran Canaria is a miniature continent rich in diversity and enjoys a consistently temperate climate with spring-like temperatures. This Atlantic island is 1532 sq km in area, 47km in length and 55km in breadth. The island is situated at the latitude 28°, more than 1000km south of Gibraltar, but only 210km from the coast of West Africa. Most of its 850,000 inhabitants live in the northeast island in the capital, Las Palmas, but the level karst terrain of the eastern island is also heavily populated. Tourist resorts are concentrated on the coastal strip, only a few kilometres in breadth, stretching from Bahía Feliz over Maspalomas to Puerto de Mogán in the southern island.

Off the beaten track of tourism, the "other" Gran Canaria begins. The island's exciting topography is best observed from a bird's-eye perspective. From the *Cumbre*, the central massif, towering almost 2000m heavenwards, gorges make their way in all directions down to the sea, and are interconnected by notches and valleys. Both geologically and climatically, the island is divided into two parts. The south appears rough and rugged, while the north boasts a smoother terrain. North of the main ridge, cutting across the island between Morro de la Armonía over the Moriscos to the Tamadaba massif, the moisture-bearing trade winds rule the weather, but to the south, it is usually sunny and dry.

The "sacred mountain" Roque Bentayga at sunset (Walk 29).

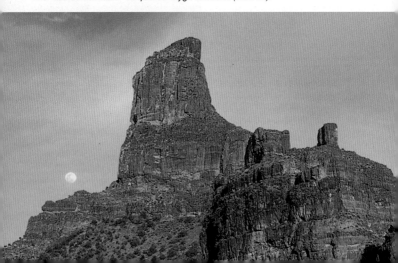

Volcanic activity

Gran Canaria is of volcanic origin: 14 million years ago, volcanic eruptions on the Atlantic Ocean floor formed a cone-shaped island. The volcanic vent, through which the magma was thrown, created a cavity into which the tip of the volcanic cone collapsed and thereby produced a steep-sided depression in the form of a basin. For this geological formation, the term "caldera" (cauldron) has come into common usage. As a result of later volcanic eruptions, the crater was filled

The "black mountain" (Montañón Negro) – only 3000 years old, a geological youngster.

with volcanic ejecta and effusion, so that a kind of mountain plateau was formed. Millennia have passed since then and through the erosive forces of rain and wind, the original topography was exposed once again.

Flora

Although the island is small, it offers a surprising variety of flora. Whether you are in the north or the south, on the coast or in the central massif (at almost 2000m above sea level), you will encounter different biotopes. Botany fans are thrilled by the numerous endemic plants (those that are only found on the Canary Islands) whose existence is based on the island's isolated location. The trade winds blowing in from the north-east (see Climate, p. 27) divides the island into two distinct parts. At a height between 500 and 1400m of altitude, these winds supply the northern island with humidity but, because of the high mountain ranges bisecting the island, the trade winds do not reach the south and, in contrast, this area is extremely dry. Additionally, flora is divided into three classifications depending on altitude: coastal, middle elevations and alpine regions. In the arid coastal region (up to 500m above sea level) aside from salt-resistant plants, the best-known representative flora of the archipelago are found: the Canary Island Date Palm and the dragon tree.

In the north, starting at 500m above sea level, is Monteverde ("Green Mountain") moistened by the trade winds, with heather, juniper and *faya* reaching up to 2m in height and, in higher elevations, these are replaced by laurel trees. The primordial vegetation, however, only still exists in Los Tilos, in the Barranco de la Virgen and in the Barranco de Azuaje (Walks 57, 58, 60). The fertile slopes in the northern island were cleared after the Spanish conquest

19

Agave and spurge in the Barranco de la Mina (Walks 23 and 24).

in the 15th century and put to intensive agricultural use since then. Starting at an altitude of 1200m, the Canary Island pine enters the floral habitat. With its long needles, the pine can "capture" moisture from the wisps of clouds. Pine forests (*pinar* in Spanish; *pino* = pine), can be found primarily in the centre of the island, and the prettiest appear in the Tamadaba massif (Walks 16–19). Above the cloud cover, trees become noticeably scarcer; primarily gorse grows in the surroundings of the "Snowy Summit" (Pico de las Nieves) at not quite 2000m. A species of *Libaetae* has also asserted itself here; because of its pale, silky leaves, it is also known as "Canary Island Edelweiss".

Numerous succulents flourish in the arid south, with fleshy leaves perfect for conserving water. Cactus-like Hercules club (*cardón*) belongs to this group, reaching up to 2m in height and growing in clusters which make them look like candelabra. They produce a toxic milky-white fluid but, when extremely diluted, this was used as a psychoactive drug and laxative in days gone by.

If it rains in the south, the usually parched mountain slopes are covered in a colourful carpet of flowers. The dominant flora here is the yellow flowering broom, interspersed with the aromatic Micromeria (with a thyme-like fragrance), wild sage and the Canary Island wallflower (*Erysimum cheiri*).

Fauna

Good news for mountain walkers: there are no poisonous snakes on Gran Canaria, nor are there scorpions. You might be surprised to find the Californian kingsnake Lampropeltis californiae (culebra real in Spanish): Some of the snakes escaped from a private terrarium and multiplied so quickly that they are now a threat to the local fauna, especially the Gran

At a Birds of Prey Show in Palmitos Park.

Canaria skink, geckos and the giant lizard reaching an average length of 50cm. Kingsnakes pose no threat to humans.

Kestrels, common buzzards and ravens are circling high above the peaks. In the pine forests of Inagua-Pajonales and Tamadaba, you can spot the grey-green canary (*Serinus canaria*) and the Great spotted woodpecker with a reddish head and breast (*Dendrocopos major thanneri*). There are only rare sightings of the Blue chaffinch (*Fringilla teydea*) – this unique species is threatened with extinction. The red-legged partridge (*Alectoris rufa intercedens*) has made its home especially in the west and centre of the island: it was probably an introduced species and usually chooses to nest in arid gorges.

12km north of Maspalomas, the Palmitos Park is a zoological and botanical garden with exotic animals from all over the world, sea lions and dolphin shows, a lovely free-flight aviary as well as a large aviary with free-flying butterflies (www.palmitospark.es). Las Palmas' latest attraction is the aquarium "Poema del Mar" (www.poema-del-mar.com).

Nature reserves

Large areas of the island are under a preservation programme and the most beautiful landscapes are protected from human intervention in 32 parks. The biggest of these is the Parque Rural del Nublo (23,300 hectares), which stretches from the centre to the west of the island. Amongst the most interesting geological formations of the park is the bizarrely shaped Tejeda caldera with the Roque Nublo and the Roque Bentayga (Walks1–4 and 25–30, UNESCO World Heritage site for "sacred mountains" since 2019). The island government has set up a number of information points illustrating the culture of the native people, the flora and the fauna, as well as the geomorphology of Gran Canaria. Open on a regular schedule is e.g. the Museo de Guayadeque (Walk 70), as well as the Centro de Interpretación del Roque Bentayga (Walk 29).

The spur of Canarian aboriginals: Almogaren, above the caves of Cuatro Puertas (Walk 68).

Museums

The most important archaeological sites include, among others, the Cueva Pintada (in Gáldar), the Barranco de Guayadeque (at Agüimes, Walk 70), the cave system Cenobio de Valeron (at Guía), Risco Caído at Artenara, La Fortaleza at Santa Lucía (Walk 39) and the burial sites of Arteara in the south (Walk 43) as well as that of Maipez (Agaete) in the north-west. As more mainstream fare, scenes from the everyday life of the native inhabitants have been reproduced in Mundo Aborígen, a reconstructed pre-Hispanic village located 8km north of Maspalomas. A more serious source of information can be found in the Museo Canario in Las Palmas: the collection of native artefacts here is the largest in the archipelago (www.elmuseocanario.com). The Columbus House (Casa de Colón) is located nearby, where the close relationship of Gran Carnaria with the New World is documented (www.casadecolon.com). For art, visit the CAAM (www.caam.net) and Castillo de la Luz (www.fundacionmartinchirino.org), for science have a look at Museo Elder (www.museoelder.org). Additional information and exhibition halls have been established in the nature reserves.

Botanical gardens

A living museum of Canarian flora is the Jardín Canario near Tafira where, in scenic surroundings, about 500 endemic species of plants are flourishing (see Walk 62; www.jardincanario.org). Commercially run gardens include the Finca Montecristo in the Barranco de Ayagaures (GC-504, km5.6; www.montecristograncanaria.com), the cactus garden Cactualdea at La Aldea de San Nicolás and Palmitos Park (see page 21).

Picnic areas

The state-run environmental protection agency has set up several picnic areas in the central mountains. They are usually equipped with barbecue sites and stone benches, and sometimes provide drinking water and sanitation facilities. The most beautiful sites are located in the central mountains on the GC-600 road, in Tamadaba (Walks 19, 52) and at the reservoir Cueva de las Niñas (Walk 33).

Beaches

Gran Canaria boasts a total of about 100 kilometres of beach. The longest sandy beaches are located on the Costa Canaria on the southern island, and in the capital of Las Palmas. Secluded beaches only still exist in the south-western and north-western parts of the island: south of Puerto de Mogán, lie the beaches of Tiritaña and Medio Almud; northwards, the bays of Veneguera, Tasarte and Tasartico. From the settlement of Tasartico, situated in the valley of the same name, a walk leads to the beautifully located Playa Güi Güi (Walk 49). The Playa Chica near La Aldea de San Nicolás is also a remote one (Walk 50) as is the beach at Guayedra (Walk 53).

Boat and ship excursions

A daily service connects Arguineguín, Anfi, Puerto Rico and Puerto de Mogán. From Agaete, a fast ferry sets off several times each day to Santa Cruz de Tenerife. From Las Palmas, ships sail to Tenerife and La Palma, Fuerteventura and Lanzarote.

Jeep safaris

You can book a jeep safari with almost every tour operator: in caravan-style, several off-road vehicles are driven about 120km along normal roads and off-road through the gorges of the island's interior. An accompanying cinematographer captures the "adventure" on film.

Mountain biking

This sport keeps growing in popularity for both Canarians and tourists. Gran Canaria offers good prerequisites for the cyclist; attractive rural roads and tracks in the south of the island have been especially waymarked for touring cyclists. The Gran Canaria Bike Week in the last quarter of the year is an important event (www.grancanariabikeweek.es).

Rock climbing

Best spots are located on the basalt rock faces towering up to heights of 230m around the mountain village of Ayacata, where clear weather often prevails. A relatively simple ascent leads to the peak of Roque Nublo, boasting a height of 65m. Also very popular are the furrowed steep rock faces of Tamadaba, Gran Canaria's oldest massif, lying in the north-western island, as well as are the numerous routes tackling the craggy fortress of Fortaleza in the Barranco de Sorrueda (Santa Lucía), in the south. If you wish to sign up for an organised rock climbing tour, contact the Patronato de Turismo in Las Palmas.

Markets

A major flea market is held every Sunday morning in Las Palmas (Santa Catalina). Handicrafts, as well as an abundance of fruits and vegetables, can be found at the weekly markets in Arguineguín (Tuesday), San Fernando (Wednesday and Saturday), Gáldar and Agüimes (Thursday), Puerto de Mogán (Friday), Teror and San Mateo (Sunday). In addition, there are numerous farmers' markets in many locations offering fresh products direct from the producer.

Information and addresses

Tourist information
The following tourist offices offer city maps and information concerning tourist attractions, cultural events and so forth:

- Patronato de Turismo, Calle Triana 93, Las Palmas, tel. +34 928 219 600, www.grancanaria.com; branch offices: Parque San Telmo, Parque Santa Catalina.
- Información Aeropuerto Gando, Terminal Internacional, the arrival hall at the airport, exit A, tel. +34 928 574 058.
- Centro Insular de Turismo, Av. de España/Av. de los Estados Unidos, Playa del Inglés, tel. +34 928 771 550.
- Patronato de Turismo, Av. de Mogán/Av. de la Cornisa, Puerto Rico, tel. +34 928 158 804.

Getting there
Gran Canaria is listed in the itinerary of numerous tour operators and can be reached from all the major airports in Great Britain. There is a ferry service to the Spanish mainland (Cádiz) and to all of the other islands of the Canary archipelago.

Driving and hire cars
The island roads are twisty, and secondary roads are also often very narrow. After heavy rainfall, there is an increased danger of rock fall in the interior and in the north-west island. The roads GC-210 Tejeda–Artenara and GC-200

View of Las Palmas from the Bahía del Confital (Walk 61).

Agaete–El Risco are often closed to traffic.

On Gran Canaria, hire cars are often inexpensive and can be booked in almost all of the larger settlements or at the airport upon arrival. A dependable hire car company is CICAR, which is represented in all of the tourist resorts, as well as at the airport and ferry harbour (tel. +34 902 244 444, www.cicar.com, info@cicar.com).

Camping

Gran Canaria boasts a number of campsites:

- Campamento El Garañón, Llanos del Garañón (approach from the GC-600, km6.9), tel. +34 928 413 282, www.vivacaventura.com.
- Camping Temisas, Lomo de la Cruz, Ctra. Santa Lucía–Agüimes (via Era del Cardón), tel. +34 928 798 149.
- Blue Ocean Camp, Playa de Tasartico (GC-204), tel. +34 828 017 515, www.blueoceancamp.com.

Romantic oasis: the Hotel Rural Las Calas in Lechuza (near San Mateo).

- Camping El Pinillo, Barranco de Arguineguín, tel. +34 629 907 826.
- Camping Playa de Vargas, Camino Vecinal de Vargas s/n, Playa de Vargas (Agüimes), tel. +34 928 188 037, www.campingplayadevargas.com.

In addition, there are attractively situated camping areas in the island's interior. Once you have a permit, you can put up your tent or park your caravan for a maximum of seven days without paying a fee. At these areas, you will frequently find barbecue sites, water and public conveniences.

You can get the permit online or from the relevant government office between one month and at least three days before the first day of camping: Cabildo de Gran Canaria/OIAC (Permisos de Acampada), Calle Bravo Murillo 23, Las Palmas (Triana), tel. +34 928 219 229, oiac@grancanaria.com.

Finca holidays

Many historical houses in the countryside (*fincas, casas rurales*) have been renovated and are available for rental through:

- Gran Canaria Natural (Patronato de Turismo), Las Palmas, tel. +34 928 334 175, www.grancanarianaturalandactive.com/de.

Opening hours

Shops are usually open from 9–13.00 (Mon–Sat) and 17–20.00 (Mon–Fri), banks and post offices, from 9–14.00 (Mon–Fri) and 9–13.00 (Sat).

Fiestas and bank holidays

Amongst the most important sporting events of the year, in addition to the island crossing in March (www.transgrancanaria.com), is the Gran Canaria Walking Festival, which takes place in October (www.grancanariawalkingfestival.es). Fiestas can be found on Gran Canaria throughout the year – the most lively occurring during carnival in Las Palmas in February. A few weeks before that, usually at the end of January, the almond blossom festival is held in Tejeda – a week later, in Valsequillo. Anchored in Canarian tradition are the festivals held at San Pedro (end of June), Agaete (beginning of August), and La Aldea de San Nicolás (September). The feast of the island's patron saint, the "Virgin of the Pine", takes place in Teror on September 8.

The most important bank holidays are: Jan 1, Jan 6 (Epiphany), Maundy Thursday, Good Friday, Easter, May 1 (Fiesta del Trabajo), Pentecost, Corpus Christi, May 30 (Día de Canarias), Aug 15 (Asunción de la Virgen), Sept 8 (Virgen del Pino), Oct 12 (Día de la Hispanidad), Nov 1, Dec 6 (Día de la Constitución), Dec 8 (Inmaculada Concepción) and Dec 25.

Hunting season

From the first Sunday in August until December 8, hunting is allowed on Gran Canaria on Thursdays and Sundays, as well as on public holidays (September 8, October 12, December 6 and 8). Many Canarians head out into the interior with their dogs and shotguns to hunt wild pigeons, partridges, pheasants and rabbits. Since there are, in Gran Canaria alone, over 20,000 hunting licenses issued, walkers should exercise some caution on these days. The only area where hunting is completely prohibited is in the Inagua Pajonales pine forest.

Climate table

Month		1	2	3	4	5	6	7	8	9	10	11	12	Year
Day	°C	21	21	23	23	23	24	25	26	26	26	24	21	24
Night	°C	14	14	15	16	17	19	20	21	21	18	17	16	18
Water	°C	8	18	19	19	19	20	21	22	23	23	21	19	21
Hours of sun/day		6	7	8	9	9	10	11	11	8	7	6	6	8
Rainy days/month		3	2	2	1	1	0	0	0	1	1	3	5	2

Spring in the mountainous interior near the Degollada de Becerra (Walk 24).

Climate

Gran Canaria, the "Island of Eternal Spring", is characterised by a subtropical climate: in the coastal areas, temperature variations between summer and winter are very low, although they are more pronounced in the higher mountain regions. Weather is determined by the trade winds, bringing mild, moist air masses from the north-east, which are blocked by the mountains and then rise up; when the air masses cool down, clouds form, rising up to a height of about 1500 m. Tiny water droplets condense on plants, and long pine needles "comb" the moisture from the wispy clouds.

The clouds are unable to fan out southwards since cold dry air descends from higher altitudes, applying downward pressure onto the massive cloud cover, thereby preventing it from rising any further.

Taxis

You will find a taxi rank in all of the larger settlements – otherwise, you can order one from a local bar. Recently, the fares have increased significantly, so it might be worth your while to negotiate a price beforehand.

Telephone

The code for Spain/Gran Canaria is 0034; the area code 928, which follows, is the former code and remains a set part of any nine-digit landline telephone number. The code from the Canary Islands to the UK is 0044. The central emergency number is 112.

Accommodation

Double rooms and apartments for 80 Euros-plus are noted by an asterisk (*).

Agaete valley

Hotel Puerto de las Nieves*, Avenida Alcalde José de Armas s/n, Puerto de las Nieves, tel. +34 928 886 256, www.hotelpuertodelasnieves.es

Casa Luna, Calle Guayarmina 42, Agaete, tel. +34 928 554 481

Roca Negra*, Av. Alfredo Kraus 42, Urb. El Turmán, Agaete, tel. +34 928 898 009, www.becordial.com

Finca Las Longueras*, Valle de Agaete, tel. +34 928 898 145, www.laslongueras.com

Agüimes

Hotel Casa de los Camellos*, El Progreso 12, tel. +34 928 785 003

Artenara

Albergue Warung, La Cuevita 38, tel. +34 656 604 290, www.facebook.com/elwarung

Ayagaures

Finca Montecristo*, GC-504 km5.6, tel. +34 928 144 032, www.montecristo-grancanaria. com

Cruz de Tejeda

Hotel Parador de Cruz de Tejeda*, tel. +34 928 012 500, www.parador.es

El Hornillo

Refugio El Hornillo, tel. +34 928 559 518, www.RefugioElHornillo.com

Fataga

Finca Tomás & Puri, Finca Capaon 30, GC-60 km35, tel. +34 928 798 681, www.fincafataga.com

Fontanales

Cabañas Valle Verde*, Calle Párroco Juan Díaz Rodríguez 3 (ten wooden cottages), tel. +34 928 620 424, valleverde@gmail.com

Gáldar

Agáldar*, Plaza de Santiago 14, tel. +34 928 897 433, www.hotelagaldar.com

Ingenio

Villa Néstor, Calle Antonio Rodríguez Medina 31, tel. +34 638 922 914, www.villanestor.com

La Aldea de San Nicolás

La Aldea Suites*, Calle Transversal Federico R., tel. +34 928 891 035, www.laaldeasuites.com

San Bartolomé de Tirajana

Hotel Las Tirajanas*, Calle Oficial Mayor José Rubio s/n, tel. +34 928 123 000, www.hotelrurallastirajanas.com

San Mateo

Hotel Las Calas*, El Arenal 36 (La Lechuza), tel. +34 928 661 436, www.hotelrurallascalas.com

Tres Almendros*, Calle La Solana de Utiaca 50 (6km west via GC-42), tel. +34 666624117, www.inzulae.com

Tejeda

Hotel Rural Fonda de la Tea*, Ezequiel Sánchez 22, tel. +34 928 666 422, www.hotelfondadelatea.com.

Apartamentos Gayfa, Calle de Cruz Blanca 34, tel. +34 928 666 230

Teror

Hotel JM El Pino, Avenida Cabildo Insular 141 (1.5km away from town on the GC-432), tel. +34 928 632 016

The Parralillo reservoir on the road from La Aldea de San Nicolás to Artenara.

18   FARO MASPALOMAS – SAN BARTOLOMÉ – AYACATA – TEJEDA*

Mon-Fri 8.00 (to Ayacata), 9.30, 11.00 (to San Bartolomé), 15.00, 19.30 (to San Bartolomé)
Sat   9.30, 15.00
       *transfer for Cruz de Tejeda and San Mateo with bus No. 305

18   TEJEDA – AYACATA – SAN BARTOLOMÉ – FARO MASPALOMAS

Mon-Fri 7.00 (from San Bartolomé), 9.30 (from Ayacata), 11.30, 14.00 (from San Bartolomé), 17.00
Sat   11.30, 17.00

30   LAS PALMAS (CATALINA)   – FARO MASPALOMAS

Mon-Fri 6.45–17.45 every 20 mins, 18.15–21.15 hourly 8.30–17.50 every 20 mins, 18.40–21.40 hourly
Sat-Sun 6.15–20.15 every half hr, 21.15   7.15, 8.00–21.30 every half hr

32/33 PLAYA DEL INGLÉS   – PUERTO DE MOGÁN

daily   about 9.00–18.00 every half hr   about 9.00–17.35 every half hr

34   SAN BARTOLOMÉ – TEMISAS –   AGÜIMES – EL DOCTORAL

daily   6.45, 9.30, 14.30, 18.00   8.00, 12.00, 16.30, 19.30

38   PUERTO DE MOGÁN   – LA ALDEA DE SAN NICOLÁS

Mon-Sat 7.00, 11.40, 16.00, 19.40   5.45, 8.00 (only Mon-Fri), 9.00, 14.05, 17.30
Sun   7.40, 18.40   9.00, 19.55

50   LAS PALMAS   – FARO MASPALOMAS

Mon-Fri 9.05–17.05 hourly, Sat/Sun 9.05–15.05 hourly,   Mon-Fri 8.05–18.05 hourly, Sat/Sun 10.05–
       16.05 (Sat), 17.05   16.05 hourly, 17.05 (only Sat), 18.05

60   LAS PALMAS (CATALINA)   – AEROPUERTO GANDO

daily   5.15–20.15 every half hr, 21.15, 22.15   6.15–21.15 every half hr, 22.15, 23.15

66   AEROPUERTO GANDO   – FARO MASPALOMAS

daily   7.30–20.30 hourly   6.30–19.30 hourly

84   MOGÁN   – PUERTO DE MOGÁN

daily   8.00–23.00 every 1–2 hrs   7.40–22.40 every 1–2 hrs

91   LAS PALMAS   – PUERTO DE MOGÁN

Mon-Fri 5.40–19.00 every 20 mins,   7.10, 7.30, 8.10–19.10 every 20 mins,
       19.30–23.30 hourly;   19.40–02.40 every 40–60 mins;
Sat/Sun 5.00–19.30 every half hr,   7–19 every half hr, 19.40–02.40 every
       19.40–23.40 every 40–60 mins 40–60 mins

101   GÁLDAR – AGAETE   – LA ALDEA DE SAN NICOLÁS

Mon-Sat 7.30, 11.15, 15.45, 19.30   5.45, 9.00, 14.05, 17.30
Sun   7.30, 15.45   9.00, 17.30

102   GÁLDAR – AGAETE   – LOS BERRAZALES/EL VALLE

daily   7.00, 10.30, 14.30, 18.30   7.35, 11.35, 15.35, 19.35

103   LAS PALMAS – GÁLDAR – AGAETE – PUERTO DE LAS NIEVES

daily   5.00–22.00 hourly   5.30–23.30 hourly

113	GÁLDAR – GUÍA	–	FONTANALES
Mon-Sat 7.00, 14.15			8.00, 16.00

116/ 117	LAS PALMAS	–	MOYA
Mon-Fri 7.45–19.45 hourly			8.15–20.15 about every 1–2 hrs
Sat/Sun 7.45–19.45 every 2 hrs			7.20–20.20 about every 2 hrs

127	MOYA	–	FONTANALES
Mon-Fri 8.45, 11.45, 15.00, 16.40			9.10, 12.10, 15.20, 17.10, 20.10
Sat/Sun 8.45, 15.00, 19.00			9.10, 16.10, 19.30

204	LAS PALMAS	–	FIRGAS
Mon-Sat 8.30, 12.30, 17.30, 21.30			10.00, 16.00, 19.00

216	LAS PALMAS	–	TEROR
Mon-Fri 6.30, 7.30, 8.00–21.00 hourly			6.00–20.00 hourly
Sat/Sun 8.00, 10.00–17.00 hourly, 20.00			9.00–17.00 hourly

220	TEROR – VALLESECO	–	ARTENARA
Mon-Fri 9.00, 11.00*, 14.15, 19.00			10.00, 16.00, 20.15
Sat 9.00, 11.00*, 16.15			10.00, 18.45
Sun 8.15*, 16.15*			10.45**
* from Las Palmas			** to Las Palmas

303	LAS PALMAS – SANTA BRÍGIDA	–	SAN MATEO
daily 6.30–22.30 every half hour			5.30–21.30 every half hour, 23.30

305	SAN MATEO	–	TEJEDA
Mon-Sat 8.00, 10.30, 12.30, 14.00, 16.00, 20.00			7.00, 9.00, 11.30, 13.00, 15.00, 17.00
Sun 8.00, 10.30, 16.00			9.00, 11.30, 17.00

311	LAS PALMAS – BANDAMA	–	SANTA BRÍGIDA
Mon-Fri 5.55–12.55 hourly, 14.05, 14.55–20.55 hourly			6.40–21.40 hourly
Sat/Sun 5.55–19.55 every 2 hrs			6.40–20.40 every 2 hrs

Las Palmas has two bus stations. If no other information is given, departure is from the Estación de Guaguas San Telmo in Triana's Old Town. The Santa Catalina terminal is in the harbour district 4km north; a bus starting off here, sets off 15 minutes later from San Telmo.

Information about additional bus service and / or cheaper multifare tickets ("Tarjeta Ida y Vuelta" are only offered for specific lines and usually only at the weekend) can be obtained from the bus company GLOBAL at the bus stations, as well as online at: www.guaguasglobal.com

The Central Island

A "petrified storm", emerald-green reservoirs, pine forests and remote canyons

This dramatic alpine terrain, sculpted by volcanic eruptions, wind and weather, is simply spectacular – it's no wonder that, since 2005, the area has enjoyed protection under the auspices of a UNESCO Biosphere reserve and has been a UNESCO World Heritage site since 2019. The landmark found here is the "Cloudy Crag" (Roque Nublo), a striking monolith that was worshipped as a sanctum by the indigenous people, and which is a destination today for many walkers. At a greater height is the "Snowy Summit" (Pico de las Nieves) at an altitude of 1949m, the source of deep gorges cutting their way down to the coast. The pine-dotted Tamadaba massif is also impressive, with steep rock faces plunging almost 1000m into the sea. Further southwards, emerald-green reservoirs shimmer on the valley floors; mountain flanks and plains are blanketed with gorse and larkspur. The mountain villages, which were cut off from the outside world until only a few centuries ago, have largely retained their traditional character. The whitewashed houses of Artenara and Tejeda cling to steep rock faces, and many of the inhabitants still devote their time to farming and the raising of livestock.

In Tejeda's village centre.

The island's most popular walk

Roque Nublo ("Cloudy Crag"), 1803 metres in altitude, is Gran Canaria's land-mark; a sanctum to the indigenous people, steeped in song and legend. This craggy finger rises like a gigantic sculpture, towering 65 metres above its base and majestically enthroned above the Caldera de Tejeda. The crag is a relic of a long-extinct volcanic pipe, laid free by erosion – only the hard rock core could resist the forces of wind and water.

Starting point: La Goleta, 1577m. GC-600, km11.2. Car park; no bus service. Approach on foot possible via Walk 3 from Ayacata (an additional 2 hrs).
Height difference: 220m in both ascent and descent.
Grade: very short, mostly easy walk, along well-laid trails.
Note: if you are approaching by bus, take the No. 18 to Ayacata and then use Walk 3 to reach La Goleta. The "Cloudy Crag" is enjoyed best in the morning and afternoon when the hordes of tourists haven't yet arrived or have already left for the day.
Alternative: from the Degollada Blanca (3), you can descend to La Culata in 45 mins and then connect to Walk 28 to Tejeda, as well as to Walk 25 that leads to Cruz de Tejeda.

Three trails start off at the rocky plateau of **La Goleta (1)** on the road GC-600, Ayacata – Cueva Grande. Take the middle trail (S-70 *Roque Nublo*), traversing the mountain slope to the left; at the outset, only a slight ascent, and later, a moderate one. South-westwards, you can spot the broad valley of Ayacata; the white houses of the village cluster around a little church. In front of you is the Roque Nublo, to the left of it, the smaller El Fraile ("the Monk"), whose silhouette brings to mind a friar in prayer. Reach this in a good 800m and, at the **fork (2)**, bear right towards *La Culata* and begin – anti-clockwise – the circular route round the Roque Nublo. The trail leads past gorse and pine trees and, 700m on, reaches the junction for the **Degollada Blanca (3)**. Ignore the right-hand fork towards La Culata and keep steadily below the steep rock face of the Roque Nublo. Past another left-hand bend, enjoy a fantastic

Left, the "Frog", right, the "Cloudy Crag".

view of the island's interior, as well as the western island: in the foreground, the *barrancos* surrounding the Roque Bentayga, behind those, the high plain of Acusa with the jagged, towering massif of the Altavista. Continue circling the Roque Nublo and then reach the junction for **Hoyetas del Nublo (4)**; a little sign proclaims *La aventura comienza en ti* ("The adventure begins within you"). Straight ahead, a sign points out the way to El Aserrador (see Walk 2). But instead, follow the trail sign for *La Goleta* to veer left. The trail ascends, temporarily steeply, and leads, 15 mins later, to the **Las Palomas pass (5)**. Here, bear left as well and follow the trail sign to *Roque Nublo* (on the return route, we will be passing this point once again). Taking an alpine path which has been cut into the rock face, keep ascending and immediately reach the extensive Nublo plateau. At the head of the plain, the "Frog" (La Rana) is crouching, and above it, the majestic "Cloudy Crag" towers to the heavens. The views are spectacular in every direction of the compass! Now head towards **La Rana**, passing it to the right, and shortly afterwards, reach the sheer drop at the edge of the **Roque Nublo (6)**. Here, too, the view is breath-taking: peeping through a window rock, take a peek down into the abyss – if the weather is clear, Teide appears on the horizon, enthroned above the neighbouring island of Tenerife.

Degollada Blanca (3) Roque Nublo (6)
1610 m 1738 m
La Goleta (1) La Goleta (1)
1577 m 1577 m
4.7 km
0 1.20 2.00 h

For the return, head back again – now enjoying a view of the jagged rock face – to **Las Palomas pass (5)**, turn left there and, at the **junction (2)** 300m on, turn right and continue somewhat precipitously to reach the saddle **La Goleta (1)**.

Alternative ascent to the "Cloudy Crag"

The classic ascent trail to the "Cloudy Crag" (see Walk 1) is Gran Canaria's most popular walking route. If you are looking for solitude, you may feel somewhat out of place. Along the walk recommended here, which approaches the Nublo massif from the south-west side, you will usually be on your own as you wander through a picturesque valley with a tiny reservoir, almond trees and scattered, rocky monoliths. At the end, the route circles the summit plateau of the Nublo in a clockwise direction and, if you want, you can take a short excursion to the foot of the Cloudy Crag. Unlike the classic version of the Nublo walk, the starting point for this route can be reached by bus.

Starting point: Hoya de la Vieja, GC-60, km12, 1418m. 3km west of Ayacata. Bus stop for line 18.

Height difference: 350m.

Grade: steep stretches are mixed with level ones; scree-slippery ones are mixed with pleasant going. Despite the moderate length of the walk, the route is strenuous, especially during exceptionally warm weather.

Note: if you choose to ascend from the Las Palomas pass to the plateau of the "Cloudy Crag" (see Walk 1), the walk is about 30 minutes longer.

Alternative: if you turn left at the Degollada Blanca (3), you will reach the village of La Culata in 30 mins, and from there, you could join Walk 28 to continue on to Tejeda or Walk 25 to continue on to Cruz de Tejeda.

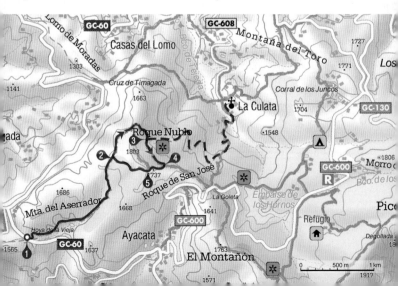

At the Las Palomas pass.

From the **Hoya de la Vieja pass**, opposite the bus stop on the **GC-60, km-marker 12 (1)**, climb up along a broad concrete ramp at the edge of a covered water reservoir (sign: *S-70 Roque Nublo*). Immediately after, pick up a dirt track which bends to the left 150m further on and then narrows into a cobblestone trail (*yellow waymarkers*). Flanked by almond trees, the trail winds upwards in bends which will put you in a sweat, most likely. After the steep ascent, the landscape changes: a tiny, green reservoir lies at the foot of black rock faces at a point where a valley sweeps ramp-like upwards – flanked, far and wide, by boulders. Climb down towards the reservoir until the trail breaks away from it.

Now the climb up begins again, but this time leading along a pleasant, moderately ascending trail that is interrupted by plates of rock from time to time – cairns help in route-finding. Scattered pine trees provide some shade on hot days. After a total of 1.1km – at about the same height as a cave to the left – the "Cloudy Crag" comes into view for the first time; in front of it, the

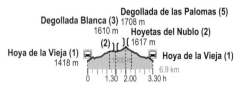

Degollada de las Palomas (5)
1708 m
Degollada Blanca (3)
1610 m   Hoyetas del Nublo (2)
(2)   1617 m
Hoya de la Vieja (1)   Hoya de la Vieja (1)
1418 m   6.9 km
0   1.30 2.00   3.30 h

unmistakable "Frog Crag" is crouching. Another 300m further on, at the **y-junction**, bear right where the route continues in a steeper ascent. At the prominent junction, **Hoyetas del Nublo (2)**, follow the sign towards *La Culata* (straight ahead) and begin the circular route round the Nublo massif, heading clockwise – later, we will return to this spot from the right.

The scenery changes yet again: looking westwards over broad valleys and gorges, you can spot the neighbouring island of Tenerife, if the weather is clear. Keeping mostly level, the trail circles pleasantly round the massif. As soon as it veers to the right, you have a possible excursion to the left, following a beaten path for a couple of minutes to reach a natural viewpoint (cairns).

However, keep to the main trail and enjoy the view, taking in pine-covered slopes and Gran Canaria's second highest peak, the "Snowy Summit" (Pico de las Nieves), easily spotted due to a globe-like military installation. Another 100m further on, at the **Degollada Blanca (3)**, ignore a trail forking left towards La Culata (see Alternative) and follow the sign, *S 70 La Goleta*, to continue the ascent. At the **junction (4)**, not quite another 700m on, turn sharp right (diagonally left leads to La Goleta) and ascend steeply for another 320m to reach the **Las Palomas pass (5)**. The panoramic view from this pass is simply fantastic: on a clear day, enjoy a view stretching from the

dunes of Maspalomas all the way to Teide on Tenerife! By following the sign to *Roque Nublo*, from there, you could pick up the route for Walk 1 and turn right to ascend to the spectacular plateau of the Roque Nublo (see Note).

If you decide against this excursion, keep straight ahead to descend towards *El Aserrador*. 40m further on, at a nondescript junction, bear right and climb down to the junction already met during the approach, **Hoyetas del Nublo (2)**. Bear left here and continue for 2.3km – this time enjoying a view of the valley, which opens up considerably, to return to the **Hoya de la Vieja pass (1)**.

Sociable companions along the return route.

Picturesque access trail with multiple connecting routes

Rugged rock faces and scattered boulders lend the Ayacata valley a dramatic touch. In the spring, the trail is immersed in a yellow sea; from Ayacata all the way up to the Roque Nublo ("Cloudy Crag"), gorse is in bloom. In winter, the valley is dressed in a white cloak; the flowers of the almond trees are unfolding everywhere.

Starting point: Ayacata, 1290m. Bus stop for line 18; parking possible opposite the bar Melo in Ayacata's village centre.
Height difference: 300m in ascent and descent.
Grade: due to the steep stretches that must be negotiated, this is a strenuous walk, although well-marked and following a restored *Camino Real*.

Refreshment: a bar in Ayacata; quite often you will find a food truck in La Goleta.
Note: for walkers dependent on buses, this route is necessary for the approach, as no bus service is provided close to the Roque Nublo nor to Pico de las Nieves. Nevertheless, the route could also be appealing for walkers with a car.
Alternatives: linking possibilities from La Goleta with Walks 1, 4 and 6.

At the church of **Ayacata (1)**, turn off onto the GC-600 towards the Roque Nublo. 15m on, turn left onto a concrete-paved trail (sign: *S-70 La Goleta*), which short-cuts a long bend in the road, approaches the road again a few minutes later, and then veers away from it once more; in front of us is the narrow, towering sculpture of the Roque Fraile and, to the right, the Montañón massif. Nestled between mammoth scattered boulders, delicate almond trees are growing; these are in bloom starting in mid-January– a fantastic feast for the eyes! At the **Finca La Huerta Grande (2)**, a good kilometre further on, reach the road again and follow this for not quite 50m to the left. Opposite **house No. 48**, pick up a path which ascends over stone steps. Another

Ascent between boulders and almond trees.

400m further, meet up again with **GC-600** near the **km-marker 12 (3)**, turn right for 200m until the *Camino Real* forks off to the left to continue the route. After not quite another 350m of ascent, reach the panoramic plateau **La Goleta (4)**. Several splendid trails offer possible variations at this point (see Alternatives). Since you may not be able to remember where the approach route was located when you return here, we will provide a brief sketch: from the three trails forking away from the stony plateau, take the left-hand one. This descends in a south-westerly direction and, a little later on, merges with the road near the **km-marker 12 (3)**.

200m on, stone walls on the left-hand side mark the spot where the trail continues. Behind a house, descend once again over steps to reach the road again; turn left and follow this for another 50m. Past the **Finca La Huerta Grande (2)** turn right onto a trail that descends, becomes a track, and then, in a bend, almost touches on the road. Now the descent continues with no further problems and the trail ends near the village church in the centre of **Ayacata (1)**.

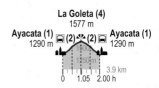

41

TOP 4 · Picturesque circular walk from La Goleta

A mostly pleasant walk off to the side of the "Cloudy Crag"

This walk runs anti-clockwise along the rim of the caldera, while opening up a splendid view of the Nublo massif. Pass a reservoir en route and then cross an open pine wood. Take some refreshment in the village of La Culata before tackling the ascent.

Starting point: La Goleta, 1577m. GC-600, km11.2; car park; no bus service.
Height difference: 550m in ascent and descent.
Grade: only the final ascent is strenuous, otherwise this walk is a real treat along renovated and waymarked trails.
Refreshment: a bar in La Culata; quite often, you will find a food truck in La Goleta.
Accommodation: a campsite and wooden huts in the Campamento El Garañón (see page 25).
Note: this splendid walk is suited for both walkers with a car and for those approach-

ing by bus. Take bus No. 18 to Ayacata and then follow Walk 3 to reach the starting point in La Goleta (1 hr). With a car, you can drive to La Goleta via Ayacata (GC-60, km14.3; Roque Nublo turn-off).
Alternatives: 1) if you want to avoid the first 400m on tarmac, follow the sign for *S-51 Llanos de la Pez* going down from La Goleta. Keep right at the following fork. 2) combination with Walk 5 near El Garañón (2). 3) a possible excursion from the Degollada de la Cumbre (5) to the panoramic plateau at the Degollada de Becerra (see Walk 25).

In **La Goleta (1)**, follow the road eastwards and 400m on, reach a little circular panoramic plateau with stone benches at the **Cruz de Juan Pérez**. Pick up a cobbled trail ("*S-51 Garañón*") and descend for 300m to reach the dam **Los Hornos**, then cross over the dam wall. Another 800m further on, reach a plateau up above, turn right onto a track and walk another 200m to reach the recreational campsite **Campamento El Garañón (2, 1680m)**. Straight ahead leads to the Cruz Grande pass (see Walk 5); but instead, take the road that forks to the left and pass by the (fenced-in) sports grounds, heading towards *Cruz de Tejeda*. 300m further on, the broad trail hooks to the right, but quickly veers again to continue in the original direction as it leads along the edge of a pine forest. 150m on, leave the road behind by turning left onto a

During the descent from the Cumbre pass.

path forking away (**3**; wooden sign): at the outset, along the right-hand bank of a dried-out stream bed, and afterwards, on the left-hand side. During the further course of the route, the correct path is flanked by tell-tale walls and cairns. Cross over two tracks, one after the other, which lead to the left to a campsite grounds, and 20 minutes later, (first descending and then ascending), reach the rather nondescript junction, **Corral de los Juncos (4)**.

A turn to the right leads to the junction, Cruce Llanos de la Pez, but turn left instead onto the cobbled trail. Ascend via steps, and afterwards, the trail is cobbled with rough stones as it continues along the slope at about the same level. From the foot of the mountain, **Montaña del Toro**, enjoy a downwards view of the hamlet, La Culata. High above,

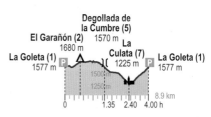

Degollada de
la Cumbre (5)
El Garañón (2)   1570 m
1680 m   La
                          Culata (7)
La Goleta (1)   1225 m   La Goleta (1)
1577 m   1577 m

1500 m
1250 m

8.9 km

0   1.35   2.40   4.00 h

Behind the Bentayga, Teide (3718m) appears on the island of Tenerife – in between the Altavista.

the Roque Nublo towers heavenwards by itself. After a descent of 10 minutes, reach the junction on the **Degollada de la Cumbre (5)**. Here, ignore the trail turning right towards the road, and instead, turn left onto the path towards *La Culata* (a trail leading to Cruz de Tejeda immediately forks to the right – ignore this trail as well).

At the western slope of the mountain, **Andén del Toro**, descend along numerous bends; ignore a right-hand fork while descending. Not quite an hour later, reach the **Finca La Palmita (6)**, the first dwelling at La Culata. Climb down another 150m along the tarmac road, turn right at the fork and continue the descent for another 200m via steps to reach the village centre of **La Culata (7)** in 10 minutes. A bar and the bus stop are located to the right, but take the main street to the left for 200m, and after passing house No. 55, turn right onto a cobbled trail. Cross through the lush undergrowth in the *barranco* and reach a cul-de-sac for a street; at this point, the trail continues to the right. This ascends for a stretch past whitewashed houses. Ignore all the turn-offs to the right, take a break on a **stone bench (8)**, and a good hour later, reach the plateau with the car park for **La Goleta (1)**.

Camino de la Cumbre: spectacular trail through the central mountains

The trail to Cruz Grande, the "Grand Cross", at the pass of the same name, leads over pine tree-dotted slopes, past rocky caves, and then skirts around petrified, multi-coloured lava flows. Breathtaking views open up again and again into the island's extensive network of gorges. The final third of the route is cobbled the entire way and flanked by stone walls: not only a classic example of a traditional Camino Real, but also one of the most spectacular descents in the entire island! Between vertiginously steep rock faces, the climb down, although a short one, negotiates 400 metres of altitude.

Starting point: Ayacata, 1290m. Bus stop for line 18.

Destination: Cruz Grande, 1249m, a breach passage for the GC-60 Ayacata – San Bartolomé, km19.5 (near the bus stop for line 18).

Height difference: 530m in ascent, 570m in descent.

Grade: the walk leads mostly along an upgraded *Camino Real* with a short stretch on a track, but very rarely along roads – somewhat strenuous due to the height differences.

Refreshment: a bar in Ayacata; quite often you will find a food truck in La Goleta.

Note: this route is best organised using bus line 18. The line runs via Ayacata, as

well as via Cruz Grande. A tip for those approaching by car: to avoid any stress involving time schedules, you could drive to the destination, Cruz Grande, park your car and, from there, take bus No. 18 to the starting point in Ayacata.

Alternatives: 1) an excursion to Pico de las Nieves with Walk 7 from Degollada de los Hornos (5).

2) at the crest of the Cruz Grande pass, you have a good choice of walking variations. To continue on to San Bartolomé, keep right along the road and, before reaching the breach in the rock, pick up the track that forks to the left, blocked for cars by a chain (sign: *S-50 San Bartolomé*, see Walk 37).

The ascent from **Ayacata (1)** to **La Goleta (2)** is identical to Walk 3. With Roque Nublo to your left, follow the road eastwards and, 400m further on, arrive at a plateau viewpoint with stone benches at the **Cruz de Juan Pérez**. Along a cobbled trail (*S-51 Garañón*), descend for 300m to reach the reservoir dam, Los Hornos, down below. Cross over the dam wall and, after another 800m, reach a plateau. Here, veer to the right onto a track which leads, in 200m, to the recreational campsite, **Campamento El Garañón (3)**. Here, at the entrance to the camp, ignore a road that forks off to the left

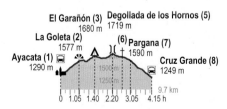

El Garañón (3) 1680 m — Degollada de los Hornos (5) 1719 m
La Goleta (2) 1577 m
Ayacata (1) 1290 m
(6) Pargana (7) 1590 m
Cruz Grande (8) 1249 m
1500 m
1250 m
9.7 km
0   1.05 1.40 2.20 3.05 4.15 h

(see Walk 4) and continue straight ahead for 50m, then turn right. A broad trail leads southwards, in 600m, to the GC-600. Cross over this road and pick up the signed trail *S-50 Cruz Grande 5.4km* to continue on. The trail runs parallel to the road, crossing through an open wood. About 600m further on, shortly before the trail touches upon the road again, turn left onto the stepped trail signed for the **Camino de Santiago (4)** to continue on. The trail runs parallel to the road, crossing through an open wood. About 600m further on, shortly before the trail touches upon the road again, turn left onto the stepped trail signed for the **Degollada de los Hornos (5)**, at 1719m – you will recog-

nise it by the concrete stanchion, tumbledown in the middle, and a nature park sign. From here, enjoy a marvellous view taking in the central mountains, including the summits of Moriscos, Roque Nublo and Pico de las Nieves – the last can be reached via the path on the left-hand side (see Alternative).

The trail keeps on a south-westerly course and descends through an open pine wood. At the junction, not quite 500m further on, continue straight ahead (here, you could follow the cairns to ascend in a few minutes to the window rock, Ventana al Nublo). Another 130m on, ignore a turn-off to the left which enters a steep secondary valley. 400m further, to the right, a **cross** (**6**; *cruceiro*) is enthroned above the trail; this was

En route along the cobbled Camino Real.

erected by a pilgrim in 1996. Where the trail crosses over a large, stony depression another 400m further on (low wall!), we recommend making a short excursion to the right to take in a dramatic panoramic view: across the terrain of a rocky abyss, gaze upon the Cloudy Crag; to the left of it, if the weather is clear, you can spot the sugarloaf summit of Teide on Tenerife.

Returning to the main trail, another 400m on, the Chira lake comes into view for the first time – far below, the lake shimmers in the distance. A little later on, reach the rocky, bitterly bleak high plain of **Pargana (7)** and then bear left from the eroded ravine. Where the trail veers off to the left, meet up with a cobbled *Camino Real* – now the dramatic part of the walk begins. In several steeply laid bends, the trail, flanked by thick walls, descends along the rim of an almost sheer rock face which is riddled with caves. Enjoy a breathtaking view of the greenish, shimmering Chira lake, the settlement of Cercados de Araña, and two small reservoirs that have been entrenched onto the sides of the rock face. Further down, the trail crosses over a little *barranco*. The trail begins to level out and then reaches, after passing an estate bearing crosses, the **GC-60**, which runs from Ayacata to San Bartolomé. Turn right here and immediately meet up with the breach in the rock, **Cruz Grande (8)** – the bus stop is situated not quite 100m on the other side of the breach.

Adventurous ascent to a secluded sanctum

Just like the Roque Nublo and the Roque Bentayga, the Montañón was a sanctum for the indigenous Canary Islanders. On the dizzying summit plateau, you feel closer to the heavens than to the earth and you can enjoy spectacular views in every direction. The first leg of the route climbs up along the edge of a labyrinth-like rock fortress with caves once used by the native inhabitants. The second leg of the walk is more relaxed. For the return route, or for a continued route, you can choose between several splendid variations.

Starting point: La Goleta, 1577m; GC-600, km11.2; car park; no bus service.
Height difference: 240m.
Grade: steep stretches and scrambling at the outset; good route-finding skills are demanded. As a whole, this is only a short walk, but with poor waymarking, and when dense clouds set in, the route is an especially difficult one.
Note: walkers can take bus No. 18 to

Ayacata and reach La Goleta via Walk 3 in 1 hr. If approaching by car, reach La Goleta via Ayacata (GC-60, km14.3; turn-off Roque Nublo).
Alternatives: from the Dogollada de los Hornos (5), use Walk 5 to head southwestwards to Cruz Grande, or use Walk 7 from Pico de las Nieves, and afterwards, via El Garañón with Walk 25 to return to La Goleta.

From the lower edge of the car park, **La Goleta (1)**, a path, protected by railings, ascends steeply (sign: *S-51 Circular Llanos de la Pez / Dgda. Los Hornos / Pico de las Nieves*). The path is waymarked by cairns and zigzags in many bends – passing pine trees and broom – upwards and veers to the right. On a knoll, meet up with a concrete **boundary marker (2)**, where the steep ascent comes to a temporary

end. The marker is the first one of several bearing the inscription *Cabildo 1953*, all of them marking the border between the communities of San Bartolomé and Tejeda. In front of us, we can spot the dome on top of the "Snowy Summit", and behind us, we observe the craggy "entourage" of the Roque Nublo.

Continue with the concrete marker on your right-hand side and, 260m further on, bear diagonally left at an inconspicuous junction. After only another 80m, meet yet another junction: from below, the towering rock face standing before us seems to be invincible, but despite appearances, there is a way to scale this! Bear right at the aforementioned junction and scramble up along the steep rock face along an alpine path, where you cannot avoid using your hands. Cairns are a help in route finding. At a little rise in the middle of the rocky terrain, we can take a bit of a breather. The path then veers to the left and leads through a breach in the rock; afterwards, turn right and cross through a rocky defile to reach a steep shelf to scramble over this up to a **breach in the rock** looming in front of us.

Scrambling stretch below Montañón.

On the summit plateau of **Montañón (3,** black/white metal sign), enjoy a stunning panoramic view: Montañón, the connecting link between the "Cloudy Crag" in the north-west and the "Snowy Summit" in the south-east, opens up a view of them both – between them lie steep, pine-covered slopes, gorges, and high terrain. Now walk on, crossing over grey basalt, peppered with rocky boulders, towards the summit column and skirt around beneath it to the right to continue (cairns!). As you walk along it, the trail becomes more and more distinct and is flanked from drystone walls as it opens to a view of the three reservoirs, Niñas, Soria and Chira. At a point where the wall is interrupted by a steep shelf, scramble carefully down over the rock – a little later, the wall begins to appear again – and then reach a **saddle (4)** at yet another concrete marker. From here, the route is simple; continue ascending along the ridge through an open pine wood. To the left, you can spot an occasional sparkle, marking the reservoir of Los Hornos. 800m on, reach the saddle and a trail junction, the **Degollada de los Hornos (5),** betokened by a boundary marker from 1953 and a sign, *Monumento Natural Riscos de Tirajana*.

If you prefer not to return along the same route back to **La Goleta (1),** you can take one of the alternative routes instead.

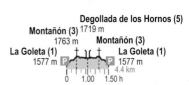

Degollada de los Hornos (5)
Montañón (3) 1719 m
1763 m   Montañón (3)
La Goleta (1)   La Goleta (1)
1577 m   1577 m
4.4 km
0   1.00   1.50 h

7 From Cruz Grande to Pico de las Nieves

Spectacular ascent to the "Snowy Summit"

A great walk: long stretches of the route are cobbled and laid out in pleasant bends as it ascends from the arid southern island to the interior through a variety of microclimates and plant communities. Even though the 1949m-high "Snowy Summit" was decrowned in 2019 when the neighbouring 1956m-high Morro de La Aguejerada was awarded the title "Gran Canaria's highest mountain", the view is still magnificent!

Starting point: Cruz Grande, 1249m. On the GC-60, Ayacata – San Bartolomé, km19.5; bus stop for line 18.
Height difference: 750m.

Grade: due to the height differences it's challenging.
Refreshment: there is often a food truck at the finish.

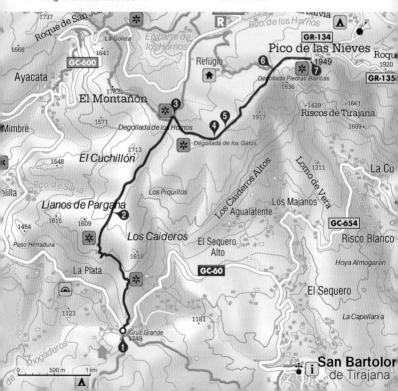

From the Mirador at the Pico de las Nieves it takes a few steps to the viewing platform.

From the breach in the rock, **Cruz Grande (1)**, head back for 50m in the direction of San Bartolomé, then turn left onto the upwards-oriented, broad trail (sign: S-*50* = *Camino de Santiago*). A little later, the trail hooks to the right and leads to a rest area with three crosses. At the adjacent house (barking dogs!), the trail becomes a cobbled *Camino Real*, then continues steeply upwards and opens a downwards view into the basin of San Bartolomé; later on, also into the La Plata valley. 20 mins later, you can catch your breath somewhat along a stretch of trail running on the level, before the dramatic ascent begins: in cleverly-laid bends, artfully cobbled, and, when necessary, flanked by supporting walls, the trail clings to the steep slope – a masterpiece of local handiwork! The abyss lies below us and gigantic boulders are posed above, thus we continue the climb upwards by the sweat of our brows. Pass a little water reservoir, cut into the rock face, then reach the **Llanos de Pargana (2)**, a reddish-coloured high plain, which we cross over with the aid of cairns and tread marks towards a pine forest.

The trail becomes distinct as it leads gently through the open wood, just slightly below the mountain ridge. 15 minutes past the high plateau, pass a **wooden cross**; to the right, a chasm opens up: the upper reaches of the deeply furrowed and rugged Barranco de Tirajana. From the wooden cross, the route keeps on the level at first, then begins to ascend over widely spaced steps leading past the left-turn to the "Nublo Window" – the hole in the rock known as Ventana al Nublo – to reach the **Degollada de los Hornos** pass **(3)**, marked by a tumbledown concrete column, placed there by the

At the Piedras Blancas pass: the last rest break before the steep ascent.

island council, as well as a nature park sign. The broad *Camino Real* leads straight ahead to the GC-600, but we change over to a forest path to the right which has been waymarked by walkers with cairns. Passing through open pine forest, the path leads, in 15 minutes, to a broad saddle, the **Degollada de los Gatos (4**; "Cats' Pass"), and from there, keeping to the left-hand side of the ridgeline, continue for 670m to reach a **junction (5)**. To the right, you could climb Campanario in an additional 30 minutes (there and back), but we continue straight ahead, crossing over a broad trail 400m further on, and after another 300m, reach the saddle of the **Degollada Piedras Blancas (6)**. From here, continue straight ahead, passing the boundary markers established in 1953. Soon, a view opens up of the military installation on the summit of the island's highest mountain. Cross over a rocky terrain, veer to the left, and pass through a breach in the wall to reach the **mirador (7**, 1939m, viewpoint plateau) on the **Pico de las Nieves**. From here or – even better – from the viewing platform that can be reached via a gentle climb, you can enjoy a magnificent view before you head back along the return route already met on the approach, to **Cruz Grande (1)**.

Short ascent to the island's highest peak

When the weather is clear, from the viewpoint plateau on the Pico de las Nieves, the "Snowy Summit", enjoy one of the most beautiful panoramic views that the island has to offer. To the north-west, the chain of mountains marking the Tejeda gorge run together like the walls of a fortress. No less dramatic is the view to the south-west, where sheer, rugged rock faces frame the Caldera de Tirajana.

Starting point: the picnic area, Llanos de la Pez, 1655m; GC-600, km8.1. No bus service.

Height difference: 320m in ascent and descent.

Grade: a moderately difficult walk, mostly along good trails; from the "shelter" (Refugio) to Pico de las Nieves, you need route-finding skills.

Refreshment: often a food truck on the viewpoint plateau of the Pico de Las Nieves or a bar in Lllanos de la Pez.

Accommodation: campsite and wooden huts in the Campamento El Garañón (see page 25).

Note: this walk is best approached by car. If you are approaching by bus, you have a choice: either take bus No. 18 to Ayacata, then via Walk 3 to La Goleta and with Walk 4 to El Garañón; or take bus No. 305 to Cruz de Tejeda and, with Walk 25, continue to El Garañón. From there, in 600m, meet the GC-600; turn left and reach the starting point in 5 minutes.

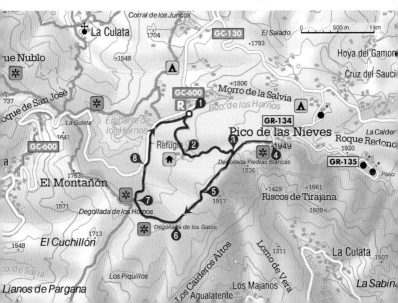

At the rest area, **Llanos de la Pez** (**1**, GC-600, km8.1) a forestry track, opposite from the wall-enclosed water reservoir, sets off into the forest (sign: *S-51 Circular Llanos de la Pez/Pico de las Nieves 2.4km*). In 700m, this leads to a **Refugio (2)** which is now a holiday home for children. Behind the first of the two houses making up the complex, take the track veering off to the left, only to leave it again, 150m further on, by turning left again onto a non-descript path, marked by cairns. This leads steeply up the slope and then merges, a good 200m on, into the dried-up stream bed of a *barranco*; take this to continue ascending. Where it levels out, 250m on, ignore a broad trail forking off to the right, and instead, continue a few paces more to turn diagonally right onto a

Sunset on the Pico de las Nieves:

narrow path (cairns) which leads into a little hollow. Above us, we can spot the destination for this leg of the route peeking out between the pine trees: the light-coloured ridgeline shimmers through. The narrow *camino* now ascends steeper upwards and brings us, in a few minutes – constantly flanked by cairns – to the **Degollada Piedras Blancas** pass **(3)**. On the concrete marker erected here you can read the inscription *Cabildo Insular 1953*. The landscape is splendid: as if cut by an axe, the rock face plunges down towards the south, a craggy monolith looms out of the abyss and, behind it, the gigantic rock face of a mountain towers up, topped by a "rock window". Turn left, ascending, and pass by several community boundary markers. If the weather is clear, a view opens up of the military installation on the island's highest peak. Afterwards, the trail winds across rocky terrain and veers to the left. Through a breach in a wall and a plank, we make our way onto the viewpoint plateau (**Mirador, 4**, 1939m) on the **Pico de las Nieves** – you will get an even more dramatic view from the viewing platform which can be reached via a gentle climb. Afterwards, head back and, in 25 minutes, return to the **Degollada Piedras Blancas (3)**. Keep heading straight on towards a rocky knoll, cross over a broad trail and, 5 mins after that, at a **junction (5)**, ignore a left-hand turn to the panoramic peak of Campanario. From this point, the pleasant and always distinct trail runs along the right-hand side of the slope – sometimes on the level, sometimes descending. 600m further on, cross

above a sea of clouds with a view towards Tenerife, reigned over by Teide.

over the crest of the pass **Degollada de los Gatos (6)**, and after a short as-cent climb down to reach the trail junction at the **Degollada de los Hornos (7)** 800m further on. This is marked by a communal boundary marker which is no longer intact, and a sign: *Monumento Natural Riscos de Tirajana*. A left turn heads to Cruz Grande (see Walk 5); straight ahead to Montañón (see Walk 6; difficult). But instead, turn right and continue descending along a well-restored *Camino Real*, the *Camino de Santiago*, for 1.3km. The final stretch leads over stone steps and then you can spot the **GC-600 (8)** in front of you.

In order to avoid walking over tarmac, veer off to the right and keep parallel to the road while crossing through a pine forest and heading for the starting point. 500m further on, at a bend in the road, ignore the trail forking off to the left towards El Garañón and, in a good 5 mins, reach the rest area **Llanos de la Pez (1)**, the starting point for the walk.

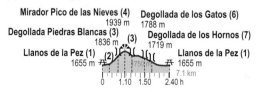

55

9 From Cruz de Tejeda to the Cuevas del Caballero

Panoramic circular walk at the central pass

This short walk offers a fabulous view over the weather-battered fortress-like mountains reaching all the way across the sea to Tenerife! Even the island's indigenous people were intoxicated by the view: at the turn-around point of the walk, hidden amongst boulders, the "Caves of the Lord" were discovered. These were decorated with triangular engravings that allude to the female sex and probably served for rites of fertility. Afternoon is the best time to go when the

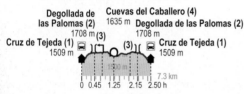

light enters the darkness of the cave. You can also watch the rocks glow at sunset. The return route leads over a forest track and, in open terrain, presents marvelous views.

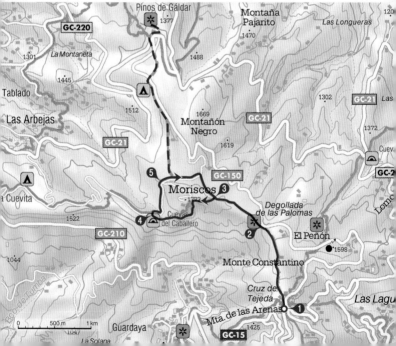

Starting point: Parador Cruz de Tejeda, 1509m. Pivot point for the island's major roads; GC-15, km24.5; bus stop for line 305.

Height difference: 360m.

Grade: only steep and strenuous at the beginning, afterwards in easy up-and-down walking along a well-laid trail and forestry track. If the wind is blowing hard and gusty and cloud cover is dense, the stretch between WP 3 and 4 is somewhat risky for the vertigo-prone, therefore it is better to keep to the forestry track instead.

Refreshment: restaurants at the Cruz de Tejeda.

Accommodation: hotel Parador in Cruz de Tejeda (see p. 28), accommodation for every pocket can be found in Tejeda.

Alternatives: 1) if you are approaching by car and you wish to avoid the steep first stretch, begin the walk at the viewpoint on the Degollada de las Palomas (2), access via the GC-150 Cruz de Tejeda – Pinos de Gáldar, near km9.2) combination with Walk 10 from the Cuevas del Caballero (4) to Artenara. 3) past the junction at the Cruz de los Moriscos (5), you can use Walk 20 to continue on to Pinos de Gáldar and, from there, to Fontanales (Walk 21) or Guía (Walk 55).

Ascent through open pine forest.

The starting point for the walk is the stone cross at **Cruz de Tejeda (1)**. Between the Hotel Parador and the souvenir stands, follow the GC-150 northwards towards Pinos de Gáldar. 200m on, reach a car park where two trails begin to the left: ignore the *Camino Real* to Teror (see Walk 22) on the right, and instead take the wide trail *S-90* which sets off farther to the left (marked, unless the signs have been removed, *S-90 Artenara*). The trail ascends steadily, soon narrows, and leads left past a water reservoir surrounded by a wall. The trail winds up the western slope of the mountain for another 5 minutes before it levels out and opens up spectacular views.

Pass black, club-shaped crags. The locals have named one of them Roque Franco – its silhouette looks like a profile of the former dictator. 30 minutes later, reach the road to Pinos de Gáldar. Turn left and follow this road for 100m to reach a roofed viewpoint, the **Mirador Degollada de las Palomas (2)**: the whitewashed houses of Tejeda lie down below, and above them, a dramatic mountain stage setting with the peaks of the Roque Nublo and Roque Bentayga.

Rock arch at the Cuevas del Caballero.

Next to the *mirador*, the trail which starts out cobbled ascends to the right. Soon the trail broadens out to become a dirt track and then levels out. 900m from the viewpoint, you have to keep an eye out because we leave the track behind at a **junction (3)** by turning left onto a narrow path; a trail sign points out the direction with *Artenara / Agaete*. The trail leads to an open col, then veers to the right and continues on from one projecting rock to the next, constantly keeping just at the edge of the precipice; a real high ramble with spectacular downwards views of bizarre rock formations.

Another 1.2km on, the trail merges into a forestry track and, a couple of paces to the left, a sign points out the way to the native Canarian "Caves of the Lord", the legendary **Cuevas del Caballero (4)**. It is worthwhile to step through the rock window and – just as the indigenous people used to do – enjoy the breathtaking panoramic view: on the opposite side, the Roque Bentayga towers heavenwards; further to the left, the Roque Nublo. To the right, you will see the fenced-off entrances to the caves which can only be reached via a precipitous alpine path (if wet or foggy, dangerous!). Looking through the grid, all you can see is darkness – the ritual triangular engravings that decorate the caves are only faintly visible if the light is exactly right. Afterwards, return to the forestry track and turn right onto it. From the pine forest, you can gaze across undulating hills to get a glimpse of Tenerife. 750m further on, pass a stone cross from the year 1913 (**Cruz de los Moriscos**) and a **trail junction (5)**: straight ahead leads to Valsendero, while a sharp right leads to a lookout tower and the aerials perched on the peak of the Morisco at a height of 1771m. But, follow the forestry road to the right to the *Cruz de Tejeda*. and 2 minutes later, ignore the left-hand fork, marked by low stone walls, that leads to Pinos de Gáldar (see Walk 20). Another 5 minutes later, also ignore the left-hand fork to Valsendero. 360m further on, reach the **junction (3)**, where our circular route first started off. Now head straight on and, at the **Mirador Degollada de las Palomas (2)**, pick up the trail already used on the approach to descend back to **Cruz de Tejeda (1)**.

Delightful pass route along the meteorological divide

This trail introduces the splendid landscape of the island's interior in a very leisurely fashion: softly rolling slopes covered in pines to the north; deep gorges and rugged rock faces in the south. Except for the steep stretch at the outset, the route mostly follows trails and forestry tracks that present only small height differences to negotiate. The destination is Artenara, Gran Canaria's highest lying settlement which sports a pretty village centre, as well as cave dwellings.

Degollada de las Palomas (2) 1708 m
Cuevas del Caballero (4) 1635 m
Cruz de Tejeda (1) 1509 m
Cruce Las Peñas (5) 1605 m
(6) Artenara (8) 1220 m
1500
1250
7.3 km
0 0.45 1.25 2.25 2.45 h

View westwards at the Cruz de Tejeda.

World of stone: a rest break at the "Caves of the Lord".

Starting point: Parador Cruz de Tejeda, 1509m. Pivot point for the island's major roads; GC-15, km24.5; bus stop (line 305).
Destination: Artenara, 1220m. End of the line for bus No. 220.
Height difference: 270m in ascent and 560m in descent.
Grade: steep and strenuous at the beginning; afterwards in leisurely up-and-down walking along forestry tracks and good trails. By strong wind, somewhat vertiginous; the northern side is often shrouded by the trade winds clouds.
Refreshment: nothing en route. Bars and restaurants at the Cruz de Tejeda and in Artenara.
Accommodation: comfort hotels in Cruz de Tejeda; *fincas* close to Artenara.
Note: from Artenara, there is no bus service to Cruz de Tejeda (only a few lines connect Las Palmas via Teror), therefore, we recommend taking a taxi back to the starting point. Or, from Artenara, you can take the route you met up with during the approach to return to Cruz de Tejeda. Due to the strenuous ascent, plan for 3 hours of walking time.
Alternatives: 1) i you wish to abort the walk at the Cuevas del Caballero (4), connect up with Walk 9. 2) if you prefer to walk to Artenara and back again from there, so as to avoid the steep first stretch, and you are approaching by car, begin the walk at the viewpoint on the Degollada de las Palomas (2), which can be reached via the GC-150, Cruz de Tejeda – Pinos de Gáldar, near km9. 3) combinations possible with Walks 11 and 13 (from Artenara).

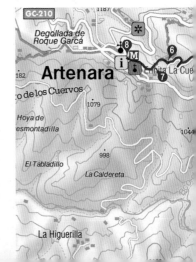

The walk starts off from the Parador, the state-run hotel at the **Cruz de Tejeda (1)**. The course of the walk via the **Mirador Degollada de las Palomas (2)** and the **junction (3**, sign: *Artenara / Agaete*) to the **Cuevas del Caballero (4)** is identical to Walk 9.

After enjoying views of the caves and caldera to your heart's content, return to the track and turn left onto it. At the junction, 600m further on, the **Cruce Las Peñas (5)**, leave the track behind by turning left onto a trail which winds downwards in many bends, then returns to the track after 700m. Subsequently, ignore tracks forking off to the right (600m on) and then forking to the left (another 240m further). 2 minutes later, watch out for a path forking off diagonally to the right and use it to short-cut a broad bend in the track.

Afterwards, return again to the track and, 5 mins later, reach a major **trail crossing (6)**. A right turn heads towards Fontanales / Teror, but turn left instead. The trail soon becomes cobbled as it descends along the slope in the direction of *Artenara*. The trail leads to the **Degollada Cruz de Toríl (7)**, a breach in the bedrock located below a cross, where a far-reaching view opens up of the mountains and the valley basin of Tejeda. Climb up the concrete-paved track past the cross, then immediately left via a stepped trail, to climb down to the viewpoint platform of the **Ermita Virgen de la Cuevita**. Usually, the meshed entrance gate to the "Chapel of the Virgin of the Cave" is only ajar, so you can take a look at the chapel which has been hewn out of the rock face in its entirety. A good 500m along the signed village street, reach the centre of **Artenara (8)** where you can find the MECCA cave museum, the Risco Caído interpretation centre, the panorama restaurant La Cilla and the Unamuno viewpoint.

Panoramic descent to the high plateau of a flat-topped mountain

Many walkers use this splendid trail as an approach route for the Acusa circular walk (Walk 12). From Gran Canaria's highest mountain village, the trail descends along the rim of a gigantic basin to the flat-topped mountain of Acusa. Almost from the outset, you have the mesa before your eyes: an expansive, high plateau that is a pillar of tranquillity in an untamed alpine world.

Starting point: Artenara, 1220m; the last stop for bus No. 220.
Height difference: 410m.
Grade: an easy walk along a steeply-laid, but well-maintained trail.
Refreshment: nothing en route. Bars and restaurants in Artenara.
Accommodation: you can rent country homes in and around Artenara on a weekly basis; there is also a cave hostel

in Artenara (see p. 28).
Note: approaching from the north, you can take the bus via Teror to Artenara, however the schedule is such that the return trip is often difficult. For walkers approaching from the south, it is best to drive there with a hire car (approach via Tejeda or La Aldea de San Nicolás).
Alternative: combination possible with Walk 12 from Cruz de Acusa.

Walk past the Arte Gaia shop (good for supplies) and the Centro de Interpretación Risco Caído to leave **Artenara (1)** behind by heading westwards along the road towards Tamadaba. At the roundabout, 400m on, keep straight ahead along the steeply ascending tarmac track towards the cemetery (*cementerio*), pass the garage for the fire brigade 5 minutes later (*Servicio Contraincendios de Medio Ambiente*) and, just a little later, reach the **village cemetery (2**; with a helicopter landing pad). Here, turn left to ascend

Flat as a tabletop: the mesa of Acusa.

along a broad dirt track (signed *Acusa*, but also *San Pedro 6.15 / Area recreativa Llanos de la mimbre 3.15*). The track leads, in 250m, to a viewpoint plateau on the **Degollada de Roque García (3)**.

Here, ignore the track leading straight ahead (Tamadaba/Agaete and Altavista/La Aldea; see Walks 13–16) and, instead, take the descending trail *S-88* diagonally left, signed for *Acusa* – down below is the Tejeda gorge and in front of us, just a little later, spot the whitewashed houses of Vega de Acusa at the right-hand edge of the flat-topped mountain. Like a monstrous stone table with a flat top, the mesa squats in the midst of a ferocious landscape: ragged ridges and arêtes everywhere you look! Sometimes descending in zigzags and sometimes cobbled, then, over huge, trodden plates of rock, the route climbs steeply down through an open pine wood. 30 mins later (from the viewing platform), cross over a **track (4)**, then the route continues via a rocky ridge.

15 mins later, circle around a farmstead in a wide bend and, at the next **junction (5)**, follow the sign towards *Acusa*. Ignore all of the paths forking off to the left or to the right and, 5 mins later, at the junction, **Cruz de Acusa Seca (6)** reach the GC-210 leading to La Aldea de San Nicolás – in front of us is the high plateau of the mesa: in the spring, this is covered in golden fields of grain; in winter, with pastureland.

Return along the approach route back to **Artenara (1)**.

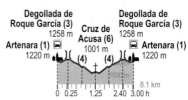

Degollada de Roque García (3) 1258 m
Cruz de Acusa (6) 1001 m
Degollada de Roque García (3) 1258 m
Artenara (1) 1220 m
Artenara (1) 1220 m
(4) (4) 1000 m
8.1 km
0   0.25   1.25   2.40 3.00 h

Panoramic trail with native Canarian cave dwellers' settlements

Our trail leads along a narrow outcrop of rock circling around the flat-topped mountain and presents one of the most remote corners of the island. The cave dwellings of Acusa Seca squat down in the shade of steeply rising rock faces and take in a fantastic view of the jagged mountain ridges of the Caldera. In the second leg of the walk, ascend along a little-used road to the parochial village of Vega de Acusa, then continue the ascent to the high plateau of the same name. In winter, the plateau becomes a lush pastureland for sheep and goats.

Starting point: Cruz de Acusa, 1001m. No bus connections, the next bus stop is in Artenara, line 220 (see Note).

Height difference: 270m.

Grade: uncomplicated walk along well-laid trails; the second leg leads over a little-used road in a picturesque landscape.

Refreshment: the next stores and inns can be found in Artenara.

Accommodation: cave-dweller lodging in Acusa Seca. You can rent country houses in and around Artenara on a weekly basis.

Notes: to approach by bus: there is no bus service from Artenara to Acusa so

you would have to combine this walk with Walk 11 (starting point and destination, Artenara). Approach by car: since the car park at the entrance to the village of Acusa Seca is only accessible via a narrow road, we recommend parking your car in front of the Candelaria church (Waypoint 7) and starting the circular walk from there. An additional advantage: because of the new alternative trail (marked on our map with a broken line), you can now walk directly from the Candelaria church to Acusa Seca (Waypoint 2) and thereby shorten the route (via the tarmac road) by 1.8km. At Waypoint 7, watch out for the sign "S-88 Acusa Seca 1km".

At the wooden cross, **Cruz de Acusa (1)**, follow the narrow, hardly used tarmac road to *Acusa Seca (S-88)*. A few minutes later, we can already enjoy a marvellous view of the settlements in the island's interior, as well as the craggy pillars of Bentayga and Nublo. The road ends about one kilometre, just before reaching the village of **Acusa Seca (2)**. Cave dwellings with whitewashed entrances squat down under amply protruding rock faces, some are still abandoned, but others have been renovated and serve

Embedded in the rock face of the flat-topped mountain: the cave dwellings of Acusa Seca.

as weekend homes. Follow the long, stony trail leading through the village. To the right leads to the entrances of the cave dwellings, but instead, we descend, while ignoring all of the paths forking off to the left. At the end of the settlement, reach the lowest-lying cave dwellings. 30 min after leaving the village behind, the trail skirts in a sharp half circle round a mighty **rocky spur (3)** on the southern side of the flat-topped mountain –the first terraced fields appear in front of us. At a chain barrier, 10 mins later on, the trail merges into a **track (4)**: in front of us, the terrain has been ploughed for potato fields, and from the dark green leaves of the trees, oranges gleam brightly. 230m further on, reach the **GC-210 (5**, La Aldea – Artenara, km-marker 16), bear right and, shortly afterwards, meet up with the hamlet of **Acusa Verde (6)**: white-washed cube houses nestle under a mighty rock face. You can refresh yourself at the spring, El Chorrillo, below the road – opposite house No. 12, steps descend to the dark cave.

Now follow the little-used GC-210, which winds up from Acusa Verde, along many bends,

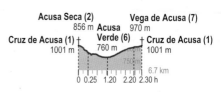

In winter, flowers festoon the high plateau of Acusa.

towards the island's interior. Above the small reservoir, La Candelaria (just past the km-marker 13), lies **Vega de Acusa (7)**, a handful of houses clustered around the Candelaria church: with the benches under Indian bay trees, this is a lovely spot for a picnic.

From here, continue along the GC-210 for another 800m to reach the cross, **Cruz de Acusa (1)**, where the circular walk around the high plateau first sets off.

Panoramic walk with attractive variation

This scenic trail leads above the road for long distances and, time and again, offers lovely views taking in the summit terrain of the north-west island, deep cut valleys and pine-covered slopes. This is the approach route to the Mirador del Sargento, where Walk 15 to Altavista begins, and to the outset of the Ring Road, where the circular route for Walk 16 around the Tamadaba starts off.

Starting point: Artenara, 1220m; the last bus stop for line 220.

Height difference: 550m in ascent and descent.

Grade: easy walk along well-maintained *Caminos Reales* and tracks.

Refreshment: nothing en route. Bars and restaurants in Artenara.

Accommodation: you can rent country homes in and around Artenara on a weekly basis; there is also a cave hostel in Artenara.

Note: approaching from the north, you can take the bus via Teror to Artenara, however, the schedule is such that the return trip is often difficult. For walkers approaching from the south, it is best to use a hire car (approach via Tejeda or La Aldea de San Nicolás). Convenient parking in front of th Centro de Interpretación Risco Caído.

Alternative: combination with Walk 16.

Well-marked: Degollada de Roque García.

Walk past the Centro de Interpretación Risco Caído to leave **Artenara (1)** behind by taking the road heading westwards towards Tamadaba. At the roundabout, 400m further on, continue on by keeping straight ahead and ascend along the steep tarmac track crossing through the district of Los Co-fritos. 5 mins later, pass the building of the local fire brigade and, a little later, reach a cul-de-sac located above the **village cemetery** (**2**; with a helicopter pad). Turn left here and ascend along a broad dirt track. This leads, 200m further on, to a viewing platform on the **Degollada de Roque García (3)**.

Ignore the trail forking diagonally left and descending towards Acusa (see Walk 11), and instead, keep straight ahead along the broad trail *S-90* towards *Tamadaba / Agaete*. At the outset, this ascends with a view of the Tejeda basin, but then continues along the ridge, opening up a view of Lugarejos and the verdant north. 10 mins later, the trail veers to the left, and a little later, peering between the branches of the pine trees, catch the first downwards view of the little reservoir, Las Hoyas, far below. When the high plateau of Acusa comes

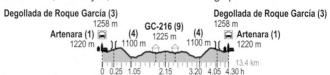

Degollada de Roque García (3)
1258 m   GC-216 (9)   Degollada de Roque García (3)
                          1225 m   1258 m
Artenara (1) (4)   (4) Artenara (1)
1220 m   1100 m   1100 m   1220 m

13.4 km

0   0.25 1.05   2.15   3.20 4.05 4.30 h

into view, begin a descent along steeply-laid zigzag bends to reach the **GC-210** down below. Cross over this road and ignore the trail towards *Coruña/Lugarejos* that forks off to the right, instead, keeping straight on, follow the sign for *Tamadaba/Agaete*. At the **road junction (4)**, a minute later, continue on along a trail that runs above and parallel to the GC-216. This crosses the road 300m further on, at first to the right, then to the left, where it temporarily ascends more steeply. Some minutes later, the trail merges once again with the GC-216 – a bench in the shade is an invitation for a rest break. Turn left onto the road and, in a good 130m, reach a charming, rustic viewpoint, the **Mirador del Sargento (5)**.

Here, too, the continuation of the route is marked by stones. A good 5 minutes of steep ascent brings us to the trail junction **Cruz de María (6)**. Turning left leads to Altavista (see Walk 15), but we ascend to the right through a pine forest. After a total of 800m, where the trail begins to drop down, pass an inconspicuous junction (cairn!) and then keep right; do the same at the more distinct junction 200m further on. Now continue along a ridge, where far-reaching views open up on either side, and then descend over steps to the road at the **Tirma forestry house (7)**. 120m further on, leave the road behind by turning left and following the sign *Agaete*.

The *camino* leads along the ridge above the road and then touches upon it, after a total of 2km, at the **Cruz de Eulogio (8)**. Afterwards, the trail veers away from the road and climbs up through an open pine wood. Another 500m further on, the trail merges into a track and the track immediately merges into the **GC-216 Ring Road (9)**, where traffic is routed around Tamadaba anti-clockwise.

If you prefer an easier stretch, leading along trails sometimes above, sometimes below the road, while circling the 1443m high Tamadaba, continue on, following Walk 16.

Otherwise, return along the approach route to **Artenara (1)**.

Descent with a view of the little reservoir, Las Hoyas.

Exploratory walk in the cloud forest

Broad and pleasant, the trail runs high above villages and two little reservoirs. At the turn-around point, pass a forestry house, then continue along a ridge-line with a far-reaching view over terraced slopes and softly undulating mountains. The trail then leads constantly through pine forests; the smell of pine sap fills your lungs. If the north-east trade winds are blowing, enjoy a real treat: on the approach, lovely wisps of cloud rise up and the scene changes into an enchanted forest; along the higher return route, these wisps usually disappear and the landscape comes alive again in the bright sunshine!

Starting point: Parking bay at the GC-216, 1110m, 800m north-west of the Acusa junction for GC-210–216–217; no bus connection. Approach possible from Artenara via Walk 13 (1.30 hrs).
Height difference: 190m.

Grade: the walk leads along a well-laid soft, spongy trail – this is one of the few island routes with a negligible difference in height.
Alternative: combination from Cruz de María (5) with Walk 15 to Altavista.

At the starting point, the **GC-216, km0.8 (1)**, and to the right of the guardrail, follow the sign *Las Hoyas / Lugarejos*. 60m on, a little stone ramp begins the descent through the pine forest. 600m further on, or 8 minutes later, pay close attention: at an inconspicuous **junction (2)**, veer off to the left and follow a lovely trail that leads parallel to the slope in easy up-and-down walking, opening up downwards views of the hamlets and the reservoirs of Coruña and Las Hoyas. After a total of a quarter of an hour (or 2km), at a **trail**

Far-reaching view from the mirador on the Degollada del Sargento.

junction (3), continue straight ahead towards *Tamadaba / Agaete* (a right turn would descend to Las Hoyas / Lugarejos). Another kilometre further on, ignore a steep descending, trodden-down path and continue again straight ahead. 8 minutes later, reach the GC-216, turn left onto it and immediately pass the **Tirma forestry house (4)**. Another 130m on, leave the road behind by turning right, following the sign for *Artenara / Cruz de Tejeda*. Now ascend along the ridgeline through an open pine wood. At the next fork, it doesn't matter which trail you choose since both merge together again just a little later on. At the following **Y-junction**, a good 100m further on, a right turn would lead to Altavista, but instead, take the left-hand lower trail and subsequently keep high above the road which appears, time and again, through the branches of the trees. 10 minutes later, the trail descends more steeply and leads, in 100m, to the junction, **Cruz de María (5)**.

Following the sign *Artenara / Cruz de Tejeda*, descend for another good 200m to reach the viewpoint **Mirador del Sargento (6)** with a fantastic 360° view. Turn right along the road, but 150m further on, at a rustic wooden bench, leave it behind again by turning right. The final stretch leads through an open pine forest – and then we arrive at the **GC-216, km0.8 (1)**, the starting point of our walk.

Casa Forestal
de Tirma **(4)** Cruz de María **(5)**
1185 m   1190 m
GC-216 Km 0,8 **(1)**   **(3)**   GC-216 Km 0,8 **(1)**
1110 m   1110 m
                                            5.8 km
0   0.35 1.15   2.00 h

A splendid walk along a mountain ridge

This is a walk that no one should miss! Pleasant and lofty, it leads to the summit of the Altavista which, as its name implies, counts as one of the island's most beautiful viewpoints. It is not rare that one will spot a brownish-grey mottled bird of prey, shooting down like an arrow from the steep faults in the rock face: the Barbary falcon, a bird whose praises are sung far and wide.

Starting point: Mirador del Sargento, 1153m, a viewing platform, 5km west of Artenara on the road to Tamadaba, GC-216, km1.4; no bus service.
Height difference: 450m in ascent and descent.
Grade: an easy walk along a *Camino Real*, a Royal Trail, which is only strenuously steep at the beginning and at the end.
Note: this walk is ideal for walkers with a

hire car; at the starting point, there are only a few possible parking spots. Unfortunately, a bus service exists only as far as to Artenara (line 220), from there with Walk 13 to the Mirador del Sargento, the starting point for the walk (1.30 hrs, one way).
Alternatives: 1) combination possible with Walk 13 from Cruz de María (2).
2) the continued route from Altavista to La Aldea de San Nicolás (4.30 hrs, 13.5km) is only a delight at the beginning. Most of the time, the walk leads along a ridge, through a pine forest at first, then through a desolate landscape characterised by spurge and broom. After about 3 hrs of walking, you reach a saddle at the Morro de las Tocinas (762m), where the weary climb down to La Aldea, lasting one and a half hours, begins: very few trees have found a niche in the barren slopes and, on the valley floor, unsightly dwellings and tomato farms covered in plastic sheeting make up the view.

From the viewing platform (parking possible on the verge) at the **Mirador del Sargento (1)**, follow the broad-laid trail that ascends to the right of the slope. After 220m of an ascent that is sometimes steep, reach the trail junction **Cruz de María (2)**. Here, bear left to continue

The view from Altavista towards the east and the Barranco de la Aldea.

the climb (to the right leads to Tamadaba, see Alternative). The trail soon runs in a south-westerly direction along the ridgeline and leads pleasantly through a pine wood. After a total of about 30 mins, the first beautiful view opens up of the mountains. Afterwards, the trail runs sometimes along the eastern side and sometimes the western side of the ridge. Pass the Risco Alto on our right-hand side and then descend via numerous bends to the saddle **Lajas del Jabón (3)** below. Cairns point out that the trail continues below the smooth boulders. 5 mins later, reach a major **junction (4)** at the foot of the Altavista: to the right, the *Camino Real* leads to Aldea de San Nicolás (see Alternative), but we continue to the left of it, ascending along the zigzag trail to the summit. The **Altavista (5)** is at a height of 1377m and you must reckon on 30 mins to negotiate the 600m long stretch, there and back. The additional effort is rewarded with a fantastic view into the rocky gorge of La Aldea: below, to the left, the high plateau of Vega de Acusa, to the right of it, the Parralillo reservoir, and enthroned above it, on a precipitous steep rock face, the houses of El Carrizal are clustered in the midst of a bizarre, forbidding mountain terrain.

Return along the approach route via the **Lajas del Jabón (3)** and the junction at **Cruz de María (2)** to arrive back at the starting point on the **Mirador del Sargento (1)**.

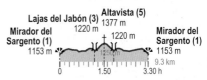

73

Panoramic trail through open pine forest

Amongst the Tamadaba walks, this one is especially recommended: the route is not very long and differences in height are minimal as it leads above, sometimes below, the Ring Road. Even when dense wisps of cloud are billowing on high, losing your way is almost impossible. The practical advantages are joined by scenic ones as well. The route leads through open pine wood and gives way to changing panoramic views: terraced slopes to the north, sheer rock faces and Tenerife to the west, and to the east, the central mountains from Roque Nublo all the way to Roque Bentayga.

Starting point: the outset of the Tamadaba Ring Road, GC-216, 1210m. No bus connections.
Height difference: about 180m in both ascent and descent.
Grade: mostly an easy walk along a well-laid and often shady trail without a great difference in height.

Note: you can park your car at the starting point for the walk. At important junctures, where you have to enter the wood from the road, a numbered point is noted on the map.
Alternatives: combinations possible at the Casa Forestal Tamadaba (6) with Walks 17, 18 and 19.

At the outset of the **Ring Road (1)**, bear diagonally to the right and head along the GC-216 anti-clockwise – don't worry: a car will be passing here only about once an hour! 620m on, leave the tarmac behind by turning left onto a cobbled trail forking off (**2**; the first entrance into the wood). A good 100m further on, ignore the left-hand fork that heads to the summit of La Bandera and then meet up with the Ring Road another 200m after that. 40m further, leave the road behind again, this time by turning right (**3**; the second entrance into the wood), and then walk on a terrain of soft, spongy pine needles, at first on the level, and then ascending, in 10 minutes, to the GC-216. On the opposite side of the road, the trail continues (**4**; the third entrance into the wood) and leads, in 300m, to a **trail junction (5)**. Follow the sign by heading straight

On the return route, pass the lovely picnic area perched on a rocky plateau.

ahead to the *Casa Forestal*, and meet up once again with the road after not quite 300m; veer left onto it. Not quite 500m further, pay close attention: leave the tarmac behind by turning onto a trail, inconspicuous at first, (fourth entrance into the wood). This leads just above the GC-216 and, 200m on, merges back into it. 200m further on, pass the **Casa Forestal (6)**, a forestry house in splendid solitude (see Alternative). A minute later, leave the tarmac behind by turning right into the wood, following the trail signs *Artenara / Cruz de Tejeda* and *Risco Faneque* (fifth entrance into the wood). 360m on, reach a **fork in the trail (7)**: diagonally right heads to Risco Faneque (see Walk 17), but instead, bear diagonally left towards *Artenara / Cruz de Tejeda*. A minute later, pass above the Cueva del Zapatero, a house with a chimney, and then ascend along a trodden path diagonally to the left. The trail becomes broad again and pleasant as it runs through numerous secondary gorges before ending up on a reddish, **rocky plateau**. Here, enjoy a marvellous view of the periphery of the Risco Faneque – a lovely spot for a picnic!

A couple of paces further, the trail merges once more with the Ring Road, then leaves it again 40m to the left (**8**; the sixth entrance into the wood). The view reaches far over the pine-covered slopes and to the "Cloudy Crag". Now the trail drops down in a wide bend back to the road. After 300m, reach the starting point at the **Ring Road (1)**.

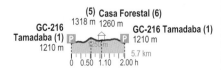

From the Tamadaba forestry house to the foot of a craggy megalith

Those who have visitied Puerto de las Nieves, have already had the chance to marvel at it: the sheer rock faces of the Risco Faneque soar over 1000 metres into the sky; further south, the coast drops in a spectacular series of zig-zags – the "Dragon's Tail" – down to the sea. But now we want to get a closer look at the Faneque while approaching from the interior: a descent through open pine wood with a constantly stunning panoramic view – you can gaze over 30 kilometres of the rugged west coast all the way to Sardina.

Starting point: Casa Forestal Tamadaba, 1260m. No bus connections; the nearest settlement is Artenara (bus No. 220), from there, approach via Walks 13/16.
Height difference: 280m.
Grade: the walk is short and well-laid, but there is an appreciable height difference to negotiate – the way back is steep and rather tiring. Be sure to avoid the midday heat!

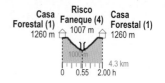

Alternatives: combinations from the Casa Forestal with Walks 16, 18 and 19.

At the **Casa Forestal (1)**, the forestry house on the Tamadaba Ring Road, continue on in the same direction as traffic. Leave the road again, 100m on, at a right-hand fork with the trail sign *S-91 Risco Faneque*. Now walking on soft, spongy pine needles, the trail leads through an open pine forest and is sometimes flanked by cairns. 5 mins later, meet up with a junction: diagonally to the left, a wooden sign points out the way to *Artenara/Cruz de Tejeda*,

Risco Faneque appears between the pines with Tenerife in the background.

but instead, follow the descending trail diagonally right towards *Risco Faneque*. Pass a stone-built house with a chimney and then a striking cave dwelling follows, the **Cueva del Zapatero (2)**; at this point, the trail (here, marked *blue/yellow*) descends sharply to the right. 50m on, the trail veers to the left and soon, the destination for our walk, the Risco Faneque, appears between the trees in front of us. At the next junction, continue descending straight ahead and, at the **junction (3)** that follows, 100m further on, bear left. A few minutes later, continue along the ridgeline and, where it ends, the rugged, gigantic crag rises up – from here, you can already spot it; diagonally left from the crag, you can see the jagged west coast. As soon as the trail continues on along the right-hand side of the ridge, the north-western tip of Gran Canaria also comes into view. Follow the trail steadily downwards and ignore a turn-off to the left. 100m further on, reach a panoramic rocky plateau and continue the descent on the right-hand side of it. After another 500m, that is a total of 2.1km, reach the **Degollada Risco Faneque (4)**. If you wish, continue along the right-hand flank of the slope to reach a rocky ledge, where the Faneque drops down vertically.

But we begin the strenuous return route instead – during the next 1.5km, we must negotiate a height difference of 250 metres. At one point, pay close attention: 1.2km past the Degollada, reach the **junction (3)**, but ignore the left-hand trail which leads to the picnic area of Tamadaba. You could continue straight ahead, but it is easier to take the trail forking to the right, along which, another 380m further on, we reach the **cave dwelling (2)** already met along the approach route. Now breathe a little easier: afterwards, meet up with a trail sign at a junction, another one at the road, and then take the road to return to the **Casa Forestal (1)**, 100m further on.

1.15 hrs

A short circular walk over spongy terrain is a constant pleasure

When the sun beats down, the dense pine forest provides refreshing shade; if cloud cover forms, the wisps are caught up in the branches of the trees, creating a cryptic ambience. Clear skies bring about splendid, far-reaching views, and time after time, the blue sea sparkles in the sunlight. The wind whispering through the pine needles produces a peculiar "musical background".

Starting point: Casa Forestal Tamadaba, 1260m. No bus connections; the nearest settlement is Artenara (bus 220); from there, approach via Walks 13/16.
Height difference: 175m in ascent and descent.
Grade: easy circular walk along a well-laid, waymarked trail.
Alternatives: combinations from the Casa Forestal with Walks 16, 17 and 19.

Next to the **Casa Forestal (1)**, the forestry house on the Tamadaba Ring Road, a cobbled trail, flanked by low stone walls, starts off towards *La Bandera*. In the shade of fragrant pine trees, ascend steeply – in front of us,

The Tamadaba forestry house at the starting point.

blocky boulders are scattered about; behind us, the sea sparkles between the branches of the pines. At the **junction (2)**, a good 900m on, veer off to the left towards *El Hornillo – Agaete* (turning right, heads towards Artenara – Cruz de Tejeda). Another 700m further on, at a **left-hand fork (3)**, cairns point out the way for an excursion to the summit of the Pico de Bandera at 1443m (there and back, an additional 10 minutes). We, however, bear diagonally right to continue along the main trail, now slightly vertiginous. Shortly afterwards, catch some views of a reservoir to the right, looming above it, the silhouette of the Roque Nublo, and in the background, the bay of Las Palmas; above us is an observation tower and, somewhat later on, a weather and radar installation.

Along broad, zigzagging bends, the trail climbs down to a **junction (4)**: to the right heads towards Artenara – Cruz de Tejeda, and straight ahead to Tamadaba – Agaete, but we turn left, heading for the *Casa Forestal*. 260m on, we are back on the **Ring Road**, **GC-216** (**5**, km6.7). Turn left onto it and another 500m further on, at a wide bend, use a trail to the left as a shortcut. Now reach a **road junction (6)**. By turning left, 5 minutes later, reach the **Casa Forestal (1)**, the forestry house at the starting point for the walk.

Ascent between pines and boulders.

A walk through a pine wood on the northern side of the Tamadaba

Circle around the panoramic summit of Tamadaba through a pine forest. In every season and all weather, this walk is simply marvellous: either sunbeams flicker through the dense treetops or wisps of cloud scurry up the slopes. Along the way, you will be delighted by a rustic picnic area, a romantic spring in a forest and a viewpoint taking in the west coast all the way over to the island of Tenerife.

Starting point: Casa Forestal Tamadaba, 1260m. No bus connections; the nearest settlement is Artenara (bus 220); from there, approach via Walks 13 / 16.

Siete Pinos (4)   Mirador El Reventón (6)
1330 m   1210 m
Casa Forestal (1)   Casa Forestal (1)
1260 m   1260 m
3.7 km
0   1.05 1.30 h

Height difference: 150m in ascent and descent.
Grade: an easy circular walk along a well-laid, waymarked trail.
Alternatives: combinations possible from the Casa Forestal with Walks 16, 17 and 18.

From the **Casa Forestal (1)**, the forestry house at the start of the walk, follow the Ring Road eastwards and, a good 300m on, reach a **road junction (2)** and bear right. A trail runs parallel to the road, but very quickly merges again into it. 500m further on, take a signed **turn-off to the right**, which ascends, in 250m, to a **trail junction (3)**. Straight on leads to Artenara – Cruz de Tejeda, but instead, follow the sign for *Tamadaba / Agaete* and ascend to the left. On the rise lying ahead, the wood opens up again and, over a rocky terrain, you descend again to the Ring Road. On the opposite side of the road, marked by a low stone wall, there is the point marked on the map as **Siete Pinos (4)**. Descend via steps and, not quite 100m further on, veer left onto a forest

Quaint stone-built house in the Tamadaba forest.

path signed for *Tamadaba/Agaete*. Passing lichen-draped pine trees, cross over narrow secondary valleys until, a good 15 mins later, you meet up with an **intersecting track**: turning right heads to Agaete (*Sendero a San Pedro*, see Walk 52), but instead, bear left towards *Tamadaba* and then pass a rustic **picnic area**. At a quaint **stone-built cottage (5)** with an information board, veer diagonally right and follow the trail sign towards *Mirador El Reventón*. 100m further on, reach the **Fuente El Reventón**, a stone circle in the wood with benches set in a wall. From this eerie spot, descend via steps to **Mirador El Reventón (6)** down below, a viewing platform presenting a spectacular downwards view of Gran Canaria's steep west coast. On a bench cut into the rock face, you can spend some time contemplating the panorama.

From the viewpoint, return along the approach route back to the **stone-built cottage (5)**. Here, climb back up a couple of metres to the track and then turn right to reach a car park on a tarmac track. A right turn would bring you to the *zona de acampada*, but instead, turn left to ascend, in 200m, to the **Ring Road (7)**. Turn right onto the road and, in a good 300m, turn right at the **junction (2)** to return to the starting point at the **Casa Forestal (1)**.

From Pinos de Gáldar via the Cuevas del Caballero to Moriscos

A long circular walk with great diversity! From a large volcanic crater, descend through pine forest and then ascend over terraced mountains into the area around Artenara. The continued walk is spectacular, leading along rugged precipices while presenting a constant view of the "Snowy Summit" and the "Cloudy Crag". Crossing over pitch-black lava fields, return pleasantly back to the starting point.

Starting point: Mirador Pinos de Gáldar, 1510m. On the GC-21, Teror – Artenara; bus stop for line 220 (very little service).

Height difference: 700m in ascent and descent.

Grade: due to the length and the great differences in height, this is a strenuous walk reserved for physically fit walkers, partially marked as *S-05*.

Refreshment: bar in Las Arbejas; restaurants in Artenara, the hotel is slightly off the trail in Juncalillo.

Note: for holidaymakers staying in the south, the approach to Pinos de Gáldar is via Cruz de Tejeda; for those in the north,

via Fontanales or Teror. Bus 220 (infrequent) ascends to the starting point from Las Palmas via Teror.

Alternatives: 1) if you wish to visit Artenara during the walk, at the junction (6), continue straight ahead and, 200m further on, reach another junction. Now pass a cross while ascending over a slope and descend along a stepped trail to reach the viewing platform in front of a chapel cave. Now take the village street for a good 500m to end up at the centre of Artenara. 2) if you prefer to end the walk in Cruz de Tejeda, at the fork in the trail (9), pick up Walk 9.

Pinos de Galdár and the sea of clouds brought about by the trade winds.

Lomo de los Galeotes (2)
1325 m
Mirador Pinos de Gáldar (1)
1510 m

Cuevas del Caballero (8)
Las 1636 m (9)
Arbejas (5)
1300 m (6)

Cruce Fontanales (10)
1700 m

Mirador Pinos de Gáldar (1)
1510 m

1500 m
1250 m

14.4 km

0   0.40   2.00 2.25   3.40 4.20 5.00 h

From the rustic viewpoint, **Pinos de Gáldar (1)** – with a plaque Monumento Natural del Montañón Negro – follow the GC-21 westwards towards Artenara. 200m on, a trail crosses the road; this is flanked by walls. Here, take the right-hand fork which descends through an open pine wood. A good 5 mins later, a lava ramp, flanked by stone walls, is left behind by turning left along a narrow trail, stepped with wooden boards, which skirts around a section of the volcanic slope in a wide bend (semicircular). Not quite 10 minutes later, the stone wall with the lava track is met again; veer left onto this and continue straight on for 400m to descend to the trail junction, **Lomo de los Galeotes (2)**: turning right leads to Fontanales (Walk 21), straight ahead to Gáldar/Guía (S-01, see Walk 55),, but we follow the sign S-05 to the left towards *El Tablado 3km/Artenara 7km*.

The trail descends through the pine forest to a ruin, and then ascends to a stone wall; there, turn left to continue while losing height. Now leave the forest behind and then the scenery completely changes: terraced slopes, where sometimes sheep and goat herds are roaming, the Tamadaba massif in the distance, and on the horizon, the sugar loaf shape of Teide's summit on the island of Tenerife. After a total of 2.4km, cross over the **GC-220 (3**, 1350m) for the first time and pick up a trail, at first cobbled, that descends to a tarmac track. Bear left onto the track, but leave it behind again only a minute later by turning sharp right onto a trail forking away. 300m further on, continue straight ahead and, after another 150m, turn left onto the GC-220, which we have already met. 5 minutes later, pass the km-marker 22. Then two minutes later, turn left onto the GC-224 and ascend towards *El Tablado* (at the junction, there is a bus stop for the lines 106 and 220, which is seldom serviced). A good 500m after that, at the junction at the village limits of **El Tablado**, take the lower trail which soon narrows, and passing cave dwellings, leads to the **valley floor (4)**. There, ignore the trail turning off to the left, signed for *Moriscos/Cruz de Tejeda*, and instead, turn right, ascending the slope to a tumbledown house – pass it by and keep towards *Artenara*. Cross over another valley notch, ignore a new turn-off to Cruz de Tejeda, and not quite 15 minutes later, reach the village limits of **Las Arbejas (5)**. Turn right onto the village street, but leave it behind again 20m on by turning left onto a dirt track forking away. This crosses over the valley floor and climbs up to the GC-21, turn right along this road (sign: *S-05 Artenara*). 60 metres on,

The cave dwellings at El Tablado.

leave it behind again by turning left onto a broad trail that is cobbled at the outset (sign: *Paisaje Protegido*). The *camino* ascends, then veers left and opens a view of the first houses of Artenara. Keeping to the same height, reach a major **junction (6)**. If you would like to take the time for an excursion to Artenara, 1km away, continue straight ahead (see Alternative). We, however, bear left at the junction and climb up the trail that has been cut into the rock face (sign: *Cruz de Tejeda*). At the junction another 80m on, turn right and, 40m after that, reach a forestry track where we turn left to continue the ascent. Yet another 220m further on, and then it is possible to short-cut a bend in the track along a *camino* forking off to the left (cairns). Naturally, you could keep to the forest trail which ascends through the open pine forest. 2 minutes after the short-cut trail merges from the left into the track, ignore a right-hand fork. 3 minutes after that, at a track junction, bear right to ascend. 600m on, leave the track behind by turning right onto a trail marked by a stone ramp (directional sign: *Cruz de Tejeda*). Immediately after, a fantastic view opens up: on the ridge opposite, you can spot the petrified exclamation mark of the Roque Nublo, further right, the Roque Bentayga, and far below, the Caldera de Tejeda. This marvellous panorama will accompany us for the next 40 minutes or so since the trail leads for a long stretch along the sheer drop at the rim. 300m further on, the trail snugs up to the track, but afterwards, begins to wind in bends, ascending the slope until, at the trail junction, **Cruce Las Peñas (7)**, it merges once again with the track: the forest trail straight ahead leads to Las Peñas; turning left onto the track leads back to Artenara. Instead, follow the track to the right towards *Cruz de Tejeda* and leave it behind again, 600m further on, at the blocky boulder of the **Cuevas del Caballero (8**; information board) by turning right onto a trail forking away. Just at the edge of the sheer drop at the rim, you can enjoy splendid downward views, as well as far-reaching ones.

Now the following leg of the route, 1200m in length, is the most dramatic of the entire walk – presenting splendid, far-reaching views and downward views, furrowed rock faces and abrupt sheer drops! Afterwards, the trail veers away again from the sheer drop at the rim and then descends along a stony ramp to a **fork in the trail (9)** down below; here, bear left onto the track (turning right heads to Cruz de Tejeda, see Alternative). Chestnuts and pine trees provide a dark and shady stretch of trail. 300m further on, ignore the turn-off to the right towards Valsendero and keep along the track towards *Artenara / Agaete*. Exactly 440m on, turn right onto the **turn-off for Fontanales (10)**, unsigned when last walked, but marked by a flanking wall. The broad trail narrows 400m further on and low flanking walls set the further course. To the right, you can spot the "Black Mountain" (Montañón Negro, see photo p. 19) that looks like a slice of craggy cake.

500m further, the trail merges into the **GC-150 (11)**; turn left and follow the road. 280m on leave it behind again by turning right onto a trail, cobbled at the outset. This leads through open groves and then crosses over volcanic scoria fields to descend to the road. Cross over the road and descend further via zigzags and over lava to the GC-21 down below. Turn right onto the road and, in a few minutes, return to the **Mirador Pinos de Gáldar (1)**.

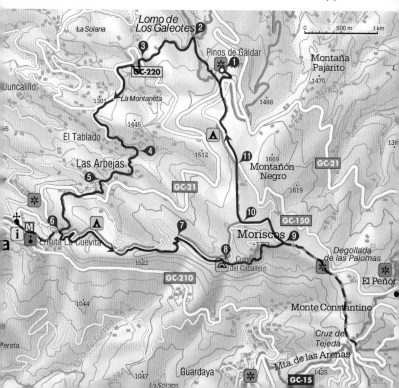

An extinct volcano, verdant grassland and fields

A tour of contrasts: the starting point is the Pinos de Gáldar crater, which, with its almost perfect circular form and its dark, gentle volcanic slope, sets a very good example of recent volcanism. It was created a "mere" 3000 years ago, the reason why the forces of erosion have had relatively little time to wash away the softer materials. During the descent to the mountain village of Fontanales, the scenery changes: after conquering the volcanic slope, you ramble over lush pasturage where sheep are grazing. The return route leads over verdant grassland with pines and chestnut trees.

Starting point: Mirador Pinos de Gáldar, 1510m. On the GC-21, Teror – Artenara; bus stop for line 220 (but hardly serviced).

Height difference: 520m in ascent and descent.

Grade: due to the differences in heights, a somewhat strenuous walk leading over scoria at the outset and then mostly along a well-laid *Camino Real*; on the return route, also along tracks.

Refreshment: bars and restaurants in Fontanales.

Accommodation: hotel and *fincas* in Fontanales (see also p. 28).

Note: the starting point is especially suited to holidaymakers approaching by car from the south or the area around Tejeda. If you are on holiday in the northern island (or if approaching by bus), best start the circular walk in Fontanales.

Alternatives: linking possibilities with Walk 20 and Walk 55 from Lomo de los Galeotes (2); Walk 58 from Fontanales (5).

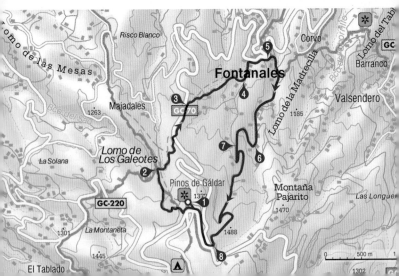

From the **Mirador Pinos de Gáldar (1)**, look down into the 100m-deep crater and also over northern Gran Canaria all the way to Las Palmas. On the western slope of the crater rim, some mighty hundred-year-old Canary Island pine trees are growing, giving the *mirador* its name: "Pines of Gáldar" (the viewpoint belongs to the community of Gáldar). From the viewing platform, follow the GC-21

Trail sign on the Lomo de los Galeotes.

westwards towards Artenara. 200m on, leave the road behind by turning right onto a trail forking away which is flanked by low stone walls at the outset. This descends through a pine forest, crossing over a terrain of soft, springy pine needles. A good 5 mins later, the trail merges into a broad lava ramp, flanked by walls, which descends steeply over the north-west slope of the crater. Since this stretch is extremely slippery under foot, it is better to take the trail, sometimes stepped with wooden boards, forking away to the left in a sweeping bend, before it merges again into the lava ramp 400m on – the ramp is more level at this point. After descending another 400m, reach the trail junction at the mountain ridge of **Lomo de los Galeotes (2**; 30 mins from the starting point). A sharp left leads to Artenara (Walk 20), straight ahead, to Guía/Gáldar (Walk 55), but instead, follow the narrow trail to the right towards *S-05 Fontanales 3km*. 5 minutes later, cross over a track. Afterwards, the trail traverses a mountain slope while keeping to the same height, then leaves the pine wood behind and meets up, 15 mins later, with the **GC-70**. Turn left onto this road for 400m, and just before reaching **km-marker 26 (3)** veer to the right and turn into the ancient *Camino Real*.

The trail climbs down the slope in broad bends and passes numerous groves of eucalyptus and chestnut. In the valley on your right, you can see pastures for grazing, and further down, a sports ground. After a good 15 mins descent, reach the valley floor: to the right, there is a picnic area; to the left, **house No. 8 (4)**, bearing the in-

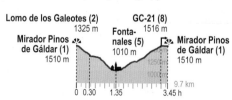

Lomo de los Galeotes (2) — 1325 m
GC-21 (8) — 1516 m
Mirador Pinos de Gáldar (1) — 1510 m
Fonta-nales (5) — 1010 m
Mirador Pinos de Gáldar (1) — 1510 m
1250 m
1000 m
9.7 km
0   0.30   1.35   3.45 h

At the Mirador Pinos de Galdár; in the background, Teide on Tenerife.

scription *Camino del Valle*. Turn left onto the track heading northwards that starts off here and, a little later, meet up with the road running from Juncalillo to Fontanales (Calle Juan Mateo de Castro). Turn right onto this street and, 10 mins later, reach the village centre of **Fontanales (5)** at the junction of the GC-70 and the GC-75.

Leave the main street behind by turning right onto the steeply ascending Calle La Montañeta. This street leads past a shrine that has been embedded in a tree and then, a little later on, you ignore the left-hand fork to Valsendero (see Walk 58). Now keep straight ahead, following the tarmac-paved *Camino de Agua de Fontanales* for 15 minutes, while slightly ascending. At **house No. 24 (6)**, bear right and the tarmac road becomes a dirt track. Past some stables built into caves (the barking dogs here are chained!), the track ascends diagonally to the left. 300m further on, ignore the fork to the right and our track veers off to the left. From now on, enjoy a far-reaching view while descending. 5 minutes later, reach a **junction on the valley floor (7)** and meet up with a broad roadway. Turn left onto this road and, at the next junction, one minute later, bear left again. The track leads along the fenced-in property of a farmstead, and after negotiating two hairpin bends, ascends to terraced pasturages up above, then winds in pleasant bends to pass a ponderous concrete building.

Passing through a terrain with open stands of eucalyptus, ascend from here, for a good half hour, to the GC-70 up above, which immediately merges into the **GC-21 (8)**. Turn right onto the GC-21 and, 600m further on, reach the viewpoint, **Mirador Pinos de Gáldar (1)**, the starting point for this walk.

Historical pilgrims' route to the village of the wooden balconies

Once this was the route taken by pious peasants from the remote mountain villages while they were on a pilgrimage to the miraculous Madonna in Teror. The restored Camino Real leads through a reforested pine wood and passes an extinct volcanic crater where sheep graze on its mossy slopes. To wrest cultivatable land from the mountainous terrain, farmers have created step-like terraces; on the little garden plots, potatoes, corn, and orange trees are growing. The destination for this walk is one of the most beautiful towns on the island: the historical pilgrimage site Teror, with feudal royal palaces and shady squares surrounding the church.

Starting point: Parador Cruz de Tejeda, 1509m. Pivot point for the island's major roads; GC-15, km24.5; bus stop for line 305.
Destination: Teror, 591m. Bus stop for lines 216 and 220.
Height difference: 150m in ascent, 1050m in descent.
Grade: despite the great difference in

height, this is an easy walk (waymarking for the trail: *RP-GC 01*) along good trails, sometimes also along tracks and tarmac.
Refreshment/Accommodation: hotels, bars and restaurants in Cruz de Tejeda and Teror.
Note: for this walk, the best approach is by bus – easy to organise from Las Palmas.

The walk begins at the road junction of the state-run *parador* **Cruz de Tejeda (1)**. Follow the road that leads to Pinos de Gáldar, the GC-150, north-westwards, and reach a car park, 200m on. On the left, two trails start off: take the *S-10* towards *Valleseco-Teror* which is cobbled at the outset: pass to the right of the little power station and then ascend along the south-east slope of **Constantino**; this is the only steep ascent during the entire walk. Head for the striking round building while crossing over water-eroded ochre-coloured bedrock. Not quite 30 mins later, at the **La Cruz Chica pass** (**2**; power pylon), meet up again with the GC-150, Cruz de Tejeda – Pinos de Gáldar. This is the highest elevation for the walk. On the opposite side of the road, a cobbled trail continues, climbing down in a northerly direction. About 15 mins later, the trail crosses over a valley floor and passes **El Peñón**, with boulders covered in rosette-shaped flora on the right-hand side; here enjoy a far-reaching

La Cruz Chica (2)
1620 m
Cruz de 🚌 Lanzarote (4)
Tejeda (1) ⎬(1160 m Barranco Madrelagua (6)
1509 m 920 m Las Rosadas (8)
747 m
🚌 Teror (9)
591 m
11.8 km
0 0.30 2.00 2.50 3.45 4.30 hrs

view taking in the northern half of the island. Now the trail steadily descends, passing pines and holm oaks. Past water basins, fields and animal enclosures, now reach the GC-21; turn right onto this road and walk for a few paces to meet up with the road junction, **Cuevas de Corcho (3)**. From the road that heads towards Valleseco to the left, turn immediately right across a ramp onto a cobbled trail and follow this for about 10 mins to reach a mountain ridge (just before, ignore a trail forking off to the right). In the circular volcanic crater, **Las Calderetas**, a farmstead with stables and storage sheds is nestled between elm and chestnut trees. Now the trail drops down and skirts to the right around the farmstead at an ample distance. Pass a livestock watering tank and, along a dirt track heading northwards (concrete along a short stretch), reach the GC-21 at the southern limits of **Lanzarote (4)**. Turn right along this road and, 100m on, pass a roofed wash-house; nowadays, you will rarely see women actually doing the washing here (**Lavaderos de Tierras Blancas**). 200m further on (a junction with a circular viewpoint), the broad GC-21 descends to the settlement's centre. We, however, bear right and pick up the GC-214 heading to *Madrelagua*. At the junction, 470m further on, continue straight ahead towards the *Centro Urbano*. After another 470m, reach the mountain ridge, **Lomo de la Rosa (5)**: past house No. 11, continue again straight ahead, but leave the (now tarmac) track behind only a few paces further on and take the trail diagonally right to descend; this is often overgrown with grass. Down below is the lovely, green **Barranco Madrelagua**. Now ignore all of the forks to the left while descending steeply to the valley floor. 15 mins later, bear left onto a narrow road which ends, 250m further on, at a house situated on the valley floor. After crossing

View into the Barranco Madrelagua.

over a small **bridge (6)**, a narrow path ascends for 5 mins through a lemon grove (sometimes via steps) to a track up above; tarmac at the outset. Turn left onto the track and cross over the western slope of the mountain **Moreno** for 15 mins 10m before reaching a **garage (7**; right-hand bend!) leave the track behind by turning left onto a vertiginous path forking away; this meets up with another track, 40m on. This track becomes a path at house No. 64, which shortly afterwards, crosses over the *barranco* floor to the left. Within 10 mins, reach the hamlet of **Las Rosadas (8)**: here, the trail merges into a tarmac track; take this for another 10 mins until meeting up with the GC-21. Turn right onto this road, but leave it behind again, a good 100m on, by turning right onto a (signed) trail forking away. 10 mins later, we are following the Calle Isla de Gran Canaria, which descends to the GC-21 down below. Turn left onto this road, but leave it behind again, 100m further on, by turning right onto the tarmac-paved Camino de Buenavista. 4 mins later, cross over the road, descend via steps to a park down below, then bear left and pick up the Calle Casa Huertas to ascend to the pilgrimage church in **Teror (9)**.

To continue on by bus: follow the Calle de los Balcones, which sets off just opposite the main entrance to the church, until it ends. At this point, turn right, and at the Red Cross, turn left. Pass the car park for the town hall and the police station to reach the bus station (a 10 minute walk).

Delightful circular walk through the island's most water-abundant gorge

The ascent through the Barranco de la Mina is a delight, both winter and summer: in the dense undergrowth of the ever-verdant gorge, mountain spring water is constantly gushing and, in many spots, waterfalls cascade from way up high, down to the valley floor. The barranco widens in the upper reaches to create pastureland where sheep sometimes graze. Along a panoramic trail, keeping to the same height, return to the starting point of the walk.

Starting point: Cruz de Tejeda, 1509m. Pivot point for major island roads; GC-15, km24.5; bus stop for line 305.
Height difference: 420m in ascent and descent.
Grade: a pleasant descent along well-laid trails until reaching Las Lagunetas; a very steep ascent through the Mina gorge along an alpine path that is precipitous in many places, requiring sure-footedness and a perfect head for heights. After rainfall, the stretch through the gorge is not recommended because the terrain is very slippery when wet.
Refreshment: bars and restaurants in Cruz de Tejeda and Las Lagunetas; a

food kiosk is often in service at the Degollada de Becerra.
Accommodation: hotels in Cruz de Tejeda (see also page 20).
Note: this walk is well-suited for both those walkers approaching by bus or by car. Parking is possible behind the Hotel Parador, 150m west of the junction, Cruz de Tejeda.
Alternatives: 1) if you prefer to avoid the stretch at the outset, take the No. 305 bus heading to Las Lagunetas; there is a bus stop directly at the entrance to the Mina gorge (WP 3). 2) from the Degollada de Becerra you could link up with Walk 25 (to La Goleta).

At the junction of **Cruz de Tejeda (1)**, between the GC-150 and the GC-15, to the right of the information kiosk, the stone-paved trail *S-15 (Las Lagunetas / Teror)* – hidden behind traffic signs and often crammed with parked cars – descends over steps heading northwards. At the outset, the trail is flanked by chestnut trees; later on, an occasional nut tree is mixed in. 430m on, the trail crosses the GC-15 for the first time and then continues on the opposite side, before it crosses the road a second time, 700m further on. The trail winds down numerous bends while passing many houses, and then is concrete-paved for a short stretch. Before a field, the trail hooks off to the left. Shortly after that, meet up with the road yet again above the **Bar Perera (2)**.

View back to the Barranco de la Mina.

Now ascend along the road for 70m, then turn left onto a precipitous track and head towards an iron gate but immediately veer off to the right. Flanked at the outset by the walls of houses, soon the trail breaks out into the open air as it leads along a railing (do not climb down to the street!). The trail passes more houses while heading south-eastwards and then merges into the GC-15. Turn right along this road (passing a picturesque house with the inscription "Estanco") and walk for 10 mins along the tarmac through a green, terraced mountain landscape. At the bus stop on the GC-15 (km19.8), just before meeting up with a narrow *barranco* bed, often flowing with water, turn right onto a narrow street which is signed **Barranco de la Mina (3)**. Pass several houses and, 200m on, past the last house, ascend along steps and then immediately bear left. 140m further on, ignore a turn-off to the left and then, at the fork after, another good 100m later, descend along a path to the left into the murky *barranco* floor down below. Moss is growing on eternally damp rock faces and gnarled branches dangle above the narrow gorge where a small stream is gushing. After rainfall, a waterfall is tumbling down here. Cross over the bed of the *barranco* and climb up the trail along the slope. Steps cut into the rock face and stairs, reinforced by wooden logs, facilitate the steep ascent on a narrow and slippery path which requires you to be sure-footed and free of vertigo.

Rocky steps in the Barranco de la Mina.

Ignore numerous turn-offs to the right – these lead to the very edge of the sheer drop and allow views of waterfalls which form here after periods of heavy rainfall. Having ascended for a good kilometre through the *barranco*, you will have managed the toughest part once you reach the **junction (4)**. Ignore the trail to the left, which is supported by low walls and leads to a concrete conduit (see Walk 24), and turn right instead. Shortly afterwards, pass a ruin which has become overgrown with flora, and then pass some **caves**, cut into the rock face. In front of us alpine pastures start to appear. A good 300m further on, yet another sign of civilisation appears. Where the stream drops down into the depths like a waterfall, in the building next to this point, there is a **water mill (5)**, which is used even today to grind *gofio*, one of the staple foods of the Canary Islanders. The *barranco* widens now and opens up to let in the sunshine once again. The vegetation changes accordingly; replacing the jungle created by the Aeonium are open, terraced pasturages where sometimes sheep are grazing. During the following stretch, cross over the *barranco* floor several times and continue by walking along a drystone wall. Near an oblong building which is fenced in, you meet a **trail junction (6)**. Turn right along the broad trail ascending to **Degollada de Becerra (7)**, a viewing platform located on the GC-150. From here, enjoy a fantastic view of the dramatically furrowed, oval-shaped, Caldera de Tejeda.

The last leg of the walk takes you northwards from the Degollada de Becerra. A well-groomed path runs parallel to and above the road and touches it twice. Afterwards, the trail merges into a track; turn right onto the track and pass a house with a fence around it. At the end, the track leads along a wall on the western slope of the mountain **Morro de la Armonía**. Along the entire stretch all the way to Cruz de Tejeda, enjoy a splendid view toward the west. Passing to the left of a restaurant, meet up with the junction at the **Cruz de Tejeda (1)**.

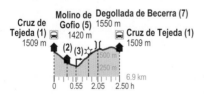

Panoramic trail around a gushing gorge

First, a descent into a valley of rushing waters, then a long, level stretch continues: the northern half of the island lies at our feet and the view reaches all the way to the Canteras bay in Las Palmas. This panorama will soon be surpassed when the view opens up of the "Cloudy Crag", reigning over a deep valley. Especially when the alpine pasturages are lush and green, when little waterfalls gurgle after the winter rains, this walk is an absolute delight.

Starting point: Degollada de Becerra, 1550m. GC-150, km2.3; approach only possible by car (car park).
Height difference: 250m.
Grade: mainly easy walk along well-laid trails and tracks. Because of the negligible difference in height, this is one of the few walks on the island that can also be undertaken by inexperienced walkers.
Refreshment: sometimes a food truck is available at the starting point.
Note: if you are approaching by bus, use the service to Cruz de Tejeda, then follow the description for Walk 25 to reach the Degollada de Becerra (an additional 1.30 hrs, there and back).

From the viewing platform at the **Degollada de Becerra (1)**, first tear yourself away from the fantastic view of the "Cloudy Crag", then cross over the road and descend along the broad trail *S-16* towards Talmulde. 260m on,

Downward view of Las Lagunetas; the bay at Las Palmas in the background.

Degollada de Becerra (1) 1550 m — Pata-burro (5) — (7) 1470 m — Degollada de la Cumbre (9) 1570 m — Degollada de Becerra (1) 1550 m

6.8 km

0   0.50 1.35   2.30 h

reach a **T-junction (2)** – in front of you is an oblong building that is fenced-in. The path on the right leads to the Degollada de la Cumbre, but you keep left and follow the *S-16* signpost towards *Las Lagunetas / Santa Brígida* which leads you downhill past low walls with railings. In spring, the terraced fields are buried in a sea of flowers; in the other seasons, blanketed by a verdant fluff. 130m further on, pass a *finca* and, after not quite another 600m, hidden away in a dense copse, pass a water mill, where the precious water cascades down like a waterfall.

300m on, you pass two caves on your right and a **ruin of a house (3)** on your left. After 60m, you reach an inconspicuous but important **fork (4)**. On your left is the Barranco de la Mina trail (compare Walk 23 in the opposite direction). Keep right here, walk past a fenced-in spring and follow a walled-in water canal. Weather-beaten rock faces which seem like gigantic sculptures tower above the canal. The view stretches across steep green slopes and a gently undulating high plateau all the way to the volcanos of the peninsula in front of Las Palmas – this panorama will be with us until the end of the walk.

About 1km from the fork we reach the small plateau **Pataburro (5)**. Here is a junction for several trails. Now leave the *S-16* behind (this continues on to Las Lagunetas), ignore the concrete track ascending to the right and, instead, turn diagonally right along the broad trail to continue. We can simply saunter along for the next 1400m: this is a marvellous stretch of trail with a view of a gently undulating slope, reigned over by a jagged mountain ridge. Pass a concrete ruin on the right and, 5 mins later, pass the entrance to a farmstead (already visible since a long time now) on the left. (Please pass by quietly and do no leave the track which is marked as private!). Shortly before reaching a **T-junction (6)**, you step over a chain that is stretched across the path. We

On the return route to the Degollada de Becerra along the rim of the Caldera de Tejeda.

veer right (arrow towards "*S-19 Degollada La Cumbre / A.R. Ana López*") to join a track which is also closed off by a chain. Count your steps, after only 20m you reach an inconspicuous path branching off to your right which is marked "*S-10 Camino Real*" and winds its way persistently uphill. A little later, the trail is flanked by a fieldstone wall and shaded by pine trees. 10 mins later, where the wall ends at a **viewing platform (7)**, enjoy a fantastic view of the settlement, Cueva Grande. Continue uphill in a south-westerly direction towards the right edge of a pine grove which will soon provide you with some welcoming shade. At the fork, follow the signpost *S-19 Dgda La Cumbre 2km*. Afterwards, pass a fenced-in property situated to your right.

The trail soon veers westwards into a narrow secondary valley and ascends along a water conduit which appears and disappears, time and again. A good 5 mins later, some distance away on your left-hand side, spot a sprawling farmstead. Now a **tumbledown house (8)** appears on the right-hand side, where the narrow trail merges into a wider one; turn left onto this trail. Between two concrete pillars, meet up with a concrete track which follows the signpost *S-19 Dgda. La Cumbre* and takes us up the street to the GC-150 in 8 minutes. Turn right onto this road and continue for 5 mins, then before reaching a chalet, turn left. At this point, the trail forks: bear right here and, only another 40m (!) on, at the so-called **Degollada de la Cumbre (9)**, turn right again ("*S-50 Cruz de Tejeda 2.7km*"). A short, but spectacular, high ramble leads along the sheer drop at the rim of the Caldera de Tejeda, back to the starting point at the **Degollada de Becerra (1)**.

Grand circular route from the Cruz de Tejeda

5.30 hrs

Panoramic walk along the sheer walls of the Caldera

At the outset, a splendid panoramic trail – the walker has a lot of time to enjoy the mountain scenery: to the right, a deeply-cut gorge; in front, pine covered slopes that sweep upwards to the highest peaks of the island. During the climb down, traverse verdant mountain flanks. The climb back up again runs through a bizarre craggy landscape.

Starting point: Cruz de Tejeda, 1509m. Pivot point for major island roads; bus stop for line 305.

Height difference: 730m.

Grade: a generally pleasant walk along broad trails and well-maintained *Caminos Reales*; only the ascent from La Culata is strenuous.

Refreshment: bars / restaurants at the Cruz de Tejeda and in La Culata; a food booth in La Goleta.

Accommodation: comfort hotels at the Cruz de Tejeda; wooden huts and tents at the Campamento El Garañón.

Note: this marvellous walk is suitable for both walkers approaching by bus or by car. Car park 200m west of the junction at Cruz de Tejeda. Since this is a circular walk, you could also start the route anywhere else along the way. If you are approaching from the south, starting in La Goleta is a good bet, but also at the Degollada de Becerra.

Alternatives: combination with Walk 1 (circling the Roque Nublo) and Walk 5 (to the Cruz Grande pass).

The trail sets off opposite the stone cross of **Cruz de Tejeda (1)**, to the right and next to the restaurant "Asador de Yolanda" (S-*50*/S-*85*). Pass the garden of the hotel, belonging to

During the circular walk, enjoy a constant view into the Caldera de Tejeda.

the restaurant, while ascending through a chestnut grove. 160m on, at the junction, bear left while climbing up the slope (*S-50*). The trail runs along a wall on the western flank of the mountain,**Morro de la Armonía**, and leads to a solitary house, bordered by a small pine wood. The higher we climb, the more overwhelmingly beautiful is the view of the central mountains: lying down below, lush pastureland and the road to Tejeda. The trail passes to the left of the house and then widens into a track which we leave behind again by turning right onto a trail forking away. 200m further on, the trail merges into a road that runs from the Cruz de Tejeda to the Pico de las Nieves, but you immediately climb over stone steps to fork to the right. The trail runs above the road, sometimes alongside it, and 800m further on, reaches the viewing platform on the crest of the pass **Degollada de Becerra (2)**. From here, follow the path marked *S-50* along the mountain ridge. Only a few minutes later, meet up with the **Degollada de la Cumbre (3)** and an intersecting trail: to the right leads to La Culata (*S-85*), but turn left instead and another 40m on, just before reaching the road, turn right onto a trail (*S-50* towards *Llanos de la Pez/Tunte*). Subsequently, the trail begins a considerable ascent. A good 500m on, it hooks to the left (conduit) and then leads, in only a few minutes, to the foot of the mountain, **Montaña del Toro**. Almost keeping on the level, the trail continues along the slope. Another 500m further on, reach the junction **Corral de los Juncos (4)**.

The trail to the left, actually continuing straight ahead, leads to the junction Cruce Llanos de la Pez, but we follow the slightly descending steps heading towards a **water reservoir**. Just before reaching it, the trail turns in a 90° angle to the right to climb up towards a pine forest. Afterwards, cross over two tracks, both leading to the campsite of Corral de los Juncos. At critical points, the course of the continued trail is constantly pointed out by stone walls. Along a stream bed, meet up with a broad roadway and turn right onto it. This leads along the edge of a pine forest, at first heading for a green iron gate, so as to skirt around the fruit tree plantation on the right-hand side. Continue for 300m along the sports grounds of the recreational campsite, Campamento **El Garañón (5)**, and then reach an obvious junction. Ignore the track that turns left towards the main entrance, 50m away (see Walk 5 to Cruz Grande), and turn right instead, passing a fruit tree plantation. About 150m further on, a clearly waymarked *Camino Real*, sets off to the left; follow it south-westwards. This leads through a young pine forest at the edge of the valley basin of La Culata. 10 mins later, veer on a westerly course and then descend to the reservoir **Embalse de los Hornos (6)**. Cross over the reservoir along the gigantic barrage wall. Afterwards, the trail winds up for 250m, ascending along zigzags, to the road leading to Ayacata. From the viewing point **Cruz de Juan Pérez** (= **Mirador Presa de los Hornos**) turn right into the "*S-51 Circular Llanos de la Pez*" which runs below the road. After 400m, just below the rock plateau **La Goleta (7)**, follow a cross path on your right which winds itself down in serpentines through the sparse pine forest to the *barranco*. Not far from a valley floor, you can spot deciduous trees close to a little spring. Shortly after that, a stone bench presents an opportunity to take a breather.

Soon after that, you can spot some caves in a rock face, where you could take shelter during fog or rain. At the end, the trail meets up with a **junction**. The fork to the left leads to the Roque Nublo, but we bear right and, 8 and 10 minutes later, ignore two turn-offs to the left. Not quite at the valley floor, after a 30 minute descent, reach the first houses of **La Ortiguilla**, an outlying district of La Culata. A concrete track leads, in 130m, to a cul-de-sac; turn left here onto a cobbled trail to descend. Cross over the valley floor and then meet up with the GC-608; turn left onto it and, 250m further on, reach the bar "Roque Nublo" in the village centre of **La Culata (8)**.

After a break in the bar, head back for a couple of metres along the village street and then immediately turn left onto the first stepped trail (*S-82*). This winds steeply upwards, protected by railings, between the houses of La Culata.

100

The Embalse de los Hornos.

5 minutes later, cross over a narrow street and, shortly thereafter, merge onto a concrete track; turn left onto this track. Only a few metres on, leave it behind again by turning right onto a cobbled path which ascends at first and then keeps on the level as it passes fields. At the end, it ascends steeply once more to reach a village street. Turn right onto this street and, 200m further on, bear left and climb up along a steep concrete track for 150m to reach (at the moment) the last house of La Culata up above; a sign proclaims this as the *Finca La Palmita*. At the **finca (9)**, a trail sets off which ascends in zigzags along the edge of the mountain into a secondary valley. The trail levels out there, so that you can catch your breath and take in the splendid scenery: to the left is a wide, open valley, to the right, a slope covered in almond trees and willows, up ahead, a copper-coloured, furrowed and steep rock face. The trail now passes a water reservoir and then crosses over a secondary valley near the mountain spring, Fuente del Ancón.

Two minutes later, pay close attention: ignore the trail heading straight on and, instead, turn right to walk beneath an aquaduct. Afterwards, a stretch follows that is, once again, strenuous and sweaty. The trail continues as it winds up in many bends. Ignore a turn-off to the left and, after a one hour ascent that started at the Finca La Palmita, suddenly meet up with the junction at the pass, **Degollada de la Cumbre** (3; just before the mountain road GC-150). Bear left onto the path marked *S-50* and, 300m further on, return to the **Degollada de Becerra (2)**. The path continues towards the north joining the road one more time before it leaves it again. Pass a *finca* and then continue along the rim of the Caldera. The walk ends at the starting point near the bus stop at the **Cruz de Tejeda (1)**.

Tranquil ascent over the north-east flank of the Caldera

Two trails descend from the Cruz de Tejeda – this is the more attractive of the two and not quite so physically demanding. At the end of this walk, you will reach one of Spain's most beautiful villages.

Starting point: Parador Cruz de Tejeda, 1509m. Pivot point for major roads on the island; GC-15, km24.5; bus stop for line 305.

Destination: Tejeda, 1049m. Bus stop for lines 18 and 305.

Height difference: 480m in descent, 20m in ascent.

Grade: a linear walk along trails and tracks; you can use the Alternative to create a longer, circular walk.

Refreshment / Accommodation: several hotels, bars and restaurants in Cruz de Tejeda; many more can be found at the destination in Tejeda.

Note: you can leave your car at the car park behind the Parador. With bus No. 305, you can return comfortably to Cruz de Tejeda. The bus departs from the petrol station on the southern limits of Tejeda.

Alternative: if you want to neither return

by bus nor walk back along the approach route, you can use Walk 27 in the opposite direction: follow the GC-60 until reaching the Artenara roundabout, bear right onto the GC-15 and then leave it behind again, 100m on, by turning left onto a concrete track. Immediately after, a dirt track forks away from this to the right and then becomes an ancient *Camino Real* as it heads left. This ascends, in numerous bends, through a beautiful landscape. 700m further on, the *camino* briefly encounters the road and then continues immediately to the left of it (low, flanking walls!). 300m after that, meet up again with the GC-15. Ascend along this road for 500m to reach a roundabout. Turn left here and low, flanking walls point out the starting point of the final leg. Climb up along a gorse-covered slope to reach the Cruz de Tejeda pass, up above (2 hrs).

Just opposite from the stone cross at the **Cruz de Tejeda pass (1)**, between the restaurant "Asador de Yolanda" and a bar, follow the trail *S-50/S-85 Tejeda (por la Isa) 3,6km*, cobbled at the outset and temporarily ascending. When you reach the **junction (2)** about 5 mins later, turn right onto the narrow trail *S-85* instead of continuing on trail *S-50* which turns diagonally to the left (heading for the Degollada de Becerra, see Walk 25). This trail descends steadily, winds through a gorge and crosses over the GC-156 several times as it opens up splendid views of the mountain sanctums of the Roque Nublo and the Roque Bentayga. The scents of sage and thyme fill the air and, in spring, bright-coloured broom and white flowering daisies surround us.

The Roque Nublo in view.

Reaching the road that runs to Cuevas Caídas, turn right onto it but then immediately turn left onto the GC-156. Follow this road for only 25m, then take the **turn-off to the right (3)**, bearing an inscription in stone, **"Finca La Isa"**, and continue for a stretch below the country cottage.

Upon meeting a right turn to the *finca*, continue climbing downwards, soon passing a small water basin and fields. At the end of a wire fence, turn left and, passing between stone walls and the house, meet up with the GC-156, cross over it, and then pick up a concrete track to reach a **helicopter landing pad (4**; *helipuerto***)**.

Bear right and continue the descent – in front of us is the Roque Bentayga. 3 minutes later, reach a little plateau, bear right and continue on; stone walls are flanking the way. Arriving at a **wooden cross (5)**, enjoy a lovely view taking in the village of Tejeda. Now descend in broad bends to the Calle Manuel Hernández Guerra, down below, which shortly thereafter, merges into the GC-156. Cross over this road to the left and then turn right onto a cobbled passageway to climb down even further. The walk ends at the viewing platform in the centre of **Tejeda (6)**, where we can enjoy a marvellous view of the mountain scenery yet again.

Cruz de Tejeda (1) 1509 m

GC 156/Finca La Isa (3) 1310 m

Cruz (5)

Tejeda (6) 1049 m

1250 m
1000 m

3.8 km

0   0.40   1.30 h

Alternative descent from Cruz de Tejeda

Especially during the first three months of the year, you find yourself walking through a sea of flowers. On the north-eastern foothills of the Caldera, you can spot lavender and dwarf broom, tree lucerne and Canary globe flower.

Starting point: Parador Cruz de Tejeda, 1509m. Pivot point for major roads on the island; GC-15, km24.5; bus stop for line 305.
Destination: Tejeda, 1049m. Bus stop for lines 18 and 305.
Height difference: 460m in descent.
Grade: despite the considerable difference in height, this tour is relatively easy and follows tracks, tarmac and trails which are currently a bit neglected.
Refreshment/Accommodation: hotels, bars and restaurants at Cruz de Tejeda and in Tejeda.
Note: by taking bus No. 305, return in comfort to the starting point at Cruz de Tejeda. The bus leaves from the petrol station on the southern limits of Tejeda.

On the Vuelta del Rincón: almond tree in flower at the end of January.

If you are facing the stone cross at **Cruz de Tejeda (1)**, starting point of the trail is to the left, somewhat hidden behind an information board for walkers. Next to the walls of the hotel "Parador", descend via a broom-covered slope to reach a roundabout in about 15 minutes; on Canarian maps, this is marked as **Vuelta del Rincón (2)**. Now follow the GC-15 downhill past km27 and after a total of 500m further on, leave the tarmac behind by turning right onto a trail at a **fork (3)**;

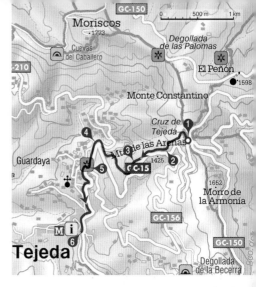

flanking walls and an almond tree point out the trailhead. Now a lovely stretch begins – flowering almond trees lend the setting white and pink highlights in January and February. 300m on, the trail touches upon the road – however, we do not tread on the tarmac, but instead, keep to the other side of the crash barrier and bear right where the trail – marked by stone plates – continues on. Now descend along numerous bends while enjoying enchanting views of the ragged rock faces of the Caldera de Tejeda. Huddled on hilltops, clusters of white houses, of the village bearing the same name, are separated from one another by short, deep valleys. 600m on, the trail becomes a dirt track (cairn). 130m after that, the track veers to the left and meets up with a concrete track that leads, in only a few paces, to the **GC-15**.

Now turn right to climb down to the gargantuan **roundabout (4)** below, where the rusty statue of a farmwoman is crouching in the middle, and turn left into the street signed for *San Bartolomé*. At the next **junction (5)**, not quite 500m further on, bear right and walk along the Avenida de los Almendros ("Almond Tree Avenue"; GC-60), continuing the descent. Just before reaching km-marker 1, pass by a viewing platform and, another 500m further on, turn right onto a steeply descending passageway (green chemist's sign!) to the centre of **Tejeda (6)**. Once again, a viewpoint awaits us with a view of the breathtaking, tower-like crags of the summit region!

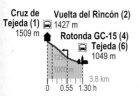

Cruz de Tejeda (1) 1509 m — Vuelta del Rincón (2) 1427 m — Rotonda GC-15 (4) — Tejeda (6) 1049 m

0   0.55   1.30 h — 3.8 km

Through almond tree groves onto the valley floor down below

Tejeda is the most beautiful mountain village on Gran Canaria: the houses of the village cling, terrace-style, to the hillside; a verdant oasis in the midst of desolate and ragged rock faces. But also, La Culata, the destination for this walk is worth visiting: a remote hamlet, buried so deep down on the valley floor that, in winter, hardly a ray of sunshine strikes it.

Starting point: the petrol station at the southern village limits of Tejeda, 1049m. On the GC-60 to Ayacata; bus stop for lines 18 and 305.
Height difference: 420m.
Grade: the ascent to Cruz de Timagada is a strenuous one, otherwise, this is an easy walk on a road at the outset, then on paths which are waymarked throughout.

In the background is La Culata.

Refreshment: bars and restaurants in Tejeda and La Culata. Tip: in Tejeda's *Dulcería*, the island's tastiest almond sweets are produced.
Accommodation: there is a lot of choice in Tejeda.
Note: this walk is suitable for walkers arriving by bus or car. There is a big car park near Tejeda's petrol station on the lower village road which turns into a limited traffic zone farther down. Bus No. 18 connects Tejeda with Ayacata and the Degollada del Aserrador; bus No. 18 and No. 305 with Cruz de Tejeda.
Alternatives: 1) the connecting walks from La Culata begin at the main street, GC-608, at the village's central square, sporting a bus stop. 50m south of the bar, a path ascends steeply to the left, passing between houses: via Walk 25, this leads to the Cumbre pass and, via the viewpoint on the Degollada de Becerra, to Cruz de Tejeda. 2) also starting in La Culata, 250m south of the square, is a cobbled trail that forks 5 mins on: bearing right, continue a direct ascent to the Roque Nublo; bearing left, follow Walk 4 to La Goleta and Ayacata.

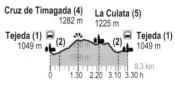

Cruz de Timagada (4)   La Culata (5)
      1282 m   1225 m
Tejeda (1)   Tejeda (1)
1049 m   (2)   (2)   1049 m
              1000 m
                           8.3 km
0   1.30   2.20   3.10 3.30 h

From **Tejeda (1)**, follow the GC-60 which runs towards Ayacata. 15 mins later, at a sharp **right-hand bend** (**2**; km-marker 3), turn left onto a cobbled track. 125m on, trail *S-80* begins sharply to the right and winds upwards along a mountain slope. Almond trees and agave cacti flank the path; in murky, rock crevices, the sage-leaved rock rose is standing its ground. Continue ascending steadily straight ahead, pass the houses on the mountain ridge (Casas del Lomo) and, to the right, enjoy a view of the craggy tower of

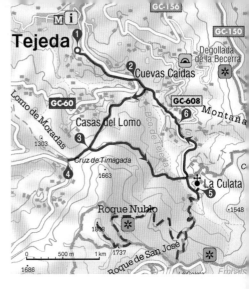

the Roque Bentayga, shrouded in legend. 1.6km further on, reach a **junction (3)**; bear right here and, 300m on, meet up with the cobblestone-paved plateau **Cruz de Timagada (4)** at the foot of the Roque Nublo, adorned with two crosses; a walled-in water source provides refreshment. After a short break, return to the **junction (3)** and then turn right, heading eastwards. The trail skirts around the Roque Nublo massif in a semicircle, keeping to the same height or slightly ascending at first and then, 20 mins later, descends. Cross over the valley floor via a bridge and then climb up to reach a road, 200m on. Now we find ourselves in the village centre of **La Culata (5)**: to the left is the church, in front of us, the bus stop, and to the right, the village bar.

The return route usually descends and is easier going: follow the main street, GC-608 in a northerly direction and, 15 mins later, leave this behind again at the start of a right-hand bend (100m past the entrance gate for "El Gran Chaparral") along a **fork to the left** (**6**; there is a breach in the crash barrier), the trail is cobbled. 100m further on, meet up with a track; turn right and follow this for 30m: a sharp right turn and the trail winds downwards, touches upon a dirt track, 4 mins later, and immediately continues to the right. After a descent lasting 6 mins, reach a junction, bear left, but then immediately turn right to cross over the valley floor. Continue along the right-hand side of the valley, descending through a trellis-like clump of bamboo. 8 mins later, cross over the stream bed again and, at the junction, change over to the track that leads, 250m on, to the **GC-60** (**2**; km-marker 3). Turn right onto the road and, in about 15 mins, return to the starting point in **Tejeda (1)**.

Ascent to a sanctum and sacrificial site for the native Canarians

Roque Bentayga, the island's third highest summit, looms spectacularly from a 600m-high, pyramid-shaped rocky peak – the site is absolutely breath-taking, and this is probably the reason it was held sacred by the native Canarians. Savour Gran Canaria's scenic mountains from a bird's eye view!

Starting point: GC-671, km-marker 0, 1150m. Approach via the GC-60 Tejeda – Ayacata at km6.3 (bus stop for line 18); here, turn onto the GC-607 and, 400m further on, turn left onto the GC-671 (towards Roque Bentayga/El Espinillo).
Height difference: 200m.
Grade: after the first leg along the road, at the visitor centre, the ascent to the sanctum sets off along a *Camino Real*: if your shoes are bearing slip-resistant soles, this is good walking.
Note: if you are approaching by car, you can begin the walk at the visitor centre, where a large car park has been built. When the centre is closed (daily 10–16.00, free admission), the approach to the summit may be closed as well.

At **GC-671, km-marker 0 (1)**, turn left onto the road leading towards Roque Bentayga. 280m on, ignore the turn-off to the left (*S-80* El Chorrillo; see Walk 30) and instead, keep walking along the road. Another 330m further on, where the GC-672 forks off to the left towards El Espinillo, follow the GC-671 diagonally to the right which ascends in 1km to the car park at the **Centro de Interpretación del Roque Bentayga (2)**, a small, but worthwhile archaeological museum with information regarding the sanctum. From there, a stone-paved trail, broad at the outset but narrowing later on, ascends, moderately steeply, along the right flank of Bentayga – the downwards views of the Caldera de Tejeda, far below, are superb! 20 mins past the visitor centre, reach a little pass – the fortress-like crag is towering directly above us now. Afterwards, ascend along the left flank of the Roque; the final metres, climb over steps cut into the rock, a stretch that is somewhat precipitous and

On the Bentayga plateau with a view westwards.

only secured by a piece of rope. Suddenly, we find ourselves standing at the **sanctum for sacrificial rites** on the natural plinth of the "holy mountain", **Roque Bentayga (3)**: the view towards the south-east of the distant hovering Cloudy Crag is absolutely breathtaking; no less splendid is the westwards view taking in the deeply-incised Barranco de la Aldea. But indeed, the scenery close by is also rewarding: the rock has been chiselled into furrows, grooves and pock-marked with holes, some of them more than 500 years old, created by the handiwork of the native people who brought libations to their god, Alcorán, here. When the sun rises on the 22nd of September, the autumn equinox, an especially beautiful event occurs on this spot: the light of the rising sun rises exactly in the frame of the V-formed notch that was hewn into the rock by the original Canary Islanders – the date was not only important for the god's cult, but also for the agricultural calendar.

After a good, long break, return along the approach route via the **Centro de Interpretación del Bentayga (2)** back to the starting point on the **GC-671, km0 (1)**.

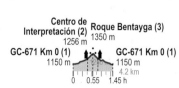

Remote hamlets and spectacular mountain scenery

Passing the rugged Roque Bentayga, a pre-Hispanic sanctum, descend along a panoramic trail via El Espinillo into the mountain village of La Solana. Slender date palm trees, crowned by gigantic fronds, cluster around the houses whilst the colourful gardens brighten the landscape. Even today, the fruits of the earth are sometimes transported by mules, and you can still meet goat herders tending their flocks on the terraced meadows. Along the return route over the northern flank of Bentayga, the scenery becomes quite dramatic: yawning chasms, fortress-like crags and ranks of mountains everywhere you look!

Starting point: GC-671, km-marker 0, 1150m. Approach via the GC-60 Tejeda – Ayacata at km6.3 (bus stop for the line 18); here, turn onto the GC-607 and, 400m further on, turn left onto the GC-671 (towards Roque Bentayga / El Espinillo).

Height difference: 500m in both ascent and descent.

Grade: the first leg mostly leads along a *Camino Real* (no shade and descending); later on, you must ascend for 6.7km along a hardly-used road (only sunny in the late afternoon).

Refreshment: bars in El Espinillo and La Solana (only sporadically open).

Accommodation: nearest holiday apartments and a hotel in Tejeda (s. also p. 28).

Alternatives: 1) combination possible with Walk 29 onto the Roque Bentayga. 2) from La Solana (5), you could turn left from the GC-607, and ascend for 1km to the village of El Chorrillo. After reaching the village limits on the other end, a *Camino Real* starts off, signed for the lovely hamlet of El Carrizall (about 2 hrs, there and back). 3) above El Roque (6), lies the Cueva del Rey, the "Cave of the (indigenous Canarian) King". Ascend along the village trail and, once above, you can spot the deep, gaping holes in the rock face far away in the distance (access is not possible).

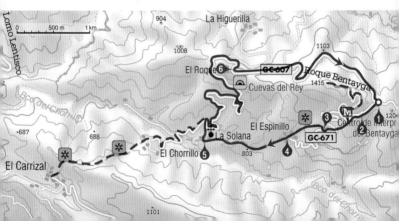

On the **GC-671, km-marker 0 (1)**, turn left onto the road leading towards Roque Bentayga. 300m on, leave the road behind by taking a **fork to the left** (**2**, *S-80 El Chorrillo*) and, just afterwards, bear right onto a path that crosses the road 10 minutes later. 5 minutes after that, pass the **Cruz de Tiznado (3)**, a wooden cross perched on a boulder. After not quite 15 minutes of descent along many tight zigzags, meet up with the village street of **El Espinillo (4)**: turn right onto the

Descent to El Espinillo.

street which leads through the hamlet, and 160m on, reach a cul-de-sac. By turning left here, you could ascend to the Mirador de la Virgen, which sports a large cross and a little chapel. We, however, continue straight ahead, following the trail sign *El Chorrillo S-80* whilst enjoying a downwards view into the valley. Not quite 100m further on, ignore a left-hand fork at a nondescript junction and then descend via numerous zigzags – passing scattered boulders – to reach a small secondary gorge after 1km. Shortly afterwards, pass a ruins and, 300m past that, cross over another secondary valley until the trail ascends to the picturesque church square of **La Solana (5)**.

After taking a good, long break on the shady square we now ascend to the **GC-607** and turn right onto it. A long ascent begins: the 500 metres of altitude, negotiated during our descent, must now be re-negotiated by climbing back up! But indeed, this height difference is spread out over a length of 6.7km and, since this stretch leads over a pleasant, narrow tarmac road, we can concentrate our attention on the splendid scenery surrounding us.

While you soon enjoy a view into the rugged Tejeda gorge to the left, to the right, the Bentayga massif rises up: numerous fortress-like crags drop down in increments to the village of **El Roque (6)** (see Alternative). We have now

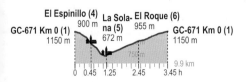

exactly 3km more to go. A level stretch follows before the road begins to twist upwards to reach the fork already met at the starting point at the **GC-671, km0 (1)**.

Panoramic circular walk through a pine forest

Sunk deep into a fold in the mountains is the quiet village of El Juncal. Opposite the village, a magnificent pine forest blankets the gently rolling slopes. From the flanks of pyramid-shaped mountains, you can enjoy far-reaching views of the central mountains with its canyons, reservoirs and monolithic crags. Unfortunately the path is not taken care of at the moment and is often marked as "closed" in winter.

Starting point: El Juncal, 1100m. Approach only possible by car.
Height difference: 380m.
Grade: the walk leads along forestry tracks and good trails, but nevertheless, route-finding skill is necessary (and a GPS device useful) since the newly established turn-offs have not yet been waymarked.
Refreshment: nothing en route – be sure to take along enough water and provisions!
Accommodation: the next nearest hotel, accommodation or holiday apart-

ments are in Tejeda.
Note: 1) according to the environmental agency, an access ban applies in the nature reserve only from June until November; this is the nesting season for the endemic blue chaffinch (*pinzón azul*). 2) the starting point is best reached by car; parking near the church. If taking the bus, use line 18 and get off at the junction on the Aserrador (GC-60, km11.4). From there, take the ancient *Camino Real* (see Walk 32) to reach El Juncal (2.6km).
Alternative: combination possible with Walk 32 from Cruz de la Huesita (3).

Across from the church at **El Juncal (1)**, follow the narrow tarmac road into the floor of the *barranco* that lies between the village and the forest. After crossing over the *barranco*, the road becomes a forest track which ascends pleasantly along the western flank of the Pajonales (1434m). Two signs announce the border of the nature reserve and, a little later, you meet up with the forestry house **Casa Forestal de Pajonales (2)**. Here, the track veers off on

a south-westerly course and leads, in 15 mins, to the major junction, **Cruz de la Huesita** (**3**; no cross in sight!). From the left, the path of Walk 32 merges into the track and continues by turning sharp left via a stone ramp. We, however, turn right where a chain blocks the way for vehicles and the walker is confronted with a restriction sign (see above). 150m on, leave the track behind by turning left onto a trail forking away which ascends steadily while passing three pyramid-shaped mountains. First, this leads along the southern flank of the **Morro de la Negra**; cairns (as well as a glance at the map) help in route-finding when confronted by confusing junctions. At a **fork** (**4**), ignore the trail forking diagonally off to the left. After a long ascent, catch your breath while walking along a level stretch, then

In the El Juncal nature reserve.

the trail veers onto the northern flank of the Carnicería and opens up a view of bleak gorges, separated from one another by rolling ridges.

Afterwards, walk along an extensive, drawn-out col which makes up the traverse crossing over to Sándara. In front of a rocky spur, keep heading straight on, then continue by ascending to the right along the mountain flank. When you spot a hamlet (Las Mesillas) on the horizon to the right, cairns tempt you to take the steep short cut to the track, visible way down below. We, however, continue following the trail for a stretch while climbing up the slope and, not until we reach the next height, take a path to the right. This path leads in a short time to the **track** (**5**) which is approaching from the west.

Turn right onto the track and, in broad bends, whilst enjoying panoramic views, head back, in 45 mins, to the junction, **Cruz de la Huesita** (**3**). From here, return along the track already met on the approach, passing by the **Pajonales forester's house** (**2**), to return to **El Juncal** (**1**).

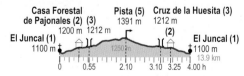

From Aserrador to Cruz de la Huesita

Splendid high alpine ascent above the Barranco del Juncal

Enjoying a view of El Juncal, a hamlet forgotten to the world, you descend into the valley, then ascend along a forestry track, shaded by pine trees, to reach the pass Cruz de la Huesita. The following stretch is the most spectacular: along a ridge, stretching for many kilometres, head towards the vast ruins of a volcano, the Aserrador. The trail changes sides numerous times along the ridge; on the right-hand side, you can spot reservoirs, back on the left-hand side, a view again of El Juncal, sunken deep into the valley.

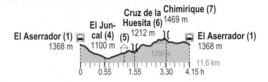

Starting point: the pass on the Aserrador, 1368m. A junction on the mountain of the same name on the GC-60, km11.4; bus stop for line 18.
Height difference: 500m.
Grade: a walk along well-laid trails and forestry tracks; however, because of the differences in height, the going can sometimes be strenuous.
Refreshment: nothing en route.
Note: equally suited for walkers approaching by bus or car.
Alternative: combination possible with Walk 31 from Cruz de la Huesita (6).

At the junction on the mountain **El Aserrador (1)**, turn onto the road signed for *El Carrizal* (GC-606) and, after a good 200m, pass over a plateau adorned with crosses – **Cruz del Carpio (2)**. 100m on, leave the tarmac behind by turning left where a track and a trail start off. Ignore the track and, instead, choose the trail that descends to the right. This twists downwards in 15 mins, passing through an espalier of agave plants, to reach the

The setting sun lights up the Aserrador.

GC-661 (3). In the distance, you can already spot the houses of El Juncal – remarkably situated at the end of a narrow valley, enclosed by pyramidal mountains. Follow the GC-661 to reach the church square of **El Juncal (4)**; here, turn left onto a track leading downwards. The track descends to a *barranco* floor and, afterwards, ascends once again. Soon the concrete-paved track becomes a dirt track which ascends in 20 mins, whilst providing pleasant shade cast by pine trees, to the forestry house, **Casa Forestal de Pajonales (5)**. Another kilometre further on, reach the pass, **Cruz de la Huesita (6)**. To the right, a dirt track forks away (see Walk 31); to the left, two cobbled trails start off: the one furthest away, which appears to descend, leads to the reservoir, Cueva de las Niñas (see Walk 33), we, however, veer onto the nearer one, which is stepped and ascending.

This ascends steeply between scattered boulder blocks, whilst in the shade of ancient pine trees – sometimes with a view of the reservoir, Cueva de las Niñas, sometimes of the high plateau situated above El Juncal. 1km further on, meet up with the first pass – there are more to follow, giving changing views southwards and to the north. The route continues steadily in constant up-and-down walking until ascending to an altitude of 1500m; the rocky terrain and the views become increasingly dramatic. This stony trail leads for a total of 2.6km along the ridge of the **Lomo de los Almacenes**, opening downwards views, time and again, of El Juncal. On the **Chimirique pass (7)**, follow the well-kept and well-marked trail *S-66* eastwards to Hoya de la Vieja along the GC-60 (km12, bus stop). From here, walk for about 500m towards the north until you reach the fork on the hill **El Aserrador (1)**, the starting point of this walk.

33 From the Presa Cueva de las Niñas to Cruz de la Huesita

2.20 hrs

Circular walk high above the "Lake of the Maidens' Cave"

At first high above the lakeshore, you then climb up along a forestry track through an open pine forest to a pass. Afterwards, along a trail sporting many zigzags – and enjoying a view of the reservoir – you return to the starting point. The walk is not spectacular, but it is easy – a picnic on the shore makes for a splendid ending! On a work day, you will have the lake almost to yourself, but at the weekend, families of Canary Islanders gather for barbecue parties.

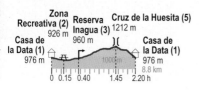

Starting point: Casa de la Data, 976m. GC-605, km8.7; no bus service.
Height difference: 300m in both ascent and descent.
Grade: easy walk along forestry tracks, a

Camino Real and tarmac.
Refreshment: sometimes, a food truck is parked on the lake front.
Alternative: combination with Walk 32 at the Cruz de la Huesita pass.

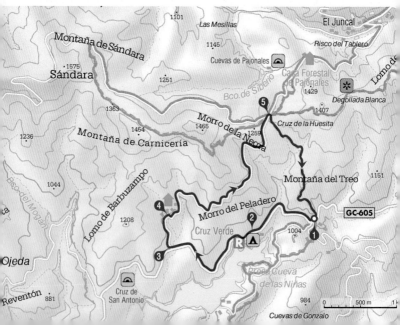

A lovely end for the walk: a picnic on the lakeshore.

From the goat farm, **Casa de la Data (1)**, walk south-westwards along the hardly used GC-605 and, 15 mins later, pass the access road to the **Zona Recreativa (2)**, the picnic area on the lakeshore (km-marker 10). A little later, pass by the entrance gate to a *Finca Privada* and then catch a glimpse, towards the left, of a massive crag with a plinth that is peppered with caves. After a total of a good 2.8km along the road, leave the tarmac behind by turning right onto a forestry track forking away that enters into the **Reserva Natural Integral Inagua (3)**. The pine forest is a highly protected nature reserve, because here, the blue chaffinch (*pinzón azul*) is nesting, an endangered endemic species of birdlife. Ancient, gnarled pines with pitch-black, resinous trunks call to mind the major forest fire that raged here in 2007 – but indeed, the trees have long since sprouted new greenery, and prove, once again, how well their thick bark protect these Canary Island pines from fire damage.

700m further on, pass a **forester's house (4)**, and immediately afterwards, ignore a left-hand fork, flanked by walls. In sweeping bends, the track twists upwards and opens up a view into the reservoir, lying far below. After a total of not quiet 2.6km, a striking black rock face appears to the left of the trail; in winter, water drips down from the rock face – a sure sign that a spring must be nearby. 800m further on, reach the pass, **Cruz de la Huesita (5)**, where there is not a cross to be seen, but to the right of the track, two cobbled trails are setting off. Ignore the trail further away which appears to ascend (see Alternative), and instead, descend along the trail closer by. Along numerous zigzags, the sometimes cobbled trail, sometimes flanked by walls, twists downwards through the open pine wood. During this stretch, the trail crosses over a series of narrow *barrancos* while opening up views of the lake from time to time. Reach the goat farm, **Casa de la Data (1)**, the starting point for the walk, and then the trail merges into the road.

A view taking in two lakes at the same time

From Gran Canaria's 69 reservoirs, the "Reservoir of the Maidens' Cave" is considered the most beautiful. The lake sprawls in a broad valley which is enclosed by pine-dotted slopes. On the northern shore of the lake lies a popular, rustic picnic area, but in the circular walk described here, the route leads along its less-known southern shoreline. From a ridge, you can get a peek into the neighbouring canyon, where a second impressive lake is situated: the Embalse de Soria. Along the way, the bleating of goats can be heard, and a legendary monumental, towering pine tree provides shade for a picnic.

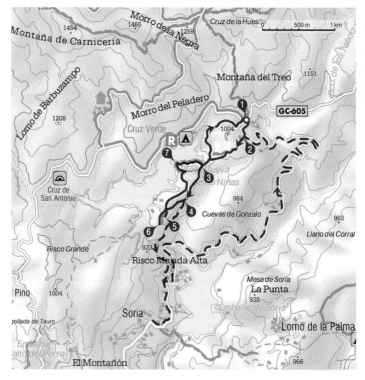

The "Lake of the Maidens' Cave".

Starting point: Casa de la Data, 976m. GC-605, km8.7. No bus service.
Height difference: 170m.
Grade: except for a short, precipitous stretch between WP 2 and 3, this is an easy walk along trails and tracks.
Refreshment: a food kiosk at the picnic area, on the northern shore of Niñas lake.
Note: by car, drive to the starting point via Ayacata, Soria/Barranquillo Andrés and Mogán. The walk is worthwhile when the reservoir is full of water.
Alternative: from Waypoint 4 via Soria to Casa de la Data (8.2km, 3 hrs).

Casa de la Data (1), the starting point of this walk along the GC-605 at km8.7, is the name given to a sheep and goat enclosure which is situated below the road (there is a sign *Pinar de Pajonales*). Ignore the tarmac road (*Camino Privado*) which is closed off by a barrier and follow the dirt track that first ascends and then descends slightly. 240m further on, you reach a bend to the left. Turn right here and follow the **path** (**2**; waymarked as *S-60 Soria/Gruz Grande*) which descends into a small and dry side valley. After 670m, take a sharp left turn (stone steps) at the fork and descend the narrow rocky serpentines. After another 210m, the path joins a tarmac track at sign *S-60* from where you can see the Cueva de las Niñas lake in front of you. Follow the track to the left and pass a **settlement boundary post (3)** which you will

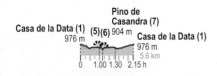

Casa de la Data (1)
976 m

Pino de
Casandra (7)
(5)(6) 904 m

Casa de la Data (1)
976 m
5.6 km

0   1.00 1.30 2.15 h

return to when you come back up from the lake. After about one minute, leave the tarmac track to the left (towards *S-60 Soria*) and ascend past an imposing boulder. 200m farther on, your path briefly touches the tarmac track but veers off again and continues at "a level lower" parallel to it. After 100m, you will get the first magnificent view of Soria village which is nestled in the adjacent canyon. A little bit farther on, the **Camino Soria (4)** with its many serpentines forks off to the left near a wooden post (indicated on the map). But you continue straight on the path which almost takes you back to the tarmac track. From here, continue on a wide *camino* passing a striking rocky hilltop on the left. This section is truly spectacular and offers a great view of Soria.

400m further on, the *camino* merges into a tarmac track, from which, the barrage wall of the "Lake of the Maidens' Cave" can now be seen; below it, you can spot the watchman's house. Afterwards, leave the tarmac behind by turning left along a path that climbs up to the highest point of the ridge: this is marked by a **cross (5)** and opens up a simultaneous view of the reservoirs Soria and Cueva de las Niñas – a wonderful spot for a break!

What follows after this, however, is also well-worth seeing: now return to the tarmac track and turn left, but leave it behind again at the next left-hand bend by turning left onto a narrow path. Crossing over rocky terrain (cairns!), the path traverses the western flank of a towering crag on our left-hand side. It heads for a power pylon and a intersecting wall (an open "portal" allows passage). At a **metal post (6)**, enjoy a splendid view of the breathtaking craggy arena of the Barranco de Soria – the centrepiece is the lake, surrounded by palm trees.

Return to the tarmac track and ascend along it – now, once again, with a view of the Lake of the Maidens' Cave. 1.2km further along, leave the track behind by turning left onto the **turn-off of a track** that is blocked by a chain (if you are tired, stay on the tarmac track).

The spurge adds green dots to the landscape.

View of the Soria lake from the mountain ridge (Waypoint 6).

260m on, we find ourselves standing in front of the **Pino de Casandra (7)**, a gigantic pine, enclosed by a circle of agave plants, situated high above the lake. The tree's mighty roots have been anchored in the earth here for over 500 years; fragrant sap gushes from the pine's "wounds", caused by violent storms and ravaging forest fires. Legend has it that Casandra was a woman who was burned as a "witch" by her own husband: supposedly, she had promised the devil the souls of her daughters. Despite this blood-curdling story, you really should while away some time here and enjoy the shade of the mighty treetop while taking in the view of the emerald waters of the lake. The shoreline opposite is far in the distance, sporting the rustic tables of the picnic area.

Now climb down to the lake and, if the water level allows, walk northwards along the shoreline until you reach the final, narrow inlet penetrating into a little secondary *barranco*. A trail ascends to the right to reach the **settlement boundary post (3)** which you passed before. Walk along the tarmac track towards the left and return to the **Casa de la Data (1)** after 1.3km.

Steep slopes and harsh highlands

This walk leads through a dramatic mountain landscape: scattered boulder blocks appear as if carelessly strewn about by a pettish act of nature and weather-beaten rock faces evoke images of rough-hewn human caricatures. Along the entire route, enjoy the view taking in the mountainous fortress-like terrain of the island's interior. But for how much longer? In the years to come, there is a chance that a gigantic hydroelectric plant will be constructed here.

Starting point: Soria, Casa Fernando, 658m. No bus service.

Height difference: 370m.

Grade: a strenuous ascent along a *Camino Real*; watch out for loose stones and scree along the way! Sure-footedness is needed!

Refreshment: nothing en route. At the starting point, in the bar, Casa Fernando, you can buy freshly squeezed juice and provisions for the walk.

Accommodation: holiday apartments in Soria (enquire at the Casa Fernando).

Note: if you get an early start, you can negotiate the strenuous ascent still in the shadow. As the sun is likely to beat down later on, you should bring along some-

thing to protect your head from the sun, as well as sufficient drinking water.

Alternative: if you would like to continue on from the high plateau to the Chira reservoir, turn right along the track, then turn right at the fork (3) 1 min thereafter, ignore numerous forks to the right, then ascend along hairpin bends to the houses situated on the mountain ridge, Lomo de la Palma. The ridge acts as a divider between the Soria gorge and the Chira gorge. Cross over a chain barrier and continue straight ahead. 300m on, ignore a left-hand fork leading to Cuevas. 10 mins later, reach a junction with a wooden cross. From this point, you could link up with Walk 36 (WP 4) to Cercados de Araña.

Behind the Soria barrage wall.

From the bar, "Casa Fernando", in the village centre of **Soria (1)**, descend along a narrow tarmac road to the barrage wall down below – a titanic construction which separates the lake from the deep-cut Arguineguín gorge. Cross over the **barrage wall** and, at its end, the **stairway (2)** that follows. Climb up a couple of steps, then back down again where a broad trail sets off afterwards. 65m further on, past a right-hand bend, leave this trail behind by turning left onto a path marked by cairns. The path ascends, at first moderately, then more steeply, into the Amácigo gorge. 20 mins later, the path veers to the left and twists up in unrelenting bends as it ascends the slope – almond trees provide only scant shade. With the aid of steps cut into the rock, negotiate some short steep sections. 35 mins later, the reservoir comes into view once more – already situated far below us. Pass a large breach in the rock and, after an hour of walking, climb up to the edge of a little **high plateau**, surrounded by mountains. Afterwards, climb down 90m to reach a **fork (3)** at a concrete foundation – a lovely spot for a picnic!

The descent leads along the route already met during the approach: in numerous bends, climb down to the **barrage wall (2)**, and then continue on to the "Casa Fernando" in **Soria (1)**.

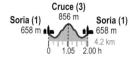

Far-reaching views over the lake and the high plateau

This circular walk is short, but rich in diversity. First, a ramble along a tarmac track on the eastern shore of the Chira lake, then cross over its barrage wall and continue along a disused canal. In the second leg, the route leads over a steppe-like plain, high above the western shore of the lake, opening a view of the fortress-like mountains of the island's interior. In the spring, with Euphorbiaceae in flower, the wasteland comes alive in green and yellow colours.

Starting point: Cercados de Araña, 925m. At the Chira lake, on the GC-604, approach only possible by car via San Bartolomé or Ayacata.

Height difference: 100m in both ascent and descent.

Grade: an easy walk without any differences in height worth mentioning; this walk is also suitable for children.

Refreshment: nothing en route. Bars in Cercados de Araña.

Accommodation: if you reserve in advance, you can spend the night in the Albergue de Chira, free of charge. Situated 5km from the reservoir is the simple campsite Morro de Santiago (for reservations, see page 25).

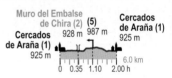

From the central crossroads in **Cercados de Araña (1)**, walk along the rarely travelled road, the GC-604, to the lake and then stroll along the idyllic shoreline for a stretch of 1.9km. At the entrance to the "Albergue de Chira", continue along the promenade-like **grand barrage wall (2)**. Walk along the entire length of the dam while enjoying the splendid 360° view, taking in the broad valley surrounded by mountains. At the end of the barrage wall, veer to the left onto a path that leads along the edge of a channel into the next

Past the Cruce de Caminos, high above one of the arms of the Chira lake.

valley notch. 500m on, where the trail has often fallen away after rainfall, continue along the dry bed of the channel. Another 100m on, climb up onto the channel and reach a second, **little barrage wall (3).** Cross over it and now continue – following cairns – in a direct course towards two **power pylons** in the area of the ridgeline. The stony slope is peppered with different varieties of Euphorbiaceae, for example, Eurphorbia regis-jubae, which is named after Juba, king of Mauritania, who commissioned an expedition to the Canary Islands in 25 AD.

Along the ridgeline, veer to the right onto a **dirt track**. This continues over a steppe-like high plateau, heading towards the central mountains; the view takes in all of the points of the compass. 200m on, when meeting a crooked **wooden cross (4)**, ignore the turn-off to the left that heads to the hamlet of Las Casas. Another 550m further on, you can either keep to the track, or leave it behind by turning left onto a **short-cut trail (5)** that is flanked by low stone walls. Continue over a stony terrain while following the power pylons, and 300m on, cross over the track. The "short-cut" (overgrown after rainfall) continues on above the lake. Some little *fincas* with lush gardens are situated on its shoreline – an idyllic scene! A good 400m further on, the trail merges again with the track at the junction **Cruce de Caminos (6)**. Here, as well as at the next fork, bear right, and then pass the house "Paraíso Vista de Chira" and the *finca* "Seeblick". Cross over a valley notch via a little bridge and, at the next junction, turn right once again and cross over a second little bridge. From the **cluster of houses (7)** that follow, you could turn right and, 2 mins later, reach the starting point for the walk. A prettier choice, however, is to turn left along the narrow road, passing flower-trellised houses, to meet up with the main road GC 604. Turn right onto the road and, at km-marker 6, pass by Señora Celia's quaint bar "Vista Alegre", then return to the junction in **Cercados de Araña (1)** 5 minutes later.

The Southern Island

Fortress-like crags, palm tree oases and quiet villages

The further that you descend from the central massif down to the southern coast, the more you will be reminded of how close you are to the continent of Africa: ochre and brown tones dominate the landscape, and on parched mountain slopes, only species of the cactus-like spurge family increase their hold on the terrain. Appearing like mirages in the desert, on the arid valley floors, oases of palm trees suddenly materialise – solely where sufficient groundwater is available, could human settlement be established. Picturesque villages, like Fataga and Soria, Santa Lucía and San Bartolomé, are manifestations of civilisation amidst a rugged and repelling mountainous terrain. On the coast, follow the shimmering, sandy dunes of the "Canary Islands Sahara", surrounded by tourist-targeted, ever-expanding, large-scale projects.

Santa Lucía: pretty quiet village at the edge of the Caldera de Tirajana.

Pleasant high mountain route and valley walk

This walk has a lot to offer: at first, breathtaking, far-reaching views into the gorges of the southern island, then a long stretch through a pine forest until reaching the Cruz Grande pass. Especially lovely is the mild downward declivity of the final leg. Steps and stone walls protect the well-maintained Camino Real from erosion. Over the tops of pine trees, enjoy a view of the mighty rock faces enclosing the valley whilst harking to the tapping of the Pica-pinos, the "pine peckers" with their red bellies and striking crowns. Crossing through abandoned plantations of almond and fruit trees, then passing the tavern/bodega of Las Tirajanas, meet up with San Bartolomé de Tirajana, fondly referred to by the locals by its native Canarian name "Tunte".

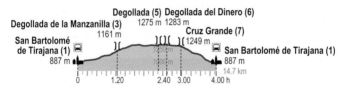

Starting point: the bus stop or the car park at the northern village limits of San Bartolomé de Tirajana, 887m. On the GC-60, Costa Canaria – Tejeda; bus stop for line 18.

Height difference: 440m.

Grade: a walk along well-laid trails and forestry tracks.

Refreshment: bars and restaurants in San Bartolomé.

Accommodation: hotels in San Bartolomé.

Note: the walk is equally suited to walkers approaching by bus or by car. If approaching by car, you could avoid the steep ascent at the beginning by parking your vehicle near the junction mentioned in the walk description.

From the bus stop in **San Bartolomé (1)**, follow the GC-60 in the direction of the central island. 180m further on, turn left onto the street signed *Mirador*. The street climbs up very steeply until, 300m on, it levels out at a **junction** (we will later return to this point along the street merging from the right). Another 260m further on, meet up with **El Mirador (2)**, a viewpoint with a view of the Tirajana basin, situated at the access road for the four-star hotel "Las Tirajanas". 3 mins later, turn right onto the signed trail towards *Degollada de la Manzanilla*, then bear left at the **T-junction**, 140m further on. 200m after that, ignore a right-hand fork, and then 300m further on, veer diagonally right onto a concrete-paved track. This ascends to a *granja*, a large hog farm exuding the usual pungent odours. Here, the track becomes a trail that veers

Backwards view from the Degollada de la Manzanilla of the route already walked.

diagonally right and twists upwards, in broad bends, along the flanks of the mountain for the next 40 mins – passing an enclosed spring, sunk into a rock face – to meet up with the trail junction on the **Degollada de la Manzanilla pass (3)**. The far-reaching view sweeps from the Tirajana valley basin in the east all the way to the gorges in the west. Southwards, the view reaches over barren, weather-flayed terrain as it takes in the coastline.

From the pass, follow the track to the right that is heading northwards (*Cruz Grande / Tunte*). The track leads almost on the level, only sometimes slightly ascending, along the western flank of the **Morro de las Vacas** ("Cow Mountain"). The view reaches over the gently dropping slopes to the upper reaches of the Barranco de Pilancones. This stretch of trail is long and pleasant, and you don't even have to pay much attention to where you're treading. Of course, if you love a shot of adventure, you have numerous opportunities for interrupting the somewhat monotonous route in order to climb up the flank at spots marked by cairns. At a **veer to the left (4)**, you could scramble up to the right to reach the viewpoint on the Rosiana pass (not signposted). 3km farther on at you reach another **pass (5)** at 1275m where you could short-cut a southwards bend by continuing straight ahead. If you have kept to the main trail, after a total of 9km of walking, a track merges from the left and, a good 5 mins after that, where the broad trail approaching from the Soria lake merges, meet up with the pass **Degollada del Dinero (6)**. Our main trail now leads along numerous bends for 20 mins to reach the road, GC-60.

Turn right onto the road, but afterwards, past the breach in the rock, **Cruz Grande (7)**, veer to the right onto the forestry track forking away (directional sign: *S-40 = Tunte*). 200m further on, leave the track behind again by turning onto the cobblestone *Camino Real*, flanked by walls (*Camino de Santiago*). This descends through open pine wood – to the right, the rocky massif of the Morro de la Cruz Grande; to the left, the broad valley of San Bartolomé. 20 mins later, pass a spring which finds its source in a narrow secondary *barranco*. Starting from the crag, El Roquillo, which we pass 15 mins later on, the trail climbs down in zigzags.

As soon as we near the village, the landscape is characterised by almond and olive trees. At the access road for the bodega "Las Tirajanas", meet up with a street and turn left onto it. At the following junction, bear left and descend along the street already met on the approach route to return to the bus stop at **San Bartolomé (1)**.

From one palm tree oasis to the next

This trail, so rich in diversity, leads from the "Valley of the Thousand Palm Trees" in the Barranco de Fataga, crosses through two remote palm-dotted hamlets, and enters the lovely mountain village of Santa Lucía. The lush vegetation owes its existence to the groundwater found here, a rarity on the island – ancient water mills along the trail are reminders of hidden springs. After the first rains of autumn, the jagged mountains come alive with flowering lavender, sage and rockrose, and the Sorrueda reservoir is filled with water. In the final stage of the walk, the trail leads over abandoned fields, where grain once grew in the midst of the huge Tirajana basin.

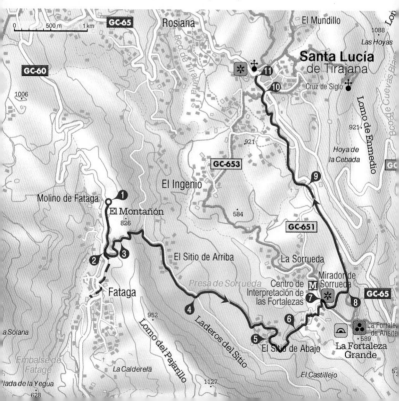

Starting point: Molino de Fataga, 716m. GC-60, km31.2, about 1.8km above Fataga; bus stop for line 18.

Destination: Santa Lucía, 709m. Bus stop for line 34 to San Bartolomé de Tirajana, from there, take bus 18 to Molino de Fataga.

Height difference: 470m in both ascent and descent.

Grade: without any shade, the route leads along a trail, a forestry track and, for a short time, tarmac; due to the height differences, somewhat strenuous.

Refreshment: nothing on the way. There are several snack bars / restaurants at the end of the walk in Santa Lucía.

Accommodation: holiday apartments in Fataga.

Alternatives: 1) if you would like to combine the walk with a visit to the lovely village of Fataga, get off the bus at the church square (or, park your car there) and then ascend along the main road for 1.2km until reaching the Molino Pequeño (2). 2) combination with Walk 39 from the Mirador de Sorrueda (7).

1.8km above the picture postcard village of Fataga, lies the palm-dotted oasis, **Molino de Fataga (1,** "Mill of Fataga"), which takes its name from a historic water mill. A bus stop for the line 18 is situated on the access road for the complex. From here, you can easily ramble down along the GC-60, during which, 200m on, to the right of the road, you can spot a historical water mill. 400m further on, directly in front of a house (and 100m further up from km32), leave the road behind by turning left onto an ascending concrete-paved trail. Shortly after, pass the second, smaller water mill, the **Molino Pequeño (2)**. Past the following house, turn left to ascend and, 70m further on, the cobbles of the ancient *Camino Real* become visible. From this point on, the trail winds up along many bends – time and again with a view of Fataga – to reach the pass, **Degollada de los Molinos (3)** up above.

Along as many bends as you have taken on the ascent, as many must be negotiated during the climb down – along a trail that is slippery underfoot. If you can manage to take your eyes away from your feet, you can enjoy a view into the Tirajana basin

Fataga is perched on an alpine knoll.

which will accompany us from now on. After a 20 minute descent, the trail merges into a **forestry track**; turn right (following the trail straight ahead will lead directly to Santa Lucía via Ingenio).

580m further on, pass the first houses of **Los Sitios de Arriba** ("the settlement above"), and a little later, other residences follow, situated in the midst of a palm tree grove. Not until 15 mins later – the track has led us in the meantime onto a high plateau, lying in the shadow of jagged mountains – bear left at a **junction (4)** and then begin a descent along the track. Not quite 500m further on, catch the first view of the Sorrueda lake to the left; to the right, the rugged rock faces of the Amurga massif tower to the heavens. 350m more, at the next junction (in front of a house), turn left and then, 200m further (house No. 36), veer off to the right. 2 mins after that, ignore a fork to the right that is usually blocked by a chain and continue descending while passing the flower-garlanded houses of the hamlet, **Los Sitios de Abajo** ("the settlement below").

Just another minute after that, at the sign *Prohibido el paso*, reach the next junction. The sign ("do not pass") acts as a deterrent to many walkers, who veer off to the right in order to leave the track behind 150m on by using a narrow path to the left. That is one possibility, but you will have a nicer experience if you ignore the sign and descend to the left to a traditional house down below, where the track suddenly ends. Señora Eva, the proprietor, allows walkers access to the private property (quote: "As long as they don't steal anything!"). Thus, you skirt around her house, treading between some old crofts, and then meet up with a path which, passing over the palm-tree dotted embankment of a *barranco*, merges, 1 min later, into the alternative trail coming from the right.

30 metres on, a **spring (5)**, on the floor of the gorge, provides some welcome refreshment: the waters of the spring feed stands of bamboo and willow, as palm trees stretch their crowns of fronds skywards. The path soon merges into a concrete-paved track; turn left onto this track to climb down to the floor of the Barranco de Tirajana. Pass the dry stream bed to the right of the mighty **barrage wall (6)** of the **Presa de la Sorrueda** and ascend steeply along zigzags for 500m to climb to the **Mirador de Sorrueda (7)**. This patch of terrain appears especially romantic after heavy rainfall, when the lake is brimming and the countless palm trees are reflected in its waters.

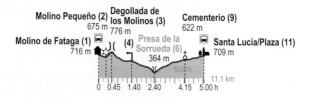

Molino Pequeño (2) 675 m — Degollada de los Molinos (3) 776 m — Cementerio (9) 622 m

Molino de Fataga (1) 716 m — (4) — Presa de la Sorrueda (6) 364 m — Santa Lucía/Plaza (11) 709 m

500 m 11.1 km

0   0.45   1.40   2.40   4.15   5.00 h

Los Sitios de Arriba with Santa Lucía in the background.

Follow the narrow road to the GC-651 which leads to the right directly towards the rocky fortress of La Fortaleza (you can make a short side trip to the visitors' center to your left, see Walk 39, WP 8). After 200m leave the GC-651 to the left onto a *Camino Rural*, which climbs up while crossing overgrown terraced fields. 400m on, the *camino* merges into the **Ansite trail (8)**. Turn left and keep to a northerly course, constantly ascending while enjoying a view of the upper reaches of the Barranco de Tirajana, with the houses of Santa Lucía in the distance.

At the junction 800m on, continue straight ahead (the Ruta de la Sal turns off sharp to the right). Another 370m further on, meet up – at the end of a wire fence – with a track which brings us to the road, **GC-651**. Turn right, pass by the superbly situated **Cementerio (9,** cemetery) and, 60m on, leave the tarmac behind by turning left onto the *Camino a Las Lagunas*. At the junction, not quite 300m on, continue straight ahead. Another 400m after that, cross over the **GC-653**. 200m further, ignore the path forking off sharp left, and a little later, the trail merges into a concrete-paved track; turn left to continue.

At the junction, 200m further on, bear left and, another 100m on, ascend steeply to the right while passing between houses built from undressed stone. Afterwards, join the asphalt road. Turn left onto the Calle Juan del Río Ayala, which merges into the GC-65 opposite the fortress-like former museum **Hao (10)**. This road leads us – passing a bakery, shops and the restaurant "El Mirador" – to **Santa Lucía's** grand and verdant *plaza* (11).

La Fortaleza and La Sorrueda: Grand route from Santa Lucía

Gigantic fortress-like crag and a romantic lake

From the lovely Santa Lucía, the walk leads over a mountain ridge covered in overgrown terraced fields, once sown with grain, while descending to two mighty fortress-like crags, towering to the heavens. During the Conquista, in 1483, these were the last retreat for the island's native inhabitants – in a natural cave, 25 metres in length, these people sought refuge from the Spanish conquerors. The return route also presents some highlights: the walk leads above the emerald-green Sorrueda reservoir, continues over palm-dotted hamlets, and then runs along a dramatic gorge.

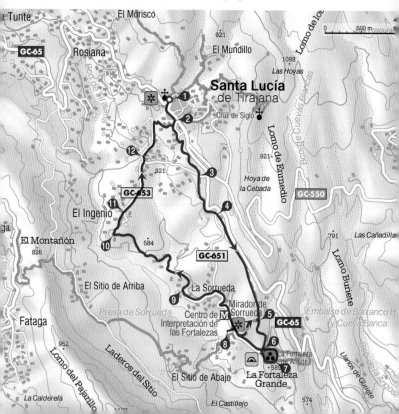

Starting point: *plaza* below the church in Santa Lucía, 709m. Car park and bus stop "Plaza" for line 34.

Height difference: 320m.

Grade: the approach is easy and descending while the return route is somewhat more strenuous due to stretches during the ascent.

Refreshment: restaurants in La Sorrueda and Santa Lucía.

Note: the walk is marked along some stretches with the directional sign *La Fortaleza*.

Alternative: if you wish to avoid the sometimes strenuous return route, walk until reaching the Mirador La Sorrueda (8), to get a view of the lake, and then connect up with Walk 38 from the *mirador* to return to the junction (5) and then Santa Lucía.

Starting point is the **plaza (1)**, in the centre of **Santa Lucía** with a large car park and a view of the church and the town hall. Walk southwards along the road, GC-65, to reach the **Hao (2)**, a fortress-like building located on the left-hand side of the street. The street, Calle Juan del Río Ayala, sets off to the right. When it ends, turn right onto a stone-paved trail. At the next junction, bear left to continue along a concrete-paved track. The track narrows immediately but widens again a little later. 30m on, ignore the right turn towards the *barranco* ground. After a good 100m, leave the comfortable levelled track at the left-hand bend. You will see two trails veering off to the right immediately next to each other. The first trail is marked with a sign prohibiting motorbikes, while our trail, the second, bears a sign towards *La Fortaleza*. Head towards a palm tree, and then cross through an espalier of cactus-like Euphorbien. A trail sign for the Fortaleza, standing at a nondescript junction, was incorrectly positioned the last time we walked this route. Please do not follow a little arrow which leads to the height, but instead, turn diagonally left to descend and, a little later, cross over the road, **GC-653 (3)**, at a traffic sign!

The trail is usually flanked by undressed stone walls, and you can enjoy a view over abandoned fields, once sown with grain, to a mountainous rock face on the horizon. About 10 mins later, the trail merges into a tarmac road; turn right onto this road and follow it to pass the **Cementerio (4,** cemetery). When the road hooks to the right, 200m further on, continue straight ahead along the dirt track. Wooden signs point out the direction for *Ruta de la Sal / Camino a Ansite*. Now pass by a fenced-in *finca* with olive trees by bearing left (the track becomes a trail at this point). At the following junction, ignore the Ruta de la Sal, which continues straight on, by

Already in view: La Fortaleza.

bearing to the right and crossing over a broad, terraced plain. At the end of the plain, you spot the towering Fortaleza Chica, the "little fortress" and, behind it, set off to the left, the Fortaleza Grande, the "big fortress". At a distinct **junction (5**; wooden trail sign), ignore the *Camino a la Costa*, forking off to the right. Instead, keep straight on (in the direction *Ansite*). 5 mins later, meet up with another junction. Continue on to the large fenced-in terrain with an **information board (6)**; reckon with 15 mins for the breathtaking excursion to the Fortaleza that follows. Ascend to the immense entrance of a **"through" cave** and, walking through it for 25m, reach the **southern opening (7)**, looking into the neighbouring gorge. This allows a spectacular view of the craggy scenery! After a break for a picnic, continue along a rocky alpine path to skirt around to the left of the "fortress" and, via the "esplanade", return to the **information board (6)**. From here, continue on to the tarmac track, 50m away, and descend along it. 200m after the *Camino Real a la Costa* (see Walk 38) has crossed over our track, turn left onto a concrete-paved track that then ends at the **Mirador de la Sorrueda (8)**: the lake with the same name is situated down below, towered over by steep, rugged rock faces, as it sprawls from the barrage wall into the *barranco*.

Afterwards, return along the concrete-paved track back to the road and then turn left, passing the "Centro de Interpretación de las Fortalezas" (Tue–Sun 10–17.00, there is a restaurant next door). A good 5 mins later, at a 180° bend, leave it to the left onto a narrow path (next to the concrete track) that shortcuts another wide bend. When the path merges into a track, ascend along this for a minute to reach a junction at a house. Turn right here and, just a little later, meet up again with the narrow tarmac road which returns us – with a view of the lake and passing restored houses of undressed stone – in 10 mins, to the *plaza* of **La Sorrueda (9)**. Afterwards, the tarmac-surfaced track becomes concrete-paved. Continue past some farmsteads for 670m and take the sharp left-hand bend. After another 130m, the concrete-paved track turns into a dirt track that leads to a small dusty car park (200m before you reach the *barranco* ground). Immediately after the car park, turn right onto a path that veers right after 100m. After another 50m, enter the wide path, which you follow to your left past a fenced-in farm. The *camino* soon narrows and then leads through an unspoilt landscape: reddish-coloured boulders, seemingly rolled here by the hand of a giant, are scattered all over the slope. The lake is situated behind us, smooth as glass and nestled between the steep mountain flanks. The trail ascends constantly, always following the edge of the slope; in case the trail seems to disappear during its course, it actually runs straight

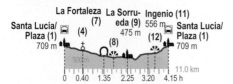

Backwards view of the Sorrueda reservoir.

ahead along a conduit, heading towards a plantation. Later, the trail levels off and then you can concentrate your attention on the canyon on your left which narrows more and more while it cuts its way into the mountain terrain. A good 20 mins later, above a round water reservoir, you reach an important **junction (10)**. A trail sign points the way sharp left and downwards (*S-47 Los Sitios / Fataga*), but we continue along our trail, still keeping on the level, by turning diagonally right and heading towards a house which we pass on the right. Soon enjoy a panoramic view that appears in front of us: in the background, a large arena of crags, in the foreground, lots of greenery, and in the valley below, lovely houses made of undressed stone. Along the trail, now concrete-paved, meet up with the junction in the village centre of **Ingenio (11)**; the left turn leads down to the Bar Silencio with a shop, however, you continue straight on the small road. After a few minutes, you can either leave the road following the sign for *S-47 Santa Lucía* or you can follow the gently ascending road. After 15 mins, you reach the **Mirador de Ingenio (12)** where you can enjoy the splendid view once again. Also, the destination for the walk, the domed church of Santa Lucía, is already in sight.

Off to the side from the *mirador*, pick up a descending tarmac track that leads in just a few minutes to a junction. Follow the concrete track by turning right towards *Santa Lucía / CR La Longuera*, but leave it again, a good 5 mins later, by turning right onto a narrow and steeply ascending path forking away. Just in front of a wall for a house, where the path merges into an intersecting trail, turn right and continue ascending steeply. At the end, the trail becomes a cobbled passageway, flanked by houses. Where this forks, bear left, and soon meet up with the GC-65, near the former **Hao (2)** museum. Turn left to reach the *plaza* **(1)** of **Santa Lucía**.

Humble trail, extreme contrasts

Pass through picturesque passageways and palm tree gardens, ascend hairpin bends along a rugged and steep rock face, then climb up to a high plateau. From there, instead of abrupt drop-offs, you'll find gentle, terraced fields of grain, laid in harmonic symmetry. They have not been cultivated for a long time and are beautifully overgrown. The highest point of the walk is the "Turn of the Century Cross", erected in 1900; here, enjoy a view sweeping over the vast Tirajana valley basin.

Starting point: *plaza* in Santa Lucía, 709m. Car park and bus stop "Plaza" for line 34.
Height difference: 270m.
Grade: except for the steep ascent along the plunging rock face, an easy walk along signed trails and tracks.
Refreshment: nothing en route. Bars and restaurants in Santa Lucía.
Note: the route has been marked by the local government with the directional sign, *Cruz del Siglo (S-40)*.

On the grand ***plaza (1)***, at the foot of the church in **Santa Lucía**, leave the street behind and head towards a reddish-coloured stone house. At the junction situated behind it, continue straight on and follow the tarmac track in the direction of *Cruz del Siglo*. This ascends steeply through a verdant garden landscape to a junction up above: straight ahead leads towards El Mundillo, but we follow the directional sign *Cruz del Siglo* and turn right onto a pretty passageway. Pass the ruins of a *gofio* and olive mill, then shortly thereafter, the junction at the **Casa El Valle 11 (2)**. Make a note of the right-hand trail, descending gently to the right, for the return route later on, but now keep straight on, veering to the left and continuing a climb upwards. Now the

trail quickly leaves the village behind while passing overgrown fields, flanked by cactus-like Euphorbia. At the following **junction**, where the entrance to the Aula de la Naturaleza Las Tederas is situated to the right and the signed *Camino a las Vueltas* sets off to the left, we continue straight off ahead. At the foot of the towering **steep rock face (3)**, ignore the unsigned turn-off to the left and bear right instead. The trail winds steeply

On the plateau below the "Turn of the Century Cross".

upwards, and the higher we climb, the tighter the switchback, and all the prettier is the view of Santa Lucía and the vast valley basin. During the flowering season, nestled between the scattered boulders, enjoy a lush display of white, yellow and violet blossoms. You can concentrate on the landscape now; en route, there is only one turn-off to be ignored (this turns right to the Cueva de la Luna/"Cave of the Moon"). Suddenly, you find yourself standing on the **pass (4)** and confronted with a completely different landscape: as far as the eye can see; gently rolling, overgrown terraced fields – no one wants to reap the harvest anymore. Keeping straight ahead along a path, you could continue on towards Temisas/Agüimes (*S-40*), but instead, we turn right and continue along the sheer edge of the rim, heading towards the striking cross, posed upon a height. Only a short time after, reach the plateau below the **Cruz del Siglo (5)**: here is a marvellous spot to picnic while enjoying breathtaking, downwards and far-reaching views! If you wish, you could scramble up the final metres to the cross.

At first, the return route is identical to the approach route: from the **pass (4)**, ignore the turn-offs for the Cueva de la Luna, for the junction at the foot of the **steep rock face (3)** and for the Aula de la Naturaleza. At the **Casa El Valle 11 (2)**, however, turn left, rambling through the picturesque passageways of this district. Then meet up with an intersecting street; turn right onto it. Pass the **Hao (6)**, a former archaeological museum, and then turn right onto the main street, GC-65. Passing shops and restaurants, return to the *plaza* (1), at the foot of the church of **Santa Lucía**.

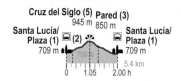

Cruz del Siglo (5) Pared (3)
945 m 850 m
Santa Lucía/   Santa Lucía/
Plaza (1) (2)   Plaza (1)
709 m   709 m

5.4 km
0   1.05   2.00 h

Pleasant ramble on the outskirts of the village

More of a ramble than a "real" walk, this tour leads into a romantic secondary gorge, reclaimed by nature. On the way, pass the ruins of numerous mills that were still in operation not so very long ago. The last molino is a good place for a picnic!

Starting point: *plaza* in Santa Lucía, 709m. Car park and bus stop "Plaza" for the line 34.
Height difference: 130m in both ascent and descent.
Grade: except for the steep ascent through the passageways of the village this is an easy walk along signed trails.
Refreshment: nothing en route. Bars and restaurants in Santa Lucía.

Note: the route is marked as the *Ruta de los Molinos* and provided with directional signs. If you wish to learn more about the mills along the way, you can pick up informational material in English at the tourist office (Casas Consistoriales, Mon–Fri 8–14.00) to the right of the *plaza*; you can also ask at the tourist office if the renovated olive oil mill can be visited from inside.

From the grand *plaza* **(1)** in **Santa Lucía**, with your back to the main street (sign: *S-40 Agüimes*), head towards a reddish-coloured stone house. At the junction situated behind it, continue by heading straight on and following the tarmac track in the direction of *Cruz del Siglo*. The track leads through a verdant garden landscape to a **junction**: straight ahead leads towards El Mundillo, but we take an excursion to the right and follow the directional sign for *Cruz del Siglo* into a pretty passageway. Just a few minutes later, meet up with the ruins of a **gofio and olive oil mill (2)**: rosette-shaped succulents are running

Molino de los Araña: at the turn-around point for the mill route.

riot on the roof tiles, whilst holes in the wall sprout lush greenery. A sign declares this to be a *patrimonio etnográfico*, but from an "ethnographic heritage" is – aside from some exterior walls and two mill stones – very little to see at the moment.

Now return to the **junction**, and then turn right into the narrow street, signed *El Mundillo*. This leads into the picturesque hamlet of **El Lomito (3)**, where the tarmac pavement becomes a cobblestone trail. The trail ascends and leads past the mill, Molino de José Pérez which is being used as a residence. Then the trail forks at the **Casa Rural El Molino**: here, bear left and then pass a tumbledown mill (**Molino de Cándido Rubio**). When the cobbled pavement ends, continue along the narrow, dirt path that leads along the rim of a little secondary gorge. At the next junction, do not continue straight on to meet up with the mill, Molino Viejo, but instead, climb up diagonally to the right, passing above the mill, Molino del Mundillo, situated on the left-hand side. The trail veers away temporarily from the sheer edge and leads in a sweeping bend, passing olive trees that are growing wild, as well as *tabaiba* bushes growing up to two metres in height. At an abandoned barn, a sign marks the end of the mill route: from here, you have a view of the white mill, **Molino de los Araña (4)** (45 mins), situated on the side of the slope opposite.

Along the return route, enjoy the panoramic view of Santa Lucía clad in the vibrant green of palm trees. One after the other, pass the mills of El Mundillo, Viejo and Cándido Rubio, afterwards, also the Casa Rural El Molino. Starting at **El Lomito (3)** the pavement becomes tarmac once again. Along the little-used street, descend pleasantly and effortlessly until merging with the intersecting street, Calle Senador Castillo Olivares. Turn right onto this street and then meet up with a mosque-like **church**, a graphic fresco for the altar is well worth seeing within. The "Matriarchat" sculpture next to the portal is a tribute to older women which seems a bit out of place. Afterwards descend a monumental flight of stairs, down to the **plaza (1)** in **Santa Lucía**.

Molino de los Araña (4)
820 m
Santa Lucía/Plaza (1)   Santa Lucía/Plaza (1)
709 m   709 m

2.8 km
0   0.45 1.30 h

3.30 hrs

Climbing up and up – always enjoying a breathtaking view!

Westwards, enjoy a view into the vast Tirajana basin, northwards, the steep rock faces of the central massif soar up and, southwards, a regiment of mountain ranges march down to the sea. The walk sets off through a typical pastoral countryside: along abandoned fields where grain once grew, the outlying dwellings of the hamlet of Taidía appear; with orange groves and goat farms. Steep stretches follow level ones en route and, just before the destination, the trail winds steeply up to reach the Altos de Pajonales, a vast, high plateau, reclaimed by nature. From here, take in the perforated crag massif "Sepultura del Gigante" ("Giants' Tomb"). At first, the descent follows the track, then use the approach route to return again.

Starting point: *plaza* in Santa Lucía, 709m. Car park and bus stop "Plaza" for the line 34.

Height difference: 350m.

Grade: steep and strenuous at the outset, in the middle section along tracks and trails in easy up-and-down walking, and then, again, a steep ascent.

Refreshment: nothing en route. Bars and restaurants in Santa Lucía.

Accommodation: country cottages in Santa Lucía; the nearest hotel is in San Bartolomé.

Alternative: from the Altos de Pajonales (5), you could keep to the trail with zigzags until reaching the Sepultura del Gigante ("Giants' Tomb"), a bizarre, cave-peppered crag (1.5km, 1 hr). Here, you are confronted with an extremely steep stretch, in a relatively short length of 1.5km, not quite 600m of altitude must be negotiated. By fog and rain, this route is very dangerous, as sometimes you are walking over smoothly polished rock. To return, you must take the very same route back to the Altos de Pajonales and, from there, join up again with the return route which is described in the main walk.

Starting point is the large **plaza (1)**, at the foot of the mosque-like church at **Santa Lucía**. With your back turned toward the street, cross over the *plaza* (sign: *S-40 Agüimes*) and, a good 100m on, meet up with a cobbled street. Turn left onto this street and head towards a yellow, two-storey house with a wooden balcony. Once there, turn onto the signed *S-43*. The extremely battered trail, strewn with scree, ascends steeply for 120m to reach an intersecting trail; turn left onto it. After about 50m (continue on the *S-43*) bear to the right where you see two wooden crosses, and 550m farther on, join a **trail junction (2)** – you are now on the lower edge of the savannah-like high plateau. Turn left for a couple of paces and then immediately continue along a broad roadway by turning right. Alternatively, you can also use the narrow path that runs parallel to the roadway.

Inspired by Moorish architecture: Santa Lucía's parish church.

The roadway soon runs along a wire fence, and then, at a **junction**, 3 min later, bear right and continue along the fence. 20m further on, turn left onto a narrow trail that, another 220m on, merges again into the track. Turn right onto the track and then ignore the path that forks away from it (we will use this narrow, overgrown path during the return route, but now, for the approach, we choose the easier track). 640m further on, at the same level as a **yellow house (3)**, the narrow path and the broad trail merge together once again. 100m after that, turn right onto a path forking away which leads between fenced-in orange trees and a stone wall. After yet another 300m, meet up with the concrete track from **Altos de Taidía**. This ascends steeply to the right – just before a **left-hand bend (4)**, the return trail merges from the right – and then, not quite 500m on, ends at a two-storey house. Directly behind the house, ascend along a stairway and meet up with the ancient *Camino Real*, which twists upwards through reddish-coloured rock, along countless bends – up above are the highest summits on the island, often obscured by clouds. After a 15 minute ascent, you have climbed up to the **Altos de Pajonales (5)**: vast, gently rounded high plains that were apparently used for agriculture in times gone by (1.45 hrs).

Altos de Pajonales: storm clouds are building.

While the zigzagged trail now leads straight ahead to ascend to the Sepultura del Gigante (see Alternative), we turn right instead, treading over the low wall and picking up a dirt track, slippery underfoot. Turn right onto the track and descend in broad bends. 930m further on, pass the entrance gate to a solitary *finca* **(6)** that we may have already spotted from the Altos de Pajonales. Past the next hillock, the track winds downwards in bends while presenting panoramic views. After passing a goat farm, meet up again with the concrete track on the **Altos de Taidía (4)** that we have already met on the approach route, and turn left. 140m on, leave it behind again by turning left onto the path forking away, continue past fenced-in orange trees, and then merge into the track once more. Now pass the **yellow house (3)**.

To vary the return route, 240m past the house, leave the track behind by turning right onto a path forking away that merges back onto the track 570m further on. Because this path leads through a romantic landscape, after 230m leave the track behind again by turning right. Immediately after, meet up with a trail junction: continue straight ahead, following along the fence, turn left 100m later and then immediately right. 5 mins later, reach the **trail junction (2)** you already came across on the approach route. Here, follow the trail sign to the right heading towards *Santa Lucía* and via the steep, battered path, return again to the **plaza (1)** in **Santa Lucía**.

Altos de Pajonales **(5)**
Altos de Taidía **(4)** 1025 m
Santa Lucía/   875 m   Casa   Santa Lucía/
Plaza **(1)**   **(3)**   Plaza **(1)**
709 m   709 m
                             8.2 km
0   1.05   1.45   2.40   3.30 h

Native burial sites and a palm tree grove

From the southern resorts, you can quickly reach the mountain village of Arteara. The water-abundant gorge, sporting palm trees, was inhabited even in pre-Hispanic times, as a large necropolis bears witness: in the rocky desert of a gigantic slope which had slipped away, 809 burial sites, dating from the 5th century BC all the way up until the 17th century AD, were exposed. The "mere mortal" dead were simply covered with stones, but those who stood higher in the social hierarchy were embalmed and wrapped in goat skins – these well preserved mummies are now on display in the Museo Canario in Las Palmas. A signed educational trail leads through an archaeological park, and the return route leads through a grove of pine trees back to the starting point.

Starting point: the village limits of Arteara, 337m. GC-60, km37.5; turn-off for the GC-601; bus stop for line 18.

Height difference: about 80m in both ascent and descent.

Grade: an easy, short walk along a village street and an educational trail. The return route leads almost on the level through a grove of palm trees.

Refreshment: en route, there is a bar with irregular opening hours. There are some restaurants in Fataga, not quite 5km north of Arteara.

Note: an entrance fee is charged, Tue–Sun 10–17.00, Jul/Aug 10–14.00; 4€/2 €.

Alternative: if you wish to experience the barren landscape for a little longer, at the *mirador* (3), if this is allowed, continue straight ahead and leave the archaeological park behind. The trail ascends over a steep slope of scree and then branches – cairns are helpful for route-finding. 10 mins later, turn right onto the dirt track Arteara – Ayagaures (GC-602) that winds along the slope in gentle bends, crosses over the *barranco* floor, and then ascends to the GC-60; turn right onto this road. 10 mins after that, you can take an excursion to the Camel Safari Baranda, where fruit juice is also served. Afterwards, return to the main road and, from there, it is a 600m walk to return to Arteara.

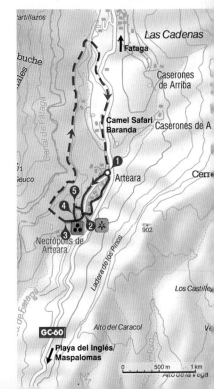

You can't miss it: Camel Safari Baranda, where freshly squeezed juice awaits us (Alternative).

From the GC-60 turn onto the narrow road GC-601 heading towards **Arteara (1)**, then continue through the sleepy little village. 650m further on, at a **cul-de-sac (2)**, reach the village limits. On your right-hand side, the little visitor centre (Centro de Interpretación) is situated, to the left, a **turn-off for a track**; make a note of it for the return route later on. At first, follow the cobbled trail straight ahead, then at the fork a good 100m further on, bear diagonally left and continue along the trail that is signed *tramo B*. Not quite another 250m after that, climb up to a ***mirador* (3)** and enjoy the sweeping view taking in the stony, desert-like terrain. Afterwards, climb back down again and turn right onto the trail already met during the approach.

There is no need to return to the visitor centre, but instead, at the **junction**, we could turn immediately to the left onto the trail signed as *tramo C*. This trail crosses directly through the burial ground – the stone plates which have been laid down to create a trail, require concentration when walking. 2 mins later, pass the **Cueva del Rey (4)**, the carefully constructed "Cave of the King". On the days of the spring and autumn equinoxes, a mysterious natural phenomena can be observed here: the archaeologist, Rosa Schlueter, discovered that when the first rays of the

Cueva del Rey (4)
365 m
Arteara (1)   Arteara (1)
337 m   337 m
2.5 km
0   0.30   1.00 h

sun appear on the dawns of the equinoxes (March 21 and September 23), it seems that the cave is directly illuminated by the light. Passing Tumuli burial mounds (signs), meet up with yet another junction: here, bear left along the *tramo D* and climb up, in not quite 100m, to the highest point of the route, with **information boards (5**, *Muralla / Los Risco de Amurga*), as well as a sweeping panoramic view taking in the gorge.

Now return to the **junction**, this time continuing straight ahead, and then a little later – after passing bee hives constructed from the hollowed-out trunks of palm trees – reach the back of the Centro de Interpretación, and the **cul-de-sac (2)** already met on the approach route. Turn right here onto the dirt track that appears to descend and, 90m on, meet up with a **junction** at the *barranco* floor. Turn left onto the track further back and then ramble through a dense grove of palm trees, casting some welcome shade. Reeds, growing high as a house, provide additional coolness and reddish-coloured, rugged mountain ridges can be glimpsed through the crowns of the palms – breath-taking scenery! A good 700m along the track, we find ourselves, once again, at the starting point for the walk, the village limits of **Arteara (1)**.

Verdant oasis in the Barranco de Fataga: Arteara is surrounded by groves of palm trees.

Coastal walk on the southern island

Holidaymakers sojourning on the Costa Canaria may get the notion to "get warmed up" in the dunes here before tackling some more demanding walks. En route, get acquainted with a small, but spectacular, landscape: a sparkling beach, 7 kilometres in length, with drifting dunes up to 15 metres high, and also, at the edge of a palm tree grove, a brackish lagoon, that serves as a migratory stopover for birds on their way south. The entire area is a protected nature reserve, however, access is allowed.

Starting point: Maspalomas, 5m. There are bus stops for lines 18, 30, 32 and 33 amongst others.
Height difference: about 50m in both ascent and descent.
Grade: an easy walk, but long, over sand, trails and promenades. Because of the intensity of the sun's rays in any sea-

son, be sure to take along some head covering; a lot of drinking water and bathing gear should also be packed! We recommend starting off in the early morning or late afternoon, when the sand is somewhat cooler.
Refreshment: beach bars (*chiringuitos*) provide refreshment until sunset.

It feels like being in the Sahara – stay on the marked route!

The lighthouse (Faro de Maspalomas) towers heavenwards on the southern tip of the island, which separates the Maspalomas and Meloneras resorts from one another. 100m eastwards, building development abruptly ends, and in front of us, an extensive nature reserve ranges on; a narrow sandbank sunders the sea from the La Charca lagoon, where our return route will lead us later on (see below).

The walk begins at the **Balneario (1)**, a round pavilion with showers and changing rooms. Now walk along the beach for more than 4km: the view reaches far over the rolling waves, whilst towards the interior, the first dunes pile up. The sand has not, as many tourist guides claim, been blown here by wind from the Sahara, but instead, was produced by the surf, which has, for millennia, crushed the coral and shellfish into fine particles. The prevailing south-west wind has carried the sand landwards, forming a lovely crescent beach. At the **Punta de Maspalomas (2)** the coastline hooks northwards. 15 mins later on, the *playa* narrows (the recreational area, Anexo II, lying before us is scheduled to be demolished). If you wish to skirt around Anexo II, at kiosk No. 5, cut away towards the interior, otherwise, at **kiosk No. 3 (3)**, you have another alternative: cross through the midst of the Anexo hustle, then the car park, and finally, via steps to the left, climb up to the promenade,

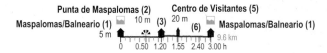

149

The lagoon, La Charca, is a little nature reserve.

Paseo Costa Canaria (4), separating the dune-peppered beach from the seaside resort, Playa del Inglés (sign *Mirador de las Dunas 1.8km*). Continue towards Maspalomas while enjoying the view of the dunes from the elevated promenade. At the same height as the **Sahara Beach Clubs** veer to the left onto a ramp trail, flanked by wooden planks, that leads, in only a few minutes, to a broad viewing platform, the **Mirador de las Dunas (5)**. You can obtain some information material from the small **visitor centre**.

Our trail sets off to the right of the viewing platform, heading straight across the dunes. There are several trails marked with wooden planks. It is best to take the main trail leading westward. Keep right at the first fork from where you can make out the towers of Meloneras. Not quite 40 mins later, following the waymarkers through the sandy terrain, meet up with a gate. Pass through to pick up the **promenade (6)** along the dry stream bed of the **Barranco de Fataga**. Bear left, cross over the valley floor via a bridge, and continue along the promenade by turning left towards the **La Charca lagoon (7)**, with a roofed viewpoint. The brackish lagoon, a nature reserve, is a nesting place for numerous seabirds, e.g., bald coots, little egrets and ringed plovers. They feed from the salty seawater, which floods over the sandbar during high tide, as well as from the freshwater provided by rainfall. The combination of the waters creates an environment for distinctive species of flora, and ensures a habitat at the edge of the lagoon that is conducive to salt cedars, Launaea and reeds.

Afterwards, follow the Paseo to the coast while passing apartment houses. The destination of the walk is the **Balneario (1)**.

The African-like mountainous terrain in the south

The walk leads for long stretches through a remote nature reserve whilst offering a great range of diversity: little reservoirs, an open pine forest, and, in an oasis of palm trees, a small "ghost town". Another marvellous sight is the Pino de Pilancones, a gigantic felled pine tree, a victim of fire and storm, whose remains have created a bizarre natural monument. The "Final Rest of the Dead" recalls the fact that this trail was once a pilgrim's way – the procession ascended from the seaside to the church at San Bartolomé high above. The landscape is characterised by water-storing flora, like Euphorbia atropurpurea and red bugloss; in the spring, white larkspur is flowering. In shady spots, you can find rosette succulents, ferns and almond trees.

Starting point: Ayagaures, 329m. Approach only by car; no bus service.
Height difference: 700m.
Grade: a long walk with very little shade; the walk is strenuous due to the height differences and some stretches that are slippery underfoot.
Refreshment: there is a village bar in Ayagaures.
Important note: at Waypoint 6 a sign saying "closed by detachment" warns of the landslide that went down behind the Descansadero de los Muertos in 2017. Experienced trekkers can take the path. At the site of the landslide, active locals fixed a rope which makes it possible to scramble across it.
Alternative: behind Waypoint 5 and at Waypoint 6, the *S-57* leads comfortably up to Tunte (2 hours).

Backwards view of the Ayagaures reservoir.

From the church square in **Ayagaures (1)**, follow the street (GC-503) for 150m northwards to the barrage wall and then turn left onto a roadway. The roadway leads above the shoreline of the lake, passing flower-garlanded houses. At the **fork (2)**, 900m further on, bear left and, another 100m further, bear right (sign: *S-57 Tunte por el Ventoso* – "Tunte" is the old Canary term for San Bartolomé) – then cross the **barrage wall (3)** that separates the Ayagaures lake from the Gambuesa lake. A picturesque, palm-dotted hamlet is situated high above the shoreline. At the end of the barrage wall, pick up a track, flanked by reeds and rushes, that winds upwards in numerous zigzags. At the top, reach a junction in **Ayagaures Alto (4)**: to the left, there is an access road leading to a fenced-in house; to the right, it leads to a walled-in water reservoir. After a few metres, turn left at the sign *S-57 Tunte* and continue along the wire mesh fence on an initially wide trail. This merges into a path which ascends doggedly upwards. This path is called the "Devil's trail" (*camino del diablo*), and this is not because of any mystical apparition, but because the path's "devilishly" slippery surface demands a great deal of concentration.

After a total of 2.45km of walking, the trail levels off, and in a pine tree grove, we can treat ourselves to a breather. But then the ascent continues and leads at the very edge of the slope. Later on, the route brings us high above a mighty gorge. The houses of the Casas de Taginastal, far below, appear like a child's building blocks; the mountain above, Punta de los Atajos, is riddled with holes. Before we pass it by, reach a **high plateau** – up and over the pine-dotted slopes, we can look back on the reservoirs of Ayagaures and Gambuesa. The next landmark is a tumbledown farmstead, which appears below us after we have skirted around numerous protruding rocks. A short ascent leads to the **track (5)**. Turn left along the track and, 300m further on, pass a cistern to our right (directly before and after this point, steep short cuts descend to the Degollada de la Manzanilla/152San Bartolomé). In gentle up-and-down walking, the track leads for 1.68km through a pine forest to meet up with a striking **junction (6**, 2.55 hrs). The trail forking off to the right (*S-57*) also leads, in 1.6km, to the Degollada de la Manzanilla (see Walk 37); straight ahead, it leads to the campsites of Los Bailaderos and El Vivero. We, however, turn left to follow the *Camino de Pilancones*, flanked by a stone wall (see note), crossing a pine forest towards the *barranco* floor.

After a steep descent, 1.7km in length, we reach the **Pino de Pilancones (7)** or better said, the remains of the "Pine tree of Pilancones". This mighty, ancient specimen, with a trunk measuring 5m in diameter, was brought down by a fire and a storm in 2008. The length of its branches can be ascertained by contemplating the wide semi-circle formed by the stone enclosure. Today, the long trunk sprawls on the ground, and a small memorial shows how it looked when it was still standing. In the background, the black, jagged rock faces of the Montaña Negra soar to the heavens. 380m further on, the trail surprises us with yet another "attraction": the **Descansadero de los Muertos** ("Resting Place of the Dead"). Funeral processions, coming from the seaside on their way to the cemetery in San Bartolomé, were accustomed to taking a break here. The coffin was set upon the stone table with the cross.

From the "Resting place", the sometimes cobbled trail climbs down in bends. Then a "ghost town" appears, boasting palm trees and picturesque ruins. 100m past the first house of **Las Tederas (8)** standing directly on the trail's edge, the trail merges into a track. Turn left onto it. 25m further on, a short-cut path branches off to the left, but it is more pleasant to keep to the track, which crosses the *barranco* floor and, 600m on, behind a barrier, merges back onto the trail. Here, do not descend to the house, but instead, follow the upper track, which leads in a wide bend to skirt around the last houses of the hamlet which are temporarily inhabited. For the next 4.6km, a good hour, continue descending along the track through the pristine mountain terrain – on the left-hand slope, we can spot the houses of Casas de Taginastal, and to the right, half way along this stretch, a solitary, gigantic pine tree catches our attention. Little by little, we come closer to Ayagaures.

The stump to the right, the trunk to the left: fire and storm felled the giant pine tree.

At the first **junction of tracks (9)**, bear left, and at the second junction, the **fork (2)** already met on the approach, turn right and then reach, just a little later, the starting point for the walk, the church square of **Ayagaures (1)**.

Austere beauty in the hinterland of the southern coast

When you are in the resort towns of the Costa Canaria, it's very hard to believe that, only 10 kilometres inland – after passing through rather unattractive settlements – a completely different world begins: dramatically steep slopes and pine forests and plenty of solitude.

Sunburnt slopes on the other side of the slate-strewn Degollada de los Tres Pinos.

Starting point: viewpoint Cima Pedro Gonzalez (often noted on maps as the "Paso de los Palmitos"), 490m. Approach only by car along the GC-503 via Monte León or along the GC-504 via Ayagaures.
Height difference: 320m.
Grade: sometimes pleasant, sometimes a steep walk, along waymarked trails and tracks. Please follow the tour description and skirt around the settlement at the outset of the trail giving it a wide berth (vicious dogs!). Sure-footedness and good

route-finding ability are useful in the later course of the walk.
Refreshment: nothing available en route, therefore, please take along sufficient drinking water for this walk, usually lacking in shade!
Note: as long as the hotel situated above the Palmitos Park remains unsold, the connecting trail noted on the map from the zoological park to the starting point of this walk (the viewpoint Cima Pedro Gonzaléz), is closed.

Whilst crossing over the Palmitos gorge.

At the viewpoint **Cima Pedro González (1**, parking possible) cross over the road and then follow it northwards towards Ayagaures. Only 100m on, at the *Paso de los Palmitos*, leave the tarmac behind by turning diagonally left onto the roadway, leading along the mountain ridge (do not descend to the hotel!). A good 15 mins later, reach a fork at the hamlet, **Casas del Lomo del Palmito (2)**: in front of us is a private property, so we bear to the right, continuing for about a minute by following the chain-link fence, and then circle around the hamlet in an anti-clockwise direction whilst ignoring all the left-hand forks, and heading directly towards a pyramid-shaped mountain situated in front of us.

At house No. 93, bear left and, 60m further on, pass the first gate, which can be opened easily (unless it has already been removed in the meantime). Another 170m on, a second gate follows. The trail, sometimes battered by storms (slippery underfoot!), leads straight ahead into the Barranco de los Palmitos and, at its eastern end, begins to ascend. 270m after having passed the second gate (8 mins of walking), cross over the *barranco* floor **(3)** where it has been visibly washed out by rain and is waymarked by numerous cairns. On the opposite side of the slope, the trail ascends steeply and along many zigzags for a good 10 minutes, leading to the slate-strewn col, **Degollada de los Tres Pinos (4)**. Cairns point out the route as it skirts around a knoll and, 260m further on, crosses over a little secondary valley. Another 8 mins later,

it leads up the slope (to the left of the valley floor), then meets up with a **fork (5)**, which marks the beginning of a panoramic circular walk. Bear left here (we will return from the right after-

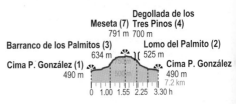

Degollada de los
Meseta (7) Tres Pinos (4)
791 m 700 m
Barranco de los Palmitos (3) Lomo del Palmito (2)
634 m 525 m
Cima P. González (1) Cima P. González
490 m 490 m
7.2 km
0 1.00 1.55 2.25 3.30 h

wards) and soon enjoy a downwards view of the untamed Barranco de Chamoriscán. 500m on, cross over a secondary valley. After another 130m, and 15m before reaching the first of two elevated heights, meet up with a confusing **trail junction (6)**: one trail heads to the left; two others, only 5m apart, head to the right. Ignore the left-hand trail, which leads in a wide bend to the second elevated height, and also ignore the right-hand trail furthest away, which provides a descent route into the gorge. Instead, take the right-hand trail nearest to you and climb up for 100m onto another **plateau (7)**, crowned with some sort of "stone pyramid". The view is stunning, taking in the houses of the hamlet of Chamoriscán down below, lying in the shade cast by the steep rock face; straight ahead, a view of the central massif, including the tip of the Roque Nublo.

From the plateau, bear right to skirt around the knoll that lies before us while ascending (Note: it is now possible to extend the walk in a northeasterly direction). On the old trail which is marked with cairns, turn right into the intersecting path 4 minutes later. 7 minutes after that, at an ambiguous **junction (8)** on rocky terrain, bear right and, 220m further on, reach the aforementioned **fork (5)** where our circular route began.

The further course of the route is already known to us from the approach: cross over a little secondary gorge, and just a little later on, we find ourselves at the end of the slate-strewn plain, the **Degollada de los Tres Pinos (4)**. Cairns point out the trailhead for the descent route: along the zigzagged path, descend steeply back into the **Barranco de los Palmitos (3)**. Cross over the *barranco* and then climb down along the scree-slippery trail. Pass the two gates and then follow the track to the **Mirador Pedro González (1)**, the viewpoint and starting point, located on the GC-605.

A sanctum for the indigenous people

On Tauro, at 1225m, the indigenous Canary Islanders once paid homage to their god, Alcorán. The mountain is shaped like a pyramid without a point, and appears like a fortress, towering out of the surrounding mountain range. Over ridges and gorges, you can take in the coast – a breathtaking view!

Starting point: the Degollada de Tauro, 914m. No bus service.

Height difference: 340m.

Grade: a short, simple walk along an ancient *Camino Real*.

Note: the approach can only be made by car. The best route is via the GC-505 towards Soria. At Barranquillo Andrés, turn off towards Mogán; the trail sets off, 3.2km further on, to the left. 200m more, a track heads to the right to the little reservoir of Salto del Perro (sign: Carretera El Pinar). At the side of the road, there are a few parking places. Another attractive approach is via Mogán: 2km north of the

mountain village, turn off from the GC-15 onto the GC-605 towards Ayacata and, 8.5km further on, turn off towards Barranquillo Andrés. 1km on, you can see the reservoir, Presa Salto del Perro, to the left and shortly after, to the right, the *Camino Real* begins the climb to the Tauro.

Montaña de Tauro (3)
1225 m

Degollada de Tauro (1)
914 m

Degollada de Tauro (1)
914 m

4.3 km

0   1.05   2.00 h

A world of stone, but softened by lakes and solitary pines: on Tauro's summit.

Leave the road behind at the **Degollada de Tauro (1)** by turning off onto the modestly signed stone ramp and climbing up the trail, flanked by gorse and lavender, to the ridge of a flank. On its southern side, descend for a short stretch, then cross over a depression and ascend to a plateau. Keeping temporarily on the level, traverse a notch in the slope before the main ascent begins. In broad, pleasant bends, the trail winds upwards to reach a **fork (2)**. Ignore the turn-off to the right to *Cortadores/La Solana* (Mogán) and follow the trail sign to the left in the direction of *Montaña de Tauro*. Ascend for a short stretch and then you are standing on the high plateau (small stone pyramid) below the summit of the **Montaña de Tauro (3)**. A tiny path leads to the inconspicuous summit on the right. Of course, the view from the **ruins** to the left of the "pyramid" is no less spectacular: the panorama sweeps to the right over the reservoirs, Cueva de las Niñas and Salto del Perro, all the way to the rugged central massif, but no matter where you look, you see a sheer drop-off! The high plateau appears very harsh, peppered with rock plates protruding askew from the terrain. Windswept pines emanate the feeling of being in the Wild West.

The return route follows the approach trail back to the **fork (2)**: here you have the option to go left for about 10 mins and reach a viewpoint offering magnificent views of the Mogán gorge. The main trail turns right down to the stone ramp at the saddle **Degollada de Tauro (1)**.

Yawning gorges, rugged ridges and little oases

This walk provides an insight into the gorges of the western island: steep, dry and barren slopes contrast with the lush green of the valleys; in the interior, the weather-beaten rock faces of the central massif rise up. Pass a "ghost town" and slopes covered in Euphorbia atropurpurea. With the starting point and the destination easily accessible by bus, the walk is simple to organise.

Starting point: the pass Degollada de Veneguera, 655m. On the GC-200 at km45.7; bus line 38 (tell or show the driver the name of the pass, as well the km-marker number where you want to get off); there is also a little lay-by for parking.
Destination: Mogán, 250m. Bus stop for lines 38 and 86.
Height difference: 620m in descent; 210m in ascent.
Grade: the route is via ancient trails without any shade; the first stretch, leading along a narrow, stony and precipitous path, demands concentration.
Refreshment: bars and restaurants in Veneguera and Mogán.
Accommodation: hotels and inns in Puerto de Mogán.

Alternative: at the windmill, Molino de Viento, 1km south of Mogán's village centre, a trail sets off on the left-hand side – at first only poorly marked – leading along the foot of the rock face, and from there, winds up steeply to the saddle at Paso de los Laderones (2 hrs). Here, enjoy a splendid view of Mogán's valley. At the pass, the alpine path also intersects with an ancient, connecting trail: turning left along this trail, in another 2 hrs, reach the mountain, Montaña de Tauro (there, possible link with Walk 47). To the right, descend, in a good hour, to the hamlet of El Cercado; from there, you can walk to the road and take advantage of the bus connection to Puerto de Mogán, Mogán and Tasarte.

The pass **Degollada de Veneguera (1)** is easy to recognise: a large sign announces the municipal limits of Mogán (*Bienvenido al municipio de Mogán*), there is a sculpture depicting a man pole-vaulting in the old Canary Islander style. If you look to the south, in the distance, you will see the destination of the first stage of the walk: the white houses of Veneguera. The trail (*S-73*), narrow at the outset, begins directly behind the walls of the sculpture and leads, in one minute, to a junction. Descend straight on here. The trail leads in zigzags, at first lightly descending, and then more steeply. Cairns help in route-finding. The view of the broadening valley and the towering fortress-like crags in the background is simply stunning. About 20 mins later, the trail crosses over a secondary valley and, shortly after, another one. Afterwards, the trail leads, somewhat precipitously, along the left-hand rim of the gorge and then

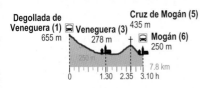

Degollada de Veneguera (1) 655 m — Veneguera (3) 278 m — Cruz de Mogán (5) 435 m — Mogán (6) 250 m
250 m
7.8 km
0   1.30   2.35 3.10 h

Near the "ghost town" La Cogolla.

reaches the palm-dotted hamlet of **La Cogolla (2)**, where not a soul appears to be living. The houses of undressed stone have been abandoned and vegetation is running rampant between the walls. Follow the trail sign in the direction of *Veneguera (S-73)* and continue descending. The trail becomes a broad, dirt track which, 5 mins later, passes by the last house of La Cogolla. Just a little later, on the right-hand side, spot a mighty, striking crag and then cross over a *barranco* floor. Afterwards, ascend slightly and then, 20 mins later, cross over another *barranco* floor, this one lushly overgrown in reeds and mighty Hercules club. Where the track becomes tarmac, it takes on the name Calle Real del Mar and, at house No. 25, meets up with an intersecting street. Turn left here to ascend whilst ignoring two passageways turning off to the right – the third one (Paseo Pantaleón) leads, in 15 mins, to the church square of **Veneguera (3)** with a bar, "Las Cañadas". Follow the descending street past the bus stop, 160m further on, and then bear left. 100m more, ignore the narrow street turning right to the Playa de Veneguera, and yet another 100m on, ignore the track climbing upwards.

At this point, the street hooks off to the right; continue following it for another 60m, but then turn left onto a provisionally-waymarked *camino*. Passing through a trellis of cacti, 130m further on, reach a fork and bear diagonally right. The trail crosses over a concrete track and then runs the whole length

Backwards view of Veneguera.

of a secondary valley. 5 mins past the aforementioned fork, pass a **right-hand bend (4)** with a sign, *Hoya de Salvia*. Just a little later, leave the track behind by forking left onto a slightly ascending trail, and continue on, past a house of undressed stone, where the trail merges into a dirt track. Follow this track along a chain-link fence, but leave it behind again, a minute later, by turning left onto a narrow path (cairn!), which is leading towards a grove of palm trees. From now on, there are no further route-finding difficulties: the trail quickly gains in height and leads over a rocky terrain into a secondary valley. Climb up to a mountain ridge, from which a far-reaching, 360° view opens up. Afterwards, the trail winds up in zigzags along the south-western side of the mountain ridge to reach the wooden cross, **Cruz de Mogán (5)** – the pass separates the two *barrancos* of Veneguera and Mogán. Ignore the ridge trail that starts off from the cross, and instead, follow the trail sign for the *S-73 Mogán* descending straight ahead. The trail is flanked by flora of the spurge family, as it winds down, in the next hour, along numerous zigzags towards Mogán.

Already nearing the settlement, pass a house with a threshing circle and cross over the **Barranco de Mogán** at a mango orchard. Only a few minutes of walking brings us to the **GC-200**. Turn left here and, 100m further on, reach the church square of **Mogán (6)**. A bus stop, bars and restaurants are all located nearby.

A remote beach between rugged mountain ridges

The nature reserve of Güi Güi is in one of the most remote corners of the island. Surrounded by high, steep cliffs, almost 1000m in height, the beach can only be accessed by boat, or on foot, along paths once used by the native inhabitants. The light-coloured sand is often washed away during the winter half-year, and thus, the beach itself isn't very attractive. At the weekend, and during Easter and summer holidays, many young Canarios come here to test what it's like to escape from civilisation. Since the police have begun to supervise the situation, and give out 500 Euro fines to those caught sleeping here, the number of these young adventurers has dropped considerably.

Starting point: Tasartico, 235m, on the GC-204, Degollada de Tasarte – Playa del Asno.
Height difference: 990m.
Grade: due to the height differences, this is a demanding walk along a steeply laid trail; because shade is almost completely lacking, it is best to begin early in the morning and to bring sufficient liquids along. Remember to wear something to protect your head from the sun!
Refreshment / Accommodation: a bar in Tasartico; a campsite on the Playa del Asno at the end of the Barranco de Tasartico.
Notes: approach by car: you can park at

The trail through the rugged massif of Güi Güi is not a piece of cake.

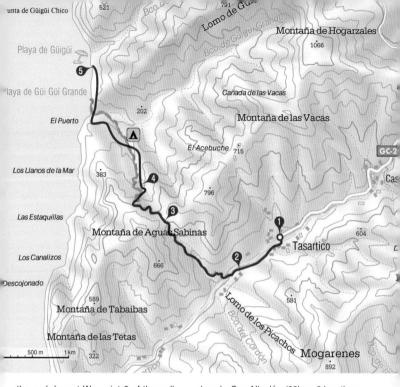

the park bay at Waypoint 2 of the walk; on foot: take bus No. 38 to Degollada de Tasarte and walk 7km to the starting point in Tasartico; Güi Güí can also be approached along a difficult trail from La Aldea de San Nicolás (22km, 8 hrs there and back), starting point on the GC-200, km32.2. Tide tables can be found on the Website https://www.tideschart.com/Spain/Canary-Islands/.

From **Tasartico (1)** follow the *Camino de la Playa Del Asno*, the gravel track heading towards the beach (GC-204). 1km further on, just past a greenhouse on the right-hand side of the track, the waymarked trail *S-79* sets off to the right, the **ascent trail (2)**, heading towards the telephone line pylon (15 mins). A sign announces the limits of the nature reserve, Güi Güí. The path skirts around some protruding rocks until it leads, in another 15 mins, into the dry stream bed of the **Cañada Aguas Sabinas**. Bear left to cross over it. From now on, we have the destination of the first stage in view before us: a distinctly notched col, situated between two needle rocks: to the right, the Cebuche (786m), to the left, the Aguas Sabinas (725m). The ascent

Along the panoramic trail to Güi Güí.

steepens and the valley steadily closes in. After a total of 1.30 hrs, reach the col, **Degollada de Aguas Sabinas (3, 547m)** and enjoy a breathtaking view of the sea and the rugged massif of Güi Güí.

After a short descent, continue for about 10 mins on the level along a panoramic rock ledge before the path begins to wind downwards in numerous zig-zags. Another 35 mins later, cross over the valley bottom, keeping constantly along the right-hand side of the slope, and return only once to the valley floor for a stretch of 60m. Shortly after this, enjoy a view of the picturesquely-situated *finca* of Señor Antonio, which we will pass to the right. He has put up a sign with the word "Beach" written on it, so that the guard dogs keeping watch on the house can be skirted around at an adequate distance. So, skirt around the *finca* to the right, descend for a couple of metres, and then meet up with a **junction (4**; sign): turning right, a long, arduous trail leads to La Aldea de San Nicolás, but we keep straight ahead. From here, it is only about 700m to the beach. From now on, the trail leads along the valley floor, crosses over it, and then reaches – passing a second house – the beach, **Güi Güí Grande (5)**: the beach sprawls 200m along the foot of the steep cliffs. In winter, the light-coloured sand is often washed away and the beach is covered with large pebbles. Only the terrain in the area of the little pier, called "El Puerto", where the fruits of the valley were once loaded onto boats, is soft, year-round. In summer, the sea brings in a new batch of sand – at low tide, you can easily wade northwards, in 20 mins, to the neighbouring beach of Güi Güí Chico. Be sure, however, that you head back again while the tide is still low, since during a strong high tide, the beach is completely cut off!

To return to **Tasartico (1)**, head back along the paths already used during the approach.

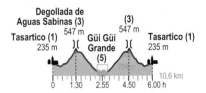

Degollada de
Aguas Sabinas (3)   (3)
            547 m   547 m
Tasartico (1)   Güi Güí   Tasartico (1)
235 m   Grande   235 m
              (5)
                                    10.6 km
0   1.30   2.55   4.50   6.00 h

A short circular walk from Puerto de la Aldea – past a cliff-enclosed bay

Climb down along slopes covered in windswept spurge – whilst constantly enjoying a view of the rugged western coastline – to a remote, sandy beach. You have to take into account that the first leg of the walk is somewhat tiresome, as it leads through a parched canyon.

Starting point: Puerto de la Aldea, 9m. Bus stop for line 101 from Las Palmas/Agaete; bus 38, approaching from the south, only services the settlement of La Aldea; it is best to get off at the junction of GC-200/201, and from there, its another 4km to Puerto.

Height difference: 210m in both ascent and descent.

Grade: mostly an easy walk leading along tracks and paths, waymarked with cairns; during the descent, route-finding skill is demanded.

Refreshment/Accommodation: you can find restaurants in Puerto, accommodation in the neighbouring settlement of La Aldea de San Nicolás.

Note: the Playa Chica is particularly beautiful at low-tide (see https://www.tideschart.com/Spain/Canary-Islands/); before you reach Punta de La Aldea, you can climb up to a deserted military sentinel.

From the bar "Avenida" on the **Paseo (1)**, the seaside promenade from **Puerto de la Aldea**, ramble over to the main village street. Cross over it, between the restaurants "Luis" and "Severo", and then ascend along the Calle Lomo del Carmen, a narrow tarmac street. On the right-hand side, there is a

Descending past sweet spurge bushes; in the background, Puerto de la Aldea.

A first view of the destination Playa Chica.

cluster of houses, and behind them, an archaeological site of indigenous Canary Islander burial mounds (*Yacimiento Aborigen de Los Caserones*). The narrow street, which soon becomes a track, leads to a **fork** – either trail will lead to a dusty plain; a walled cave is located on its left-hand side, from where you can get a magnificent view of the coastline.

The track veers to the right into a valley notch, the **Barranco del Perchel**. At the **fork (2)**, ignore the track that is ascending from down below (this will be our return trail later on) and turn right instead, climbing up through the stony, desert-like terrain. Another 700m further on, meet up with a **trail junction (3)**: here, leave the track behind by turning left and crossing over the valley floor. Every additional metre of altitude improves on the view: at first, we can spot the Aldea basin, then the rugged western coastline. A good 400m further on, the broad, track-like trail levels out and a high mountain ramble begins that skirts around a number of rocky knolls. 300m further, just before a right-hand bend and the end of the track at the **Punta de la Aldea (4)**, it's time to pay attention: to the left of the track, low walls have been placed to flank the outset of our descending path which, from now on, is waymarked with cairns. Not only botany buffs will be enchanted by this stretch of trail. Windswept spurge, flowering in pale grey and pink, sprawls along the slope; with their scraggy and branching finger-like stems, they look like miniature sculptures. The most prevalent is the "sweet" balsam spurge (*Euphorbia balsamifera*). It

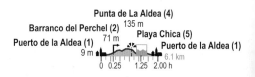

has been so named due to the fact that its latex-like juice, unlike other subspecies, is not poisonous. The view over the slopes all the way to the coast is just as stunning! At first, the path leads eastwards, parallel to the track already used (which is above us), but 60m further on, it hooks to the right and, another 300m further, crosses over a little secondary valley. Here, continue diagonally to the right while ascending, at first gently. Past a left-hand bend behind two boulders, the path again descends and, 200m further on, crosses over yet another secondary valley – from here, you can already catch a glimpse of the Playa Chica, the destination for this walk. After another 200m, at a **barranco floor**, the path merges onto a trail; turn right onto it to reach the **Playa Chica (5)**: a little sandy beach, surrounded by cliffs, which is usually deserted on weekdays!

From the beach, head back along the *barranco* floor to the spot where we have made our descent. Ascend to the right, using one of the trodden paths to return to the track that climbs up again to the **junction (2)** already met during the approach. Here, bear right and ramble back to the starting point of the walk in **Puerto de la Aldea (1)**.

Refreshing cool-off on the Playa Chica.

The Northern Island

Under the spell of the north-easterly trade winds: pine forests and pastureland, volcanic craters and subtropical barrancos

The northern island is mellow, charming and green – but in the coastal areas overdeveloped as well. The walks presented in this guide are targeted to the nature reserves, and mostly lead along heights between 500 and 1500 metres of altitude. They take in pine-dotted lava fields on their way to lush green pastureland, where sheep and goats are grazing. Terraced fields, wrested from the mountain slope, provide ground for the cultivation of fruits and vegetables; even coffee and grape vines are flourishing. Here and there, relics of a certain unique laurel forest still exist, which had covered most of the northern island before the coming of the Spanish conquerors. Holiday-makers can truly savour walking in the north: bright sunlight is intertwined with the shade cast by passing clouds, and the sea breeze provides a pleasant coolness.

The hamlet of San Pedro, splendidly situated on a slope in the fertile Agaete valley.

A short circular walk in the Agaete valley

Through a subtropical, cultivated countryside

Due to the abundance of water in the Agaete valley, oranges, papayas, avocados, and Europe's only coffee, are growing almost year-round. To the right and behind the terraced-formed gardens, the weather-battered slopes of the Tamadaba soar heavenwards; the steep rock face to the left is not quite so dramatic. This walk is ideal as a "warm-up route" for the grand circuit (Walk 52), which also includes the upper Agaete valley and the Tamadaba forest.

Starting point: San Pedro, 200m. The bus stop for line 102 is nearby. If approaching by car, it is easy to find parking at the starting point.
Height difference: 400m in both ascent and descent.
Grade: a simple walk along a well-laid *Camino Real*; only at the height of the hotel is it strenuous; on the return route, sometimes you follow tracks and a hardly-used road.

Refreshment: a bar in San Pedro; a hotel café in Los Berrazales (currently closed).
Accommodation: hotel, private rooms and holiday apartments in Agaete.
Note: bus 102 sets off only every 4 hours into the valley; if you are approaching by bus, the best link up with the walk is at the bus stop "Casas del Camino" (2) (be sure to tell the driver in advance where you want to get off!).

In the village centre of **San Pedro** (**1**; bar "La Palma"), to the left of the bridge, follow the railing-secured trail *S-97*, running parallel to the *barranco* floor. This veers diagonally to the right and then becomes a track. The track leads straight ahead to the sports ground in San Pedro; cross over this by heading south. At about the same height as the rear goalpost for the football field, ascend past an electricity pylon via a stepped trail, passing two houses and keeping parallel to the street lanterns. The trail passes on the right-hand side of some ruins and leads, in not quite 15 mins, to a cluster of houses, **Casas del Camino (2)**, where we meet up with the road Agaete – Los Berrazales (bus stop). Turn right, but 200m further on, leave the road behind again by turning right onto a track, the *Camino Agrícola de la Peña* (the sign has been removed). Before this track crosses over a valley floor, about 250m on, leave it behind by turning left onto a cobbled trail, ascending between the walls of two *fincas*. This track

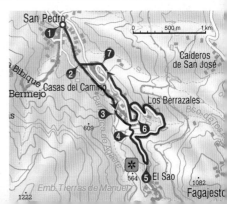

At the valley head of the Valle de Agaete.

leads, for 700m, to reach a **bridge (3)**; by crossing over it, you meet up with the road Agaete – Los Berrazales. We, however, continue straight ahead, passing a *finca* while ascending. Soon, the trail is flanked by cypress trees. Terraced fields are lying to the left and below us, with plantations of oranges and lemons. The trail leads above the (former) hotel in Los Berrazales and then winds upwards in comfortably-laid bends along the steep slope of the **Montaña de las Vueltas** ("Mountain of the Bends"). On the **crest of the ridge (4)**, an electricity pylon is standing, snug up to a tarmac track, which we can reach via a trodden path, forking off to the left, after only a few paces. If you prefer, you can, however, remain on the pretty, only slightly descending, trail for another 350m, until it reaches the narrow, hardly-used, road, **GC-231 (5)**, that connects Agaete with El Sao. We take this road back to the **ridgeline (4)**, where there is a rustic viewpoint with a wooden table and bench, perfect for a breather. From here, the view is marvellous: far below lies the Agaete valley, winding its way to the coastline, next to us is the basalt colossus of Tamadaba, and in front of us, the pyramid shape of the Roque Cumplido, surrounded by steep, rugged rock faces.

Afterwards, pick up the tarmac track, which descends in many broad bends, passing pine and almond trees. A good 1km on, pass the **Casa de Esperanza** ("House of Hope"), where alcoholics make use of the seclusion found in the mountains to rid themselves of their addiction. At the next bend of the trail, meet up with the hotel in **Los Berrazales (6)**: from the terrace for the café, you can get an overview of the route already travelled and be amazed at the steep rock faces you have just climbed. Here, along the hardly-used mountain road, continue down the valley. 1.2km further on, at a striking left-hand bend, a long stretch of road can be short-cut by leaving it behind via a descending, cobbled and **stepped trail (7)**.

Passing lovely houses, the trail merges, shortly after, into the road again, at the same height as the hamlet, **Casas del Camino (2)**, already met on the approach route. Cross over the road and follow the trail used during the ascent, to continue down the valley: parallel to the lanterns, this leads to the football pitch, which we cross to return to **San Pedro (1)**.

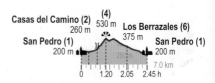

Casas del Camino (2) 260 m — (4) 530 m — Los Berrazales (6) 375 m — San Pedro (1) 200 m — San Pedro (1) 200 m — 250 m — 7.0 km — 0   1.20   2.05   2.45 h

An adventurous pilgrim's path and a dramatic barranco

A splendid walk! At first, it leads through the rugged upper reaches of the Valle de Agaete to the remote mountain villages of El Sao and El Hornillo; then pass by an emerald-green reservoir and climb up through an open pine wood to a rustic picnic site. The dramatic final stretch leads along the steep rock faces of Tamadaba in many zigzags, and passes a disused threshing circle, as it descends into the valley. During long periods of the walk, you can enjoy panoramic views, taking in Gran Canaria's northern region. At the end of June and beginning of August, the trail becomes the stage for the Bajada de la Rama, the "Festival of the Branches": the valley's inhabitants ascend in a torchlight procession to collect branches in the Tamadaba forest, and then, at the crack of dawn, carry them back into the valley to the beat of an archaic rhythm.

Starting point: San Pedro, 200m. If approaching by car, parking spots are easily found at the starting point. The bus stop for line 102 is nearby (only every 4 hrs in the valley); if approaching by bus, get off at the stop "El Lomo de San Pedro" and descend, in about 5 mins, to the bar La Palma in the village centre.
Height difference: 1230m.
Grade: The walk leads along well-laid trails; also along little-used roads for some short stretches. Very strenuous, due to the height differences. After storms or heavy rainfall, it would be better to postpone this walk because of the danger of rockfall and/or slippery conditions!
Refreshment: bars in San Pedro; and a bistro in El Hornillo. If you reach San Pedro before 5pm, visit the Finca La Laja for some good wine, local cheese and Agaete coffee (tel. +34 628 92 25 88,

www.bodegalosberrazales.com, daily. 10–17, wine tasting 8 € per person).
Accommodation: hotel, private rooms and holiday apartments in Agaete. B&B in El Hornillo, camping possible in the picnic area of Tamadaba, if you pre-register.
Alternatives: 1) if you find the Grand Circuit to be too strenuous, you may be contented with the shorter Agaete Valley Circuit (see Walk 51).
2) if you have a hire car and wish to restrict yourself to the prettiest stretch of the walk, drive up the valley to the car park at El Sao (6) and walk from there to El Hornillo and back again.
3) holidaymakers, sojourning in Tejeda or Artenara, will find it best to drive to the picnic area Tamadaba (10) and link up there with the valley circuit route.
4) it is possible to do another walk from Roque Bermejo (12) to Agaete via the *S-90* (2 hrs).

The outset of this walk is identical to the shorter valley circuit (see Walk 51): from **San Pedro (1)** via **Casas del Camino (2)**, passing the **bridge (3)**, where you can reach the road Agaete – Los Berrazales, and ascending the **Montaña de las Vueltas** to reach the **crest of the ridge (4)**. 350m past the crest of the ridge, turn right onto the **GC-231 (5)** which is coming from

Ascent to El Hornillo.

Agaete; this leads, in 5 minutes, to the car park below the village of **El Sao (6)**. At this point, the modern road network connecting us to civilisation comes to an end: for centuries now, the steep section of the *barranco* has been negotiated by a cobbled *Camino Real* – the only connecting route between the mountain villages of El Sao and El Hornillo.

Following the *S-97*, take the steps which ascend to the first houses up above (from the cement track, immediately turn off to the right), afterwards, the trail leads on the level in a wide bend skirting along a protruding rock face. Now pass the water mill **Molino de Abajo**, built around 1900, which is no longer in service.

The trail winds doggedly upwards, passing yellow-coloured rock faces of tuff and uninhabited cave dwellings. At a fork, bear left and then reach the church square of **El Hornillo (7)** – the terrace of the bistro is a great spot for a break! From here, follow the street southward (sign: *S-97 Lugarejos / Artenara*) and, 20 mins later, at a confusing junction, turn right onto the descending road that, 250m further on, reaches the dam wall of the **Presa de los Pérez (8)**.

Siete Pinos (9) 1330 m · Tamadaba (10) 1215 m
Presa de los Pérez (8) 825 m
El Hornillo (7) 750 m · Mirador Vuelta del Palomar (11) 868 m
Montaña de las Vueltas (4) 530 m · Roque Bermejo (12) 643 m
San Pedro (1) 200 m · San Pedro (1) 200 m
16.8 km
0 1.20 2.20 2.50 4.30 5.45 6.15 7.15 h

Cross over the dam and continue on along the broad trail between the water channel and the rock face. The trail winds upwards in many bends through a pine forest. At the **fork**, 1km further on, bear right (towards *Tamadaba*). The trail crosses through a valley floor and then continues an ascent along bends. At the edge of the trail, you can often spot tree moss, hanging like tinsel from the branches of the trees – a sure sign of the humidity brought to this area by the trade winds. The higher we climb, the more spectacular the view. Before the trail reaches the Tamadaba Ring Road, meet up with the little plateau, **Siete Pinos (9)**, where a number of trails come together. Turn right here onto a forest trail (*S-90 Tamadaba/Agaete*), that merges 1km further on at the Tamadaba **picnic area (10)** onto a track.

Turn right onto this track (towards *Agaete*), pass a chain barrier, 200m further on, and then after 250m more, turn left onto the waymarked trail to *San Pedro/Agaete*. Descend through an open forest, and at forks, low walls set the course for the continued route. The trail leads northwards at the outset, but later on, turns to the north-west and leads along the eastern slope of the mountain, Las Presas, 1083m at the summit. The marvellous views begin to appear more often. On a hairpin bend at the **Mirador de la Vuelta del Palomar (11)** (the name is not posted anywhere), enjoy a view of the sheer slopes of Tamadaba all the way down into the Guayedra gorge.

Taking a break above the reservoir of Los Pérez.

Cult site at the Roque Bermejo.

Afterwards, the cunningly-laid trail winds downwards in many hairpin bends along the steep rock face. After the zigzag stretch, lasting 1km, comes to an end, the trail meets up with abandoned terraced fields at a disused threshing circle, a round, cobbled plateau. This is marked on maps as the Era de Berbique (or Bibique); the knoll, situated in front of us, carries the name **Roque Bermejo (12)**, "Reddish Rock". The sometimes stepped trail continues precipitously at the eastern side of the plateau and passes towering, bizarrely-shaped crags. More than 50 caves have been carved out of the volcanic tuff found here. These are connected by steps and passageways, and are called the **Cuevas de Berbique**.

The trail descends to the right of the caves and, after many bends, meets up with the valley floor, where a **spring** provides refreshment. Soon afterwards, to the right, we can spot the first almond and palm trees – San Pedro is not far away now. The trail now leads parallel to the *barranco* floor and then descends along a mountain ridge. At the end, near a cluster of houses, reach a towering eucalyptus tree, which bears a sign with the inscription *Camino de los Romeros* ("Pilgrims' Way"). Return back to the starting point, the village centre of **San Pedro (1)**, via the road that starts here and runs past the access road to the Finca La Laja (see refreshments).

Over barren slopes to a remote playa

At the foot of mighty cliffs, little gorges merge to meet the valley at Guayedra which then opens up broadly to the sea. The valley floor is a verdant oasis – after the Conquista, Guanarteme from Gáldar, the dethroned king of the indigenous Canary Islanders, lived here. There is still a finca (Redondo de Guayedra), that sprawls almost the entire way to the seaside. The isolated beach is open to the public, but is usually only used by the Canarios at the weekend.

Starting point: GC-200, km-marker 0, 33m. Turn-off of the road to La Aldea de San Nicolás at the halfway point between Agaete and Puerto de las Nieves; bus stops for lines 101–103.
Height difference: 350m.
Grade: an easy to moderate walk along a mostly well-marked trail with a short stretch along a road.
Refreshment: in Agaete and Puerto de

las Nieves, there is also an expensive garden restaurant in Guayedra (book in advance! tel. +34 636 51 86 55).
Accommodation: apartments and hotels in Agaete and Puerto de las Nieves.
Note: the walk can be approached by bus or by car. Bus stop in front of the church at Agaetes: follow the road for 600m towards Puerto de las Nieves. By car, park at the nearby residential area.

The walk begins at the turn-off of the road towards La Aldea de San Nicolás (**GC-200, km-marker 0**). Right of the **Casa de los Huevos (1)**, a striking house, decorated with immense eggs, a cobbled track (sign: *SL-01 Guayedra 2.4km*) ascends up the slope and, 50m further on, turns off sharp left onto the *Camino Real* towards Guayedra. The track is reinforced with steps at longer intervals and leads, in a good 15 minutes, to a striking left-hand

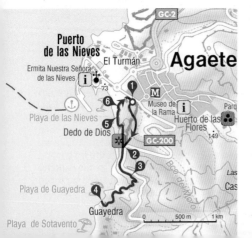

bend on the GC-200 (Agaete – La Aldea). 100m before the road, at a **fork (2)**, the path for the return route merges with ours. But for now, follow the road by turning right, soon enjoying a splendid view of Puerto de las Nieves and the remains of "God's Finger" (*El Dedo de Dios*), docked in 2005 by a tropical storm. 460m along the **GC-200**, pick up a **right-hand turn-off (3,** there is a gap in the crash barrier): leave the road behind via a reinforced trail (sign: *Guayedra*) which descends over numerous steps. The steep slopes are covered in shrub vegetation; in some spots, mighty *tabaiba* plants with gnarled stems stick out. About 45 mins later, only the mouth of the *barranco* separates us from the bright green Guayedra *finca*. Here, the trail veers to the right and winds down the slopes in tight bends. At the end, you have to use your hands to scramble down the smooth surface of the rock, then you reach the broad **Playa de Guayedra (4)**. The beach is dark-coloured and stony; longer stretches of sandy beach are located on the north side of the cove. Heaps of stones have been piled up for protection from the wind. A life saver, dangling from a

Cooling off at the beach of Guayedra.

post, is a reminder that the rip currents are powerful here and have already swept swimmers out to sea.

After a long break, at first, return along the path already used on the approach. This leads us back up again to the **GC-200 (3)**; turn left here and keep to the tarmac for 5 mins, until the descent via the left-hand turn-off begins. We don't wish to return along the same trail, and therefore, 100m further on, turn left at the **fork (2)** already passed along the approach, onto a **path** which descends into a narrow secondary gorge and, 270m afterwards, crosses over a track. 3 mins later, in front of a fenced-in **water reservoir (5)**, the path merges into an intersecting trail. Turn right onto it, but leave it behind again, 40m further on, by turning left. Now keep left again, descending into the valley floor, and shortly after, meet up with an esplanade. Turn right and ramble through **La Palmita (6)**, a "native Canary Island" village with typical rotunda-like houses: the picturesquely situated Casas Hondas serve as a hostel for Canarian youth groups. The palm-flanked trail leads to the restaurant, "La Palmita", and passes it to the left – the dragon trees and the colourful geometric sculptures are simply wonderful. Now we reach the street, turn right onto it and 140m further on return to the **Casa de los Huevos (1)**.

Playa de Guayedra
(4)
Bifurcación GC-200 (3)   Casa de los Huevos (1)
180 m   33 m
Casa de los Huevos (1)
5.3 km
0   1.05   2.15 h

Pleasant seaside ramble to some cliffs and rocky coves

The views of the cliffs along the coast in the north-western island are stunning: the sheer, plunging basalt rock faces appearing as though split by an axe. In the distance, they drop from rugged spikes at an altitude of almost 1000m all the way down to sea level. Between the rock faces, deep gorges have found their way, with their estuaries forming small coves – like in El Juncal and La Caleta. Here, you could take a little break for bathing when the sea is calm (be aware of the tides)! Unfortunately, you will pass some half-finished residential areas at the start of this walk.

Starting point: the village district of El Turmán, Agaete, 61m. Bus stop for lines 101–103; El Turmán is signposted from the major roundabout on the GC-2, ascend from there to the smaller roundabout where the walk sets off (here is also a small car park).

Height difference: 180m.

Grade: easy coastal walk, following trails and tracks without any considerable height differences. No shade! Don't forget drinking water and something to protect your head from the sun!

Refreshment: bars and restaurants in Agaete and Puerto de las Nieves.

Accommodation: apartments and hotels in Agaete and Puerto de las Nieves.

Note: the descent to the coves are not included in the height profile. The cove of La Caleta can only be visited during low tide (*bajamar*). Be careful that your return route is not cut off by the rising tide (see https://www.tideschart.com/Spain/Canary-Islands/Provincia-de-Las-Palmas/Agaete/)!

Alternative: from El Turmán, walk along the coast to Puerto de las Nieves: follow the road (signed) to the Hotel Roca Negra in a few mins. From there along a concrete-paved zigzag trail to the Piscinas Naturales, the natural swimming pools of Puerto de las Nieves (with terrace bar). Along the promenade you can reach the harbour (it's 400 m to the bus from here).

Tidal pool at the rugged, rocky cove of La Caleta during low tide.

From the roundabout in **El Turmán (1)**, ascend along the street, decoratively lined with palm trees, with Agaete's school lying to the right. 150m further on, at the cul-de-sac, leave the tarmac behind by turning left onto a trodden, barely visible path forking away, and then, 40m on, turn right onto a track (a house to the left). The track veers to the left and sometimes leads parallel to the motorway.

After 500m pass a non-descript **fork (2)** on the left that we should take note of for the return route (excursion to La Caleta). Only 80m further on, leave the broad trail behind by turning left and, one minute later, reach a fork: turn left onto the narrow trail that crosses the *barranco* floor, then veers to the left, and finally, becomes a trodden path that leads parallel to the *barranco*. 3 minutes later, the path merges into a track. Turn left onto it and continue on in a wide bend along the sheer drop at the rim of the plateau. At the **fork (3)**, 650m further on, bear left onto a trail only to leave it again, 30m on, by turning left again – here, the loveliest stretch of the walk begins: the trail leads along a slope, flanked by cactus-like spurge vegetation, opening views of the "Seagull Rocks" lying far out to sea, and of the steep, cliff-lined coast – heaven and sea seem to merge as one. 400m further on, to the right of the trail, you can spot a cave. The **Cueva del Muro (4)** was established by the native inhabitants and is used today as a shelter.

Only a few strides further on, turn left onto the trail forking away, and at the trail junction, another 110m on, turn left, heading towards the towering "Seagull Rocks" lying in front of us. Now descend into the depression and enjoy the first spectacular downwards view of El Juncal: a fjord-like bay, surrounded by high cliffs – many an anchor has been weighed with pleasure in this natural harbour. Afterwards, continue along a narrow, precipitous alpine path to the summit of "Seagull Cliff" up above – on some maps, this is marked as **Punta Gorda (5)**. Awaiting us are breathtaking downward views from all sides, and the haunting cries of seagulls!

Punta Gorda (5) La Caleta (6)
El Turmán (1) 80 m 2 m El Turmán (1)
61 m

5.1 km

0   0.45   1.50 h

The 25-minute side trip down to the fjord-like bay of El Juncal is definitely worth it.

During the descent and 280m on, you could decide to turn left when the trail forks, to head to El Juncal: the path descends, in 25 mins, to the pebble beach cove down below, protected by offshore rocks, where bathing and snorkeling are possible. We, however, bear right and follow the path to traverse the slope. 170m further on, pass by the **Cueva del Muro (4)** already met on the approach, and after another 400m, meet up with a track that forks, and descend along this to the right. A 650m long descent and then we must watch out for the path forking off to the right – two stones mark the "entrance". The path leads along the rim of the *barranco*, crosses over it, and then leads to the right to meet up with the broad trail from the approach. Only 80m on, at the **fork (2)**, choose the narrow trail to follow the path along the left flank of the valley. At the fork, 150m on, bear left, pass by a **breach in the wall**, and then veer to the right. The path brings us again to the very edge of the sheer drop. In front of us is the residential area, El Turmán. A couple of minutes later, meet a stairway which leads in numerous zigzags down the slope to reach the rocky cove **La Caleta (6)** with marvellous breaking waves, as well as tidal pools and semi-enclosed natural bathing pools (5 mins of descent). If you prefer not to climb down, follow the track, which begins at the top of the stairway, for 330m to return to the roundabout at **El Turmán (1)**.

A day trip through a Central-European-like alpine terrain

From the interior to the northern coastline: after a descent over pine covered volcanic slopes, the view opens up even more – sheep graze on lush alpine pastures, and over the gently rolling slopes, you can see all the way to the northern coast. At the end, climb down along an untamed gorge to reach Guía. At the end of the walk, treat yourself to a serving of "flower cheese"!

Starting point: Mirador Pinos de Gáldar, 1510m. On the GC-21, Teror – Artenara; bus stop for line 220 (bus service is pretty rare).
Destination: Santa María de Guía, 180m. Bus stop for lines 103 and 105.
Height difference: 1350m in descent; 50m in ascent.
Grade: the walk is long and the steep descent is hard on the knees.
Refreshment: bars in Saucillo, Hoya de

Pineda and Guía; "flower cheese" (*queso de flor*) is sold at the destination in the Bodega de Guía (Calle Marqués del Muni/corner of Médico Estévez).
Accommodation: a hotel in Anzofé.
Note: for this linear walk, the bus is the best transportation. Bus 220 starts from Las Palmas and Teror to ascend to the starting point, buses 103 and 105 leave every 30 mins from Guía to return to Las Palmas.

From the viewpoint plateau of **Mirador Pinos de Gáldar (1)**, follow the GC-21 westwards towards Artenara. 200m further on, leave the road behind by turning right onto a trail forking away that descends through a pine forest with soft, springy pine needles to walk on. This leads to a volcanic ramp which descends steeply and is enclosed by walls on each side. This used to be the descent trail. As the ramp is very slippery, it is better to walk down the descent trail on the left which is partially fixed with wooden boards before you reach ramp. This cuts a broad bend before it merges onto the volcanic ramp 400m further on. At this point, the ramp is more level.

After another 400m of descent, reach a **trail junction (2)** on the mountain ridge, **Lomo de los Galeotes**. To the right heads towards Fontanales

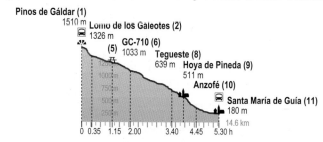

183

From the stone cross, Cruz del Cabezo, catch a view into the next valley notch.

(Walk 21); sharp left to Artenara (Walk 20). We, however, continue straight ahead towards *Guía / Gáldar* along the path *S-01* forking away, which soon leads below a mountain ridge that is crowned by a stone wall. Pass the stone cross, **Cruz del Cabezo (3)**, and at **Majadales (4)**, meet up with the **GC-702** Juncalillo – Fontanales (directional sign: *Santa Cristina SL-1*). Turn right along the road and, 700m further on, in a pronounced right-hand bend with the **picnic area Risco Blanco (5)** to the right, turn left onto a narrower road (direction: *Monte Pavón*). Leave this behind again, 400m further on, at a slight right-hand bend, but heading westwards (straight ahead) along a dirt track to continue the route that leads across a meadow landscape. A good 100m further on, the track is cement-surfaced for a short stretch. Ignore a fork to the left (a stone house). Not quite 100m more, the dirt track narrows and becomes a cobbled trail, which shortly after, is cement-surfaced, but later, becomes a tarmac track. Follow this track northwards while enjoying a sweeping view taking in the verdant slopes of the northern island, as well as the sea.

15 mins later, cross over the **GC-710 (6)**, and not quite 10 mins after that, turn left onto a concrete track (power pylon). At the hamlet, **Caideros de San José**, ignore a trail turning left to a cluster of houses, and shortly afterwards, pass by a number of caves. Another 100m further on, at a pronounced left-hand bend, turn right onto a track only to leave it behind again, not quite 30m further on, by turning right onto a trail forking away – in front of us, to the left, is the mountain Acebuche, to the right, the terraced sheep pastures of Troya. The trail narrows temporarily before it becomes a tarmac track, which meets up with the **GC-220 (7**; bus stop for line 106 Galdár – Fagajesto). Turn right onto this road for 1.9km via **Saucillo** and then use two short cuts for the road, one after the other and both at pronounced right-hand bends. 10 mins later, reach **Tegueste (8)**.

Continue descending along the road for a good 5 mins, then turn sharp left (to the right, an eroded reddish slope) onto a broad trail. This veers, 25m further on, to the right and short cuts a broad bend before it also merges again onto the road. Cross over the road and, next to the bus stop, descend along a tarmac track. A good 300m further on, meet up with **La Degollada**, an outlying district of **Hoya de Pineda (9)** at the foot of the conical mountain Guía. Ignore two roads forking off to the right and keep steadily on a northerly course. A few minutes later, the tarmac track becomes a trail (directional arrow: *Anzo SL 4 1.5km*) that narrows and descends along the right-hand side of a splendid, untamed *barranco*.

20 mins later, the narrow trail broadens again and becomes a track. 10 mins after that, reach the first houses of the hamlet **Anzofé (10)**. The track is tarmac from now on.

Ignore all the forks to the left towards Gáldar. Behind the **chapel** turn right and head north-eastwards towards **Guía**. Cross over a bridge near the sports ground (with a neighbouring hostel) to reach the **church square (11)**.

Pleasant walk through the Barranco del Laurel

This barranco is also a delightful scenic attraction – no wonder that a number of ancient fincas have been converted to Casas Rurales here – and for "Country Holidays", the valley is a very good bet. The same goes for the one on the way to the coast, the Barranco de los Tilos. Here is also the laurel forest of the same name, for which, an individual walk has been dedicated in this guide.

Starting point: Fontanales, 1010m, at the road junction for the GC-70/GC-75. Bus stop for line 127 Moya – Fontanales, to Moya with bus 117 from Las Palmas or bus 113 from Gáldar.

Destination: Moya, 490m. Bus stop for line 127 at Fontanales.

Height difference: 660m in descent; 140m in ascent.

Grade: for a long stretch, the route descends pleasantly and leisurely; the narrow roads en route are hardly used by traffic.

Refreshment: there are restaurants only at the starting point/destination in Fontanales and Moya.

Accommodation: wooden cottages Sibora in Fontanales; Casas Rurales in the Barranco del Laurel.

Alternative: at the Casa Amarilla (4), you could use Walk 57 to add a short walk through the laurel forest, until reaching the fork to the north of the Casa de los Tilos.

In the village centre of **Fontanales (1)**, where a number of streets meet, descend along the Calle Párraco Juan Díaz Rodríguez to the historical centre. Keep always straight ahead, pass the smaller of the two churches, and then take the narrow passageway to descend further. The passageway merg-

Country cottages en route: the Casa Rural Los Arcos del Laurel.

es into a major road; turn right onto this road. Only 30m on, at house No. 6 (**Casa de Cho Juaa**), leave the road behind by turning onto the tarmac Calle La Feria, which soon becomes a trail and, passing a wayside cross, climbs down into the scenic **Barranco del Laurel**. Cave dwellings have been carved into the rock face to the left, and cactus-like Euphorbien, up to two metres in height, are flanking the trail on both sides. On the **valley floor**, veer left onto a track and ramble downwards. A good 20 mins later, the track merges into the **GC-704 (2)**, which is approaching from the left. Now continue by taking the narrow street (*Camino de Laurel*) straight on – and constantly descending. Cottages are nestled in the lush greenery and vegetables are being cultivated in the fields. There are also a number of Casas Rurales here, i.e., the Casa Rural "Los Arcos del Laurel" (No. 24) and the Casa Rural "El Laurel" (No. 20). Following to the right, house No. 11, the seat for the *Asociación de Vecinos* "El Laurel Noble", and at the turn-off for the Casa Encarnada, 2 mins later, house No. 9, the humble **Ermita Immaculada** (**3**, " Chapel of the Immaculate Conception"). A good hour later, where a yellow house is situated

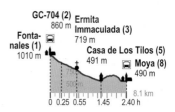

GC-704 (2) Ermita
860 m Immaculada (3)
Fonta- 719 m
nales (1) Casa de Los Tilos (5)
1010 m 491 m Moya (8)
490 m
8.1 km
0 0.25 0.55   1.45   2.40 h

Here's the way to go: the cobbled trail to Moya.

to the left, the **Casa Amarilla (4)**, an educational trail approaching from Los Tilos (see Walk 57), intersects our street. Along the GC-704, descend for another kilometre until reaching the **Casa de Los Tilos (5)**. At a small visitor centre, the flora and fauna of the laurel forest is on display (Mon–Fri 9–14.00), and the forest nature trail sets off (*Sendero del Bosque*, see Alternative).

Follow the road for another 100m towards Moya, and then leave it behind by turning right onto the trail that begins ascending next to the information board. 3 mins later, meet up with a **fork**: ignore the *Camino de la Laurisilva* forking off to the right, and instead, take the *Camino a San Fernando* heading straight on. The trail leads between a rock face and an espalier of fragrant eucalyptus trees, high above the road to Moya. In the distance, you can spot the village's multi-steepled church, situated boldly on top of a precipice. At the outset, the trail ascends gently, then continues in hairpin bends, climbing up to a **junction of tracks** (**6**; to the left, 100m away, a house with a garden): here, leave the trail behind by turning left and then veering to the right into the track, which ascends gently to pass to the left of the grounds of the *finca* (house No. 36). At the property limits, pass through a chain barrier, which prevents cars from driving through, and then turn left onto a narrow road. In 20 mins, descend steeply to reach the village limits of **Moya**. To the right, the **GC-75 (7)** heads to Fontanales, straight ahead, leads to the **village centre (8)** with the church, and the first turn-off to the right leads to the bus station.

Along the educational nature trail near Moya

For holidaymakers wishing to take a daytrip to discover the north, this walk through the nature reserve of Los Tilos is highly recommended. The height differences are negligible and the entire family can take part! The short, sometimes shady, circular walk leads through the remains of a laurel forest which once covered most of the north – the Spanish conquistadors deforested here to allow for the cultivation of sugar cane.

Starting point: Casa de Los Tilos, 491m. From Moya 2km on the GC-700 towards Guía/Gáldar (*S-8 Moya/Los Tilos de Moya*), then turn left and continue on the GC-704 to the starting point of this walk.
Height difference: 60m in both ascent and descent.
Grade: easy walk along a well-laid trail.
Refreshment: nothing en route.
Note: if approaching by car, you can park for free at the visitor centre. When the centre is closed, you can climb over the barrier and reach the nature trail with-

out any difficulty.
Alternative: the circular walk through the laurel forest of Los Tilos can be combined with Walk 56 approaching from Fontanales through the Barranco del Laurel. The walk leads via Los Tilos to Moya.

Entering the thicket of the laurel forest Los Tilos.

At the Casa de Los Tilos.

In the **Casa de los Tilos (1)**, built with undressed stone, you can gather information regarding the laurel forest and the on-going reforestation programme (Mon–Fri, 9–14.00). Behind the building, the *Sendero del Bosque* starts off, a signed, attractive and informative nature trail. Crossing over a wooden bridge, enter a woodland area, open at the beginning, where a variety of laurel trees are growing – these are signed with their Spanish and Latin names. This is an idyllic landscape: passing a shady spot at the edge of a cleft in the rock, continue with the valley road (GC-704) nearby and then cross over it at the **Casa Amarilla (2)**, the "yellow house" (No. 16).

The trail now ascends for the moment and, in the next 5 minutes, passes a water hole, a little rest area, and a **cave (3)**. 10 minutes later, ramble along an outcrop of rock located high above the Barranco de los Tilos and, from the so-called **Zona Mirador (4)**, enjoy a sweeping view of the steep, wooded slopes. Another 400m further on, meet up with a **fork (5)**: the *Camino a San Fernando* turns off to the right, a leg of Walk 56 leading to Moya (see Alternative); but we, instead, bear left at this point and descend over steps to the GC-704 down below. Turn left onto this road and, 100m further on, return to the **Casa de Los Tilos (1)**.

Fields, pastures and farmsteads: a tour through pastoral Gran Canaria

This walk, so rich in diversity, leads from the mountain village of Fontanales into the water-abundant "Valley of the Virgin" (Barranco de la Virgen): after the first stage of the walk along a ridge, descend along a romantic Camino Real, passing laurel trees and other lush flora. At the ever-verdant valley floor, pass gardens where papayas, lemons and oranges are cultivated. This is followed by the "untamed" final stretch via a steep slope.

Starting point: Fontanales, 1010m, *plaza*. At the junction of the GC-70/GC-75; bus stop for line 127, Moya – Fontanales, to Moya with bus 117 from Las Palmas or bus 113 from Gáldar.
Height difference: 550m.
Grade: moderately difficult walk along reinforced paths and tracks; between the watercourse and house No. 48, the *Camino Real* is sometimes ill maintained.
Refreshment: nothing en route. Bars

and restaurants in Fontanales.
Accommodation: Cabañas Valle Verde and *fincas* in Fontanales.
Note: the walk is equally suited to those approaching by bus or by car, however, if approaching by bus, you should be sure to read the timetables carefully, since connections are seldom.
Alternative: from Fontanales, link up with Walk 21 to the Mirador Pinos de Gáldar.

Idyllic countryside: in the "Valley of the Virgin".

A rising mist over Fontanales.

The starting point in **Fontanales (1)** is the little *plaza* on the main street, 50m above the restaurant "Sibora". Here, follow the signs for *Valsendero / Teror* along the narrow Calle La Montañeta that ascends steeply at the outset. Past the highest point, a statue of the Virgin, set into a tree, imparts a blessing to everybody travelling along this route. Ignore the narrow street forking off to the right, and after a total of 260m, past **house No. 7**, turn left onto a trail, concrete and cobbled at first, narrower later on, that ascends along the western slope of the **Lomo del Marco**. At the point where it broadens again, ignore the roadway ascending from the left, and continue climbing up straight ahead, following a conduit. 100m further on, in front of **house No. 9**, meet up with a tarmac track and turn left onto it. Follow it for one minute and then leave it behind again by turning right (trail sign: *Valsendero / Teror*). 300m further on, ignore the turn-off to the right at **house No. 33 (2**; later on, the circular route will come to a close here). 2 mins later, also ignore the left-hand fork at the transformer tower and continue straight ahead towards the north-east. During the next 15 mins, the trail leads parallel to the GC 75 (Fontanales – Moya), merges into it for a short stretch, only to leave it again, a little later, at house No. 117 in the district of **Corvo (3)**. The trail is tarmac at the beginning, and then, concrete. At the fork by the house, "El Mirlo" (No. 30–32), bear right and follow the track for half an hour along a mountain ridge until meeting **house No. 37**, situated to the right, below the trail.

Here, leave the tarmac behind at the **wooden sign (4**, *Corvo / Lomo de la Data*) by turning right onto the *Camino Real*, forking away, which winds downwards in panoramic bends to the valley floor. At one time, the *Camino Cuevas de Acero* ("Trail of the Steel Caves") was hailed as a perfect example of traditional construction technique: steep stretches were made more level by chiseling steps, precipitous stretches protected by flanking walls. In the winter months, the slopes are covered in lush vegetation; eucalyptus and ferns line the cobbled path, Canary bellflowers blaze out in bright red. Enjoy a downwards view into the "Valley of the Virgin", and you can spot the manor house, Casa de la Marquesa, once a prosperous grain-producing hacienda, now owned by the powerful water cooperative.

At the valley floor of the **Barranco de la Virgen (5)**, turn right onto the track heading towards *Valsendero* (southwards). The gravel track soon becomes a tarmac road, but

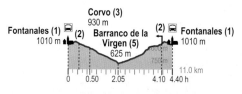

is hardly in use. The road ascends slightly and leads past *fincas* where fruit and vegetables are being cultivated. After a total of 50 mins, at **house No. 58 (6**; across from No. 63), leave the road behind by turning right onto the roadway forking away (sign: *Fontanales*). 75m further on, this becomes a steep, ascending, sometimes cobbled, *Camino Real*. Passing beneath a watercourse, the ascent continues. In many bends, the trail winds up the slope and is then flanked by eucalyptus trees, later, also lemon trees. The trail crosses over a track and then continues along the slope; ignore all of the turn-offs towards the houses.

After a 45-minute ascent, the path merges into a narrow road which, at **house No. 48 (7**, the number is not visible), bends to the left and descends. At the fork, follow the trail sign to the left (*Fontanales/Artenara*) for 1.3km through two verdant valley notches. At **house No. 33 (2)**, meet up with the trail already met on the approach, turn left onto it, and ascend along the narrow street. Shortly after, reach the mountain ridge, **Lomo del Marco**, turn left and, 100m further on, turn right to continue (trail sign). In 20 mins, you have returned again to **Fontanales (1)**.

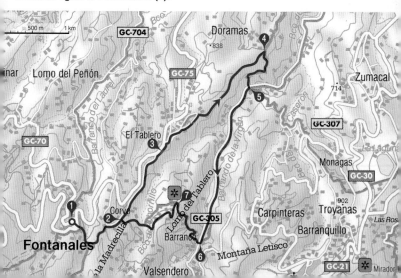

Through green valleys to a place of pilgrimage

This trail leads, numerous times, down into the valley and then back up to the mountain ridge, and the natural scenery changes repeatedly. You will see eucalyptus groves and the remains of the laurisilva forests, then green fields, sweet chestnut and fig trees. Situated at the edge of the trail are little hamlets with overridingly traditional Canarian architecture. At the destination, Teror awaits with its beautiful church square.

Starting point: Corvo, 930m. Bus stop for line 127, Moya – Fontanales; to Moya with bus 117 from Las Palmas or bus 113 from Gáldar.
Destination: Teror, 591m. Bus stop for lines 216 and 220.
Height difference: 630m in descent;

300m in ascent.
Grade: moderately difficult walk along trails, tracks and narrow roads.
Refreshment: bars and restaurants in Fontanales and Teror.
Alternatives: combination with Walk 58 to Fontanales and Walk 60 to Firgas.

Along the descent trail into the "Valley of the Virgin".

From the bus stop in **Corvo (1)**, Fontanales' lower district, follow the narrow road northwards, passing colourful village houses. At the **fork**, 250m further on ("Casa El Mirlo"), bear right to descend effortlessly along the precipitous track. Soon, the track leads along a narrow mountain ridge, planted with eucalyptus trees, and opens up sweeping views to the left and to the right: a pastoral scenery with verdant slopes and solitary houses. Not quite 1.4km further on, in the bushes to the left, spot a private,

Well-marked: the trail from Barranco de la Virgen to La Laguna.

improvised **campsite** ("Raíces de Corvo"). Continue along a track to reach **house No. 37** (**2**; wooden sign: *Corvo/Lomo de la Data*) to the right, below the trail. At this point, leave the tarmac behind by turning right onto a *Camino Real*, forking away, that descends along the steep slope in cobbled bends. On the edge of the trail, cactus-like Euphorbia, fig trees and Bambusinae; further below, ferns and agave, sporting huge flowering, stems. Time and again, enjoy deep-reaching downwards views into the "Valley of the Virgin", which is dressed in lush greenery from autumn until spring. After an hour's descent, reach the valley floor of the **Barranco de la Virgen (3)**. Turn left onto the gravel track, but leave it behind again after 1 min by turning right onto the trail to *La Laguna*. The trail is now flanked by dense greenery as it ascends, passing restored country cottages. Lecterns provide information concerning the "arid laurel forest" which, in pre-Hispanic times, covered the flanks of this *barranco*. 2 mins later, in front of a house, our path merges into a broad trail; turn left onto it.

600m further on, the path becomes a narrow, tarmac street in the hamlet of **Carpinteras** and leads us through the hamlet of **Las Tasquillas**. At the next **fork (4)**, turn left to continue to La Laguna (signpost), passing a lovely, historic estate with the chapel of **Ermita Virgen de la Silla**.

400m further on, cross over the **GC-307** and keep straight ahead along a concrete track ascending steeply. A good 600m more, meet up with an intersecting road, turn left and immediately after, below an old cross, turn left again onto a broad trail. Once again, pass by pretty cottages, sweet chestnut and fig trees. 6 mins later, meet up with a narrow road, turn right, but leave it behind again only another 30m further on by turning left onto a narrow, apparently ascending, concrete track. At the junction, 70m on, leave this behind as well by keeping straight on along a trail leading between fenced-in fields. A sign announces the *Espacio Natural Protegido Parque Doramas* and then continue the climb up in zigzags – a romantic stretch of trail through an ancient laurel forest. Cross over the **GC-30 (5)** and follow the trail sign, *La Laguna*, ascending. At the fork, not quite 100m further on, continue along a broad trail heading straight ahead, passing a round, dried-out lagoon (bird sanctuary!). Shortly after, reach the road at the picnic area, **La Laguna (6)**, turn left and, 140m further on, when the road forks, bear right.

After a descent for 160m, reach the **GC-21** (**7**; bus stop) and cross over to the other side – there's a breach in the crash barrier – to descend via a eucalyptus trail. Immediately, the first view opens up of the pilgrimage site of Teror, situated in a broad valley. From now on, the trail crosses over the GC-21 a half a dozen times, as the road drops down in broad bends. The fourth time this happens, you have to follow the road for 30m to the left in order to continue along the trail to the right. After a good 20 mins of descent, reach **Teror** at the **Estadio Insular** (**8**), continue climbing down and meet up with a bigger street to descend along it even further – a terraced house complex to the left. 130m further on, leave this street behind by turning left along the street forking away (*Camino de los Castaños*). Descend easily for 500m along this street and then turn right onto the cobblestone Calle Herrería, which climbs down to the ambience-rich **church square** (**9**) of Teror.

Historic estate at the trail's edge during the ascent from the "Valley of the Virgin".

From a water-abundant town into an evergreen gorge

If you are driving along the barren and desolate northern coast, it would be hard to believe that only a few hundred metres landwards, fertile barrancos are issuing forth. One of them is the nature reserve of Azuaje: a gorge enclosed by towering, steep rock faces and boasting almost jungle-like vegetation of Bambusinae and laurel trees, willows and ferns. Further upwards, the barranco broadens into the "Valley of the Virgin" (Barranco de la Virgen), where oranges and lemons are flourishing.

Starting point: Casas de Matos, 520m.
Bus to Firgas: from Las Palmas, take No. 204; from Arucas, bus No. 211.
Height difference: 460m.
Grade: uncomplicated walk along well-laid trails and tracks; at the end, it leads along tarmac.
Refreshment: there are bars and restaurants in Firgas.
Note: the walk is suitable for both walkers approaching by bus or by car. If approaching by car, park near the garage with the inscription "El Trapichillo". If by bus, from the bus station in Firgas walk 1.5km along a little-used road to reach the starting point.
Alternatives: 1) the tourist office in Firgas is promoting an adventurous alternative route and provides a brochure re-

garding it: instead of following the main route at the fork (before Waypoint 3) to the left, follow the trail sign and turn right into a jungle-like gorge. En route, steep stretches are negotiated using a wooden ladder and aided by an affixed cable (dangerous after rainfall!). The trail leads past the ruins of the onetime health resort of Balneario de Azuaje, via a steeply-laid rock face alpine path (*Camino de la Capellanía*) to return again to Firgas (about 2 hrs; difficult).
2) Firgas – Corvo/Fontanales a good 5 hrs; moderately difficult): linear walkers follow the main route to the house with the sign "Camino de la Data 2" (6), and then continue straight ahead to Corvo (using a stretch of Walk 59 in the opposite direction).

Begin the walk at the (unsigned) dispersed settlement of **Casas de Matos (1)**, or to be more exact: on the **GC-305** Firgas – Las Madres, 1.5km on (that is, 250m past house No. 34), just before a striking left-hand bend, where a narrow and precipitous tarmac road turns off to the right. 140m further on, at a garage with the inscription "El Trapichillo", leave the tarmac be-

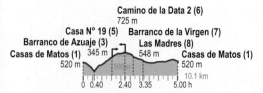

Camino de la Data 2 (6)
725 m
Casa Nº 19 (5)   Barranco de la Virgen (7)
Barranco de Azuaje (3)   Las Madres (8)
Casas de Matos (1) 345 m   548 m   Casas de Matos (1)
520 m   520 m
300 m
10.1 km
0 0.40   2.40 3.35   5.00 h

hind and continue straight ahead along the concrete track. A good 100m past the garage, near a fenced-in house, the track makes a bend to the right. A few metres after

Lush greenery: the floor of the Barranco de Azuaje.

that, watch out for a cobbled trail turning off to the right that is often overgrown with grass in winter (sign: *Reserva Natural Especial de Azuaje*). Descend along this trail, flanked by a stone wall. 150m further on, just past a little power station, the trail merges into a concrete track; descend along this track. Now pay attention: another 200m on, ignore the trail heading straight on, newly-laid by the local government, and veer off along a sharp **fork to the left (2)** towards a majestic eucalyptus tree, where a sign marks the limits of the nature reserve, Azuaje (*Reserva Natural Especial de Azuaje*; about 15 mins from the starting point). The *barranco* that we are climbing down into is simply splendid: the steep flanks are overgrown in vegetation; in the springtime, a multitude of Canarian endemic flora is blooming here. Now the trail winds down in zigzags to reach a fork down below, situated 300m past the last left-hand turn-off; turning right, you could continue via Alternative 1. We, however, bear left and a few minutes later reach the floor of the **Barranco de Azuaje (3)**, densely covered in reeds. After crossing over the *barranco*, the trail continues along the opposite flank and, at **house No. 8 (4)**, merges into a narrow tarmac road. Follow this road for 290m and then turn left, between two houses, onto a concrete track, which is ascending steeply. Just a few paces afterwards, directly past **house No. 20**, veer left onto a narrow concrete trail, which climbs up along a fenced-in garden. Soon this becomes a dirt trail and leads snug up alongside a rock face, before merging into an intersecting trail. Climb up along this trail, but leave it behind again a minute later by turning sharp right onto an ascending path forking away. 4 minutes later, we are standing at the foot of the sheer rock face where we veer to the right. The path now leads us almost on the level, passing a cave dwelling with a water reservoir to the right. Just afterwards the path forks; bear left and, 70m further on at the next fork, left again.

Ascend again for 30m onto a small plateau, follow the track further upwards, and then leave it behind again, 100m on, by turning onto a path that passes to the left of a concrete cistern. The path crosses over a dirt track and, 150m further on, merges into a broader track which leads to **house No. 19 (5)**. At this point, turn right onto the narrow road that crosses over the ridge and follow this southwards while enjoying constant far-reaching views taking in the secondary gorges.

Descent overlooking the valley with our hiking track in the background.

Along the next 1.4km, we can relax, since there are no turn-offs to pay attention to. During the first stretch, fruit trees have been planted to the side of the trail; afterwards, the terrain is dominated by young eucalyptus trees: their rapidly growing, robust trunks make ideal supports for tomato plants. Past the house with the sign "**Camino de la Data Nr. 2**" (**6**) turn left onto a track and descend past **house No. 37**. The track soon narrows to become a classic *Camino Real*. Climb down via numerous bends along a splendidly cobbled trail and, a good 15 mins later, reach the floor of the **Barranco de la Virgen (7)**. Here, meet up with a broad track and turn left onto it. 100m on, ignore a *Camino Real* turning right towards Teror (see Walk 59, from WP 3), and continue instead – passing a walled-in property – constantly downwards. After a good 1km, meet up with the road from **Las Madres (8)**.

If you are lucky, you may be able to catch one of the rare buses that, in the evening, are driving to Las Palmas via Firgas. Otherwise, you have to walk along the picturesque country road, **GC-305**, usually only frequented by a few lorries servicing the water bottling plant, Agua de Firgas. In a little more than an hour, you will return to the starting point of the walk at the **Casas de Matos (1)**. At the end, a jaunt through the pretty little town of Firgas is worthwhile: on the *plaza*, a splash fountain is burbling and along the Paseo de Canarias, a stepped promenade, flanked by flower beds, a stream is cascading downwards.

Wildness on the La Isleta peninsula

Almost in the city and already a completely different world: directly north of Las Palmas, patches of white sand, rocky skeleton-like reefs in the breaker waves, and cliffs, riddled with caves. The reason why Las Palmas is called the "City of the Two Seas" becomes clear when reaching the highest point of the walk: to the left, the harbour bay with cranes and huge ocean liners at anchor, in the middle, a densely settled isthmus, and to the right, the sweeping, sandy bay of Las Canteras. La Isleta, "the small islet offshore", has not yet been developed for tourism – thanks to the military, stationed on the island's north and east.

Starting point: Las Palmas, La Puntilla, 4m, at the northern end of the Canteras promenade; several bus lines from the city, i.e. No. 12.
Height difference: 140m.
Grade: a short walk along a promenade, a track and lava; a short stretch demanding sure-footedness.
Refreshment: restaurants at the starting point, as well as en route in Las Coloradas.

Note: Gran Canaria's capital is serviced by a bus line from almost every other settlement; you can park a hire car, for example, in the multi-storey car park, La Puntilla, at the outset of the walk. During Easter and summer holiday seasons, as well as on bank holidays, El Confital bay is "under siege" by large families of Canary Islanders; on working days, only a few anglers and joggers are about.

From **La Puntilla (1)**, the "little cape" at the northern end of the Canteras promenade, head northwards along the street between the row of houses and the large square with the wind chimes. Past the restaurant "Amigo Camilo" the scenery changes: black headlands, where fishermen are casting their fishing rods, are followed by cliffs and surf-battered pebble beaches. Plates of undressed stone, making up the promenade, and viewpoints precariously perched

Along the delightful coastal trail to Confital bay.

above the precipice, emphasise the untamed ambience. After leaving the final terraced restaurant behind us, continue high above two bays until reaching the end of the Paseo at the **Rondell Pepe el Limpiabotas (2**, "Pepe the shoeshine boy"). From here, a dirt track leads, in only a few metres, to a **cliff trail**, flanked by walls of undressed stone. Adorned with artificially rusted iron plates and handrails, the trail nicely compliments the weathered, brown to black-coloured, gleaming cliff walls. The view sweeps over the El Confital bay – from the rocky skeleton-like reef, battered by waves, over the white sandy plain, all the way to the sheer, towering remains of a volcano. The waters are so clear that you can see deep down, below the breakers, even the smallest of crevices. When reaching the level of the sea, the trail merges into a broad promenade made from wooden planks, interrupted by sun decks. From a little **viewing platform**, almost at the end of the bay, a look back is worthwhile; the city already seems far, far away. Continue on along a gravel track. (Note: Where the crash barrier begins, adventurous souls could, if the tide is low, continue walking near the sea along the rocks, and a little later, at the ruins, pick up the track again.)

At the **northern end (3)** of **El Confital**, where the track takes a hook to the right, the scenery changes: over a dark, fractured volcanic plain, a view opens up of the open sea. Holding their ground on this malpaís, "badlands", are spurge (*euphorbia*), sea-lavender and Launaea arborescens, which can also withstand the strong, salty winds. 200m further on, a **wooden espalier (4)** points to the right where soon a trodden path takes shape, heading along the slope. A good minute later, meet up wit

El Confital Norte (3)   Altos del Confital (5)
                  15 m   117 m
Las Palmas/   Las Palmas/
La Puntilla (1)   La Puntilla (1)
4 m   5.6 km
        0   0.40 1.10 2.00 h

The cross on top of the Altos del Confital; below it, the Cuevas de los Canarios.

distinct junction; turn diagonally left here to climb up the slope. 200m on, where the trail seems to end at a rock face, scramble through a notch to reach the high plain up above. Here, you will often see hang-gliders taking flight, situated to the left, Las Coloradas, a non-assuming settlement with a good seafood restaurant "El Padrino" (closed Mon). Bear right and then meet up with a tiny **picnic area**. Our next destination is easy to spot from here: the **cross (5)** crowning the **Altos del Confital** ("Confital Heights"). It takes 10 minutes to get there and then we can enjoy a superlative view, taking in the city and also the mountainous interior.

Past the cross, descend to the south-east. 160m on, a trail, marked by iron rods, turns off sharp right to reach the **caves** (**6,** *Cuevas de los Canarios*) once inhabited by the indigenous people. If you are not quick on your feet, you can turn left to use the road instead. We, however, descend straight ahead. 145m further on, skirt around a tiny cirque via a trodden path to the left. Now ascend for a short stretch, afterwards keep parallel to the road, situated to the left – to the right, the mountain forms a sheer drop down to the Playa del Confital. Where the path leads snug up to the road (a good 100m before a little plateau, blocked off by stones), change over to the pavement. Descend pleasantly for 500m, then turn right towards *Canteras*, and another 50m on, turn towards *Confital* (Calle Coronel Rocha). All at once, we find ourselves on the **roundabout (2)** of "Pepe the shoeshine boy", already met on the approach route. Turn left onto the promenade to return in 1.1km to the ~ting point, **La Puntilla (1)**.

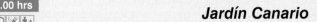
A circular walk through Spain's largest botanical garden

This destination is worthwhile the entire year round: taking up an area of 27 hectares, the Jardín Botánico Canario Viera y Clavijo stretches from the damp valley floor all the way to the sun-drenched, steep flanks of a rock face. The biotopes are so varied that the entire palette of Canarian flora are flourishing here – from the desert-loving Hercules club to the "cloud combing" laurel tree. Nowhere else on the island can you find so many dragon trees in one spot! In addition, there is a large cactus garden and a Palmetum, with rare specimens from all over the world, also, waterfalls and ponds with koi carp. In winter, a migrating crane may appear; canaries warble in the trees, and in the under-growth, you can spot lizards. If you are interested in nature, you can easily spend an entire day here. The walk is also suitable for children.

Starting point: Jardín Canario, 330m, the upper entrance (poorly signed) in Tafira Baja on the GC-110, km1.7. Bus stop for lines 301–303.
Height difference: 100m.
Grade: mostly an easy tour. If you tend to suffer from vertigo, you should de-scend to the left from the *mirador* (2).
Refreshment: restaurant "Jardín Canario" at the upper entrance.
Note: if you drive up from the south, take the lower entrance to the park on the GC-310 (La Calzada). The botanical garden is open daily from 9–18.00; the exhibition centre is open on working days from 9–14.00. The entrance is free at the mo-ment; the gates close punctually! The numbering system in situ is not in sync with that of the overview maps, and this can be confusing – the best thing to do is to keep to the walk description given here, which will allow you to "take in" all of the interesting sites!
Alternative: on the Plaza de los Nenú-fares (4), you can extend the walk by tak-ing an excursion to the attractions in the south-western area of the garden; plan for at least an extra 30 mins Crossing over a

stone bridge, meet up with the Plaza de Matías Vega (with a pavilion and sur-rounded by palm trees), then veer to the left and pass by a rock face. After this, bear left and reach a cactus garden, boasting more than 2000 species. Via the Plaza Fernando Navarro and a *Tagoror*, a "native Canary Islander meeting site", meet up with the Palmetum, which in-cludes palm trees from every continent; continue on to the ornamental garden and to the koi pool. Passing natural olive trees, return back along the foot of the rock face.

Kiosk / pavilion at the lower entrance.

From the upper **entrance (1)** to the **Jardín Canario**, a palm-lined boulevard leads, in not quite 200m, to the car park, where the **gate** to the botanical garden is situated. Past the wrought-iron portal, sporting images of euphorbias, continue on along a cobbled trail to descend to the **mirador (2)**, a viewing platform with the bust of the Canarian philosopher in the Age of Reason, Viera y Clavijo: from here, you have a good overview of the botanical garden, which takes up the entire upper reaches of the Barranco de Guiniguada. Two trails set off at the viewing platform: via the left-hand one, we will make our return ascent, but now, we take the right-hand one, which leads – passing rosette-bearing Aeonium species – to the **Arco del Viento**, a picturesque "Wind Arch". Shortly after, the ambience of the route changes: via a steep and narrow zigzag trail, descend (without any safety railing!) along the rock face for 5 mins to reach a **fork**. Here is the outset of a somewhat labyrinth-like stretch of trail – but no worries: even if you take a wrong path, you will still end up in the valley!

At this fork, as well as on the following three, always turn right to continue, then, for a change, bear left at the fourth. A little later on, when you meet up with a level, intersecting trail, bear left again, and at the next fork, bear diagonally right. Passing palm trees, reach a fork at the **Cueva de Sventenius (3)**, a large cave construction. Ignore the left-hand trail (leads to the cave entrance) and also the right-hand one. Instead, continue straight ahead to a pond (*charca*) covered in plants. Cross over it along a little dam and then bear left. Subsequently, pass a museum piece, traditional Canarian stall (*alpendre*), and then meet up with the circular **Plaza de los Nenúfares (4)**, the "Square of the Water Lilies". Sitting on the bench circling the square is a bronze statue of the park's founder, Sventenius, and across from him, in

Impressive dragon trees in the botanical garden.

front of an exhibition centre, is the marble sculpture of woman potter. Continue by passing to the right of the Centro de Exposiciones, heading towards *Bosque de la Laurisilva – Acebuchal*, and cross through a dark, wooded area full of laurel trees. At the square with the **Fuente de los Sabios (5)**, the "Spring from which the wise men drank", you could turn right to reach the pine wood (*pinar*), but we continue our ramble straight ahead, towards *Guiniguada*. Also at the next fork, continue straight ahead, and 2 mins later, veer to the left to reach the **Paseo de los Dragos (6)**.

After a steep ascent lasting 50m, turn left and walk past magnificent dragon trees. Afterwards, in zigzag fashion, head towards the twin dragon trees (*Dragos Gemelos*): first right, then left, and then right again, finally left, below the impressive rock faces. Now continue straight ahead to return to the **mirador (2)**, already met on the approach route. To the right, the cobbled trail to the **gate** at the car park, from where you walk along the palm tree boulevard to return to the upper **entrance (1)**.

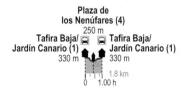

Plaza de
los Nenúfares (4)
250 m
Tafira Baja/   Tafira Baja/
Jardín Canario (1)   Jardín Canario (1)
330 m   330 m

1.8 km
0   1.00 h

Descent over volcanic ash into the island's prettiest crater

The crater at Bandama provides the very best example of the most recent volcanic activity on Gran Canaria, which ended about 1800 years ago. Slopes of black lava contrast with green carpets of foliage; steep, weather-beaten hillsides are peppered with caves. Tourists usually drive the 2km up to the conical summit and only take a quick look into the crater lying far below; it is definitely worthwhile, however, to descend along the "Camino Fondo de la Caldera" and, 200 metres in altitude further down, spend a few hours on the valley floor, a remote oasis under environmental protection, with groves of olive and palm trees. Today, the large farmstead is no longer inhabited; but in the little house next door, Señor Agustín, a hermit, used to spend his days in heavenly seclusion until a short while ago.

Starting point: the hamlet, Casas de Bandama, 450m. Bus stop for line 311 (from Las Palmas or Santa Brígida).
Height difference: 270m.
Grade: via a reinforced trail leading over volcanic ash; strenuous due to the ascent. Be sure to avoid the midday heat!
Refreshment: nothing en route. Near

the bus stop, restaurant and *bodega*.
Note: the walk is suited to both those walkers approaching by bus or those who are taking a car. The gate for the crater is closed at 17.00!
Alternative: combination possible with Walk 64 from the little bus stop shelter in Casas de Bandama.

At the little bus stop shelter for the hamlet, **Casas de Bandama (1)**, on the GC-802, turn off onto a tarmac track that passes by some houses and then leads through a wrought-iron gate to a terrace viewpoint. To the left of the terrace, pick up a descending trail, flanked by walls of black rock, which is soon surfaced with volcanic gravel. At a fork, a few minutes later, bear right and head towards the circular viewing platform of the **Mirador del Cornical**; from here, enjoy the first view taking in the entire crater. Afterwards, the trail winds downwards in many bends, flanked by gorse and lavender. At the junction known to the

The Bandama crater is vibrantly green in winter.

Canarios as **Las Tres Piedras (2)**, due to the towering crags here, just before reaching the floor of the crater, bear left (later on, we will return along the *Camino Fondo de Caldera*, approaching from the right). 2 mins later, pass the **first threshing circle**, with an ancient winepress and an abandoned farmstead to the left of it. Continue to the right of the ruins, passing fields that were cultivated by Señor Agustín until a short while ago, and begin the circumnavigation of the crater in a clockwise direction. After walking a total of almost 35 mins, reach a **second threshing circle** (**3**; Spanish: *era*). A shady grove is located below it (an information board there commemorates the *Día del Árbol*, "Arbor Day"). 400m further on, keep straight ahead and, afterwards, ascend to the left. 5 mins later, we are standing directly on a terrace of solid bedrock, from which two **caves (4)** penetrate into the mountainside – a lovely spot for a picnic; even a barbecue site is provided!

Then the trail leads us, in 2 mins, to a **fork** where we climb down to the right, along a somewhat slippery path. The path immediately merges onto a broader trail; turn left. Continue on, passing a mighty boulder, and then meet up with the crossing at **Las Tres Piedras (2)**, where the circuit route comes to a close. The trail leads to the left, climbing up via sweat-provoking bends, completely lacking in shade, passes a dizzying viewing platform (**Mirador del Cornical**) and then the terrace platform met before. Now return to the little bus stop shelter at the **Casas de Bandama (1)**.

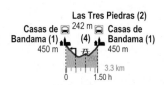

Dizzying high mountain ramble

The descent into the crater is unique; however, it is also exciting to walk a circular route along its upper edge. The entire time, you can enjoy a downwards view into the maw of the abyss and a view taking in half of the island. On the horizon, the sea lies shimmering, sprinkled with ships. The trail is posted as the "Camino Borde de la Caldera" (Trail on the Crater Rim) and is waymarked with directional signs.

Starting point: the hamlet Casas de Bandama, 450m. Bus stop for line 311 (from Las Palmas or Santa Brígida).
Height difference: 160m.
Grade: easy up-and-down walking along a trail that is sometimes laid with step-like reinforcement. During a short, precipitous stretch, vertigo could be a problem to walkers prone to acrophobia. If the wind is blowing in strong gusts, this walk shouldn't be undertaken.
Refreshment: a little inn and a *bodega* next to the bus stop; en route, a bar / café at the Bandama golf course.
Note: the walk is suited for both those approaching by bus or by car.
Alternative: combination possible with Walk 63 from Casas de Bandama.

View from the upper rim into the Bandama crater.

From the little bus stop shelter in **Casas de Bandama (1)**, head for a couple of paces northwards to the km-marker 0 of the GC-822 and follow this road in the direction of *Pico Bandama*. The road to the "summit" (*pico*) ascends along the flank of the cone, while far below, the crater opens up. Erosion has created rills in the black lava, proving how porous its composition really is in some areas. 470m on, turn right onto the **trail (2)** forking away – a wind-tossed pistachio tree (*Pistacia lentiscus*) reminds us of how strong the wind can blow here. At the outset, the trail climbs down, parallel to the road, and opens views, sweeping from the peninsula, La Isleta to the north, all the way to the

Gando peninsula to the east; in between, lie gently rolling mountain folds and sprawling residential complexes. 400m further on – in the meantime, we have drawn closer to the crater's rim – reach a **fork (3)** and take the trail to the right to ascend. The trail is flanked by agave plants and olive trees, lavender and spurge. Rammed into the porous volcanic rock, reddish, basalt rock faces appear, created during much older geological periods. Wind and water have sculpted some of them into rock windows and spires.

After circumnavigating half way round the crater, the neighbouring gorge of Barranco de las Goteras shows its sheer, plunging slopes – spoilt, at the outset, by a stone quarry, but later on, appearing in all its natural splendour. After a short, precipitous stretch, descend steeply to the deepest point of the crater circuit and then just as steeply back up again – wooden steps facilitate the climb. Suddenly, meet up with a track at a tee-off, surrounded by dragon trees, at the edge of the Bandama golf course, which leads to the **Bandama Golf Hotel (4)**. Afterwards, continue along a track between the golf course (left) and the crater (right) for a good 500m to meet up with a narrow tarmac road, which merges, a minute later, onto the **GC-802**. Enjoying a view of the heights and the valleys of the Monte Lentiscal, this road leads us, in 200m – passing the *bodega*, "Hoyos de Bandama" – back to the little bus stop shelter at **Casas de Bandama (1)**.

65 *Atalaya circular walk*

2.40 hrs

Through the Goteras gorge to the ceramic centre

A short, but rewarding walk: descending through the verdant Barranco de las Goteras, reach a chapel, then climb steeply up to La Atalaya, (in the language used by the indigenous Canary Islanders, this means "viewpoint"). But it is not only the far-reaching views that will please you; a visit to the ceramic centre, where pottery is created using ancient techniques, provides amusement!

Starting point: Bandama, 500m, GC-802, km4.3. Bus stop for line 311, near km4, 300m from the starting point.
Height difference: 350m.
Grade: the steep descent and ascent is

relieved by stretches of leisurely walking. Due to the extreme differences in height along some short stretches, physical fitness is an advantage.
Refreshment: bars in La Atalaya.

The walk sets off in **Bandama (1)**, along the GC-802 at km4.3. Turn off onto the Calle Tabaiba, flanked by palm trees and villas, as it passes the riding area for the "Club de Hípica". At the fork, 270m on, bear left onto the *Camino Las Cordilleras*, which skirts around the golf course. Another 370m further on, where the narrow street snuggles up to the sheer drop at the rim of the gorge, turn sharp right in front of a house onto the **Camino Caraballo (2;** *Las Cordilleras*): a precipitous concrete track, which a little later on, bends to the left and then becomes a broad, volcanic scree-covered trail. From here, you have an overview of the upper reaches of the Barranco de las Goteras,

penetrating into the central mountain range. To the right, you can spot gently rolling slopes, as well as the colourful houses of La Atalaya, which we will be ascending to later on. At first, however, we will be descending. At the fork, a few minutes later, bear left; to the right, the trail is signposted as private. The following stretch is a wonderful experience: via the ancient cobbled *Camino Real*, descend in zigzags, surrounded by agave plants sporting flowering stems that tower metreshigh, lush spurge and delicate olive trees. Enthroned above us is the spiked crown of the crag El Roque.

Wild and idyllic stretch of trail in the Barranco Las Goteras.

500m further on, reach the **Ermita del Carmen (3)**, a Neogothic-embellished chapel from 1774 with an open courtyard, giving a view of palm trees, which serves as an ideal spot for a picnic. Now descend along a stepped trail to reach the track on the floor of the **Barranco de las Goteras**.

Turn right along the track and enjoy a view of the greenery: small fields, meadows and groves of olive trees (the sign, *Camino Privado*, only pertains to vehicles). 1.2km along the track, tarmac at the end, reach the hamlet of **Las Goteras (4)** and a little bus stop shelter on the GC-80. Below the shelter, you'll find a small *plaza* with a domed pavilion and a spreading Indian bay tree. Turn left along the road, but 20m on, turn right onto a narrow street, the starting point for the pilgrimage route, P'Al Pino. The concrete track winds up in exhausting sweat-provoking bends, passing houses as it ascends. A backwards look takes in the yawning Barranco de las Goteras. 1.15km further on, the concrete track merges into an intersecting road; turn left onto it. You can breathe a sigh of relief as it is all downhill or level on this road that runs parallel to the *barranco*. Not quite 600m on, past **house No. 6**, bearing the inscription "**Lugar El Peñón" (5)**, turn right onto a concrete track. 50m on leave it behind again by turning left onto a stepped trail. The trail climbs up in zigzags along the steep slope; bear left, then right, in a steady ascent. At **house No. 54**, bear right again, at **house No. 42**, meet up with the village street *Camino El*

Centro Locero (6)
549 m GC-80 (7)
Ermita del Carmen (3)   516 m
296 m
Bandama (1) 🚌   🚌 Bandama (1)
500 m   500 m

6.7 km
0   0.40   1.55   2.40 h

Backwards view of Atalaya from the Cuesta Caraballo.

Chorro, which ascends to the Bar Cafetín, est. 1948 (Calle Picota 5, Tues–Thur, 12–14.30, Fri–Sun, 11–15.30). The Calle Picota, a narrow passageway, which we follow to the right, with its colourful *casitas* and cave dwellings, is reminiscent of Atalaya from before. A few paces further and we are standing in front of the Centro Locero in **La Atalaya (6)**. This ceramic centre, with workshop, store and ancient kiln, maintains the traditional pottery handicraft which has made Atalaya famous for centuries; just next door, the Casa/Museo Panchito, named after a well-known potter, opens its doors to the public (Calle Picota 9–11; closed from Sat–Mon). 20m further on, the Calle Picota forks: bear right here, then immediately left, and meet up with a lovely *mirador*. From the north-east corner, at house No. 6, continue along the "passageway of the tumbledown caves" (*Camino de Cuevas Caídas*) to reach a street down below. Turn right along this street to reach a junction on the **GC-80**. A **stone cross (7)** commemorates the pilgrimage trail, P'Al Pino. At the little bus stop shelter, you could wait for the bus that runs to Las Palmas.

Instead, we ascend along the **GC-802** (Calle Juan Bordes), passing a residential area of terraced houses. 500m further on, leave the tarmac behind by turning right onto the trail, *SL 07 Cuesta Caraballo* (to the right, house No. 2). This leads under the shade of trees between the walls of the houses and the sheer drop at the rim of the Barranco de las Goteras. When the trail approaches very near to a road, 130m on, continue straight ahead. After another 400m, at a height, veer to the left and pass by a copse of pines trees. At the cul-de-sac, continue straight ahead for another 30m (to the right, house No. 26), to veer left onto the Calle Tabaiba. This leads us past the fork already met during the approach, to return to the starting point of the walk in **Bandama (1**, GC-802).

Rediscovery of the viticulture tradition

This short walk passes through Gran Canaria's traditional wine-growing region which, since the end of the 19ᵗʰ century, has become a popular residential area for the well-to-do. Thus, vineyards are side-by-side with the villa gardens, and ancient connecting trails are mixed with quiet streets.

Starting point: Arco de Atalaya, GC-80, km1.1, 554m. Bus stop for line 311, with service from Las Palmas via Casas de Bandama to the starting point.

Destination: Bodegón Vandama on the GC-802, km2.4, 425m. Bus stop for line 311.

Height difference: 280m in descent; 160m in ascent.

Grade: easy walk, which is mostly descending; somewhat slippery along precipitous stretches.

Refreshment: en route, some bodegas may be open "when fancy strikes". The Finca El Mocanal (Mon–Fri 10–12; guid-

ed tours at 10.30 and 12.30, available for 10 € per person, www.bodega-sanjuan. com) as well as the Bodegón Vandama at the destination of the walk (Weds–Sat 13–16, 20–24, Sun 13–17.30; www.bodegonvandama.com) are reliably open.

Note: if you are approaching by car, you can return to the starting point by taking bus 311 on the roundabout at the Vandama access road (direction Atalaya).

Alternatives: at house No. 26 (8), you could ascend in just a few minutes to Casas de Bandama, acquaint yourself with the Bodega Hoyos de Bandama and then tackle Walk 63 or Walk 64.

Along the Ruta del Vino; in the background, the houses of Monte Lentiscal.

From the bus stop near the **Arco de Atalaya (1)**, an aqueduct spanning the road, descend along the tarmac-surfaced *Camino El Roquete*. Lush violet bougainvilleas are draped over walls and fences. 700m on, the narrow road becomes a dirt track, which immediately bends to the left and then narrows down to become a trail. While descending along the steep and sometimes slippery trail, the houses of Monte Lentiscal pop up in the background. A little later, pass the abandoned **Bodega Camino de Roquete (2)**, a 19th century wine-growing estate. With its walls of undressed stone, a mighty winepress, and a courtyard overgrown in vegetation, the *bodega* is lovely, even in its tumbledown condition.

Below the *bodega*, the trail broadens out to become a concrete track. 150m on and at a tall monkey-puzzle tree, the track hooks to the left and, to the right, you'll find the access road to the former Bodega Viñedo Rosa Caballero. In the background, there is a vineyard with a grove of palm trees. Our concrete track now becomes the tarmac *Camino Fuente de los Berros*. We leave it behind again, 150m further on, by turning right onto the Calle El Reventón. Pass a few terraced houses, and after 240m join a junction with a rotunda covered in greenery with the statue of a female winemaker. Before turning right onto the street Cuesta El Reventón take an excursion by heading straight onto the tree-flanked access road for the **Finca El Mocanal (3)**. With its display of ancient equipment, this bodega dating back to 1912 seems like a museum – and the wine is delicious (GC-802, km0.9).

Afterwards, climb steeply up the traffic-pestered Cuesta El Reventón, but 300m on, leave it behind again by turning left onto the Calle Mirlo. Turn left again at the next fork and follow the street for 150m, until it ends at the car park for a tennis club. At the rear end of the car park (street sign: *La Curruca*)

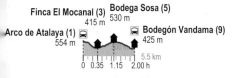

Finca El Mocanal (3)
415 m

Bodega Sosa (5)
530 m

Arco de Atalaya (1)
554 m

Bodegón Vandama (9)
425 m

5.5 km

0 0.35 1.15 2.00 h

a **stairway (4)** begins: in the shade of medlar trees, ascend 110 steps to the street up above and then turn left onto it (a small shopping centre is located to the right). 4 mins later, the street merges onto the Calle Hubara; turn left and, 200m further on, directly past **house No. 17**, turn into a rather neglected trail that ascends along the high walls encompassing several estates. 90m on, ignore a turn-off to the right and continue along the trail, which has become even narrower. At the next **fork** (massive Yucca palm!), turn left onto the *Camino Las Arenillas*, which leads on the level between tidy houses. 350m further on, the track, Viticultor Ricardito Sosa, forks away; take this for 50m until meeting up with the **Bodega Sosa (5)**. Posted on Señor Antonio's gate is the inscription: *Prohibido fumar y mujeres* ("smoking and women prohibited"). Hidden away indoors, there are barrels full of wine that Antonio is pleased to offer for a free wine tasting – naturally, he hopes that his guests will buy a bottle afterwards (usually open from 12–15.00).

Return to the Camino Las Arenillas and continue the walk whilst taking in a new landscape. The view over the verdant slopes is a far-reaching one and the trails forking off to the right have been given cute names, such as "Grape Farmer" and "Fruit Wine". 300m on, ignore the *Camino de Los Toscones*, forking off to the left, and instead, turn right along the narrow road "Winepress" (*Lagar*), along which, to the left, the access road to the **Bodega Montealto (6)** can be found. From here, it's wonderful to take in the view over a vineyard-blessed valley to the dome of the Bandama.

This breathtaking view will accompany us for the next 500m, until we reach the junction, **Tres Cruces (7)**, on the GC-802. Here, turn left onto the *Camino Enmedio*, a concrete track that, 5 minutes later, we will leave behind by turning right onto a descending trail, leading above a natural basin planted in grape vines. 400m further on, at a solitary **house, No. 26 (8)**, turn left to continue and, along a dirt track, reach a roundabout with a round water reservoir. Bear left here and turn onto the access road to the Bodegón Vandama. Passing through vineyards, a volcanic track ascends to the **Bodegón Vandama (9)**, where you can enjoy a good glass of red wine and a marvellous meal.

Bodegón Vandama at the end of the walk.

A circular walk around Santa Brígida

When the rains of winter have turned the Barranco de Santa Brígida into a flowering garden, this short walk is twice the fun! Christened by the local government as the "Water Route" (ruta del agua), "Adam's ale" is not as physically present as the exuberant flora being nurtured by it. At the end of the walk, a botanical garden, as well as a wine tasting, is awaiting at the Casa del Vino.

Starting point: the bus stop and car park at the "Casa del Vino" on the GC-15, km3.9 in Santa Brígida, 509m. Bus 303 from Las Palmas; there is a car park at the starting point.
Height difference: 120m.
Grade: short and easy walk along well-

laid trails and tracks; via tarmac at the end.
Refreshment: bars and restaurants in Santa Brígida, e.g., the Casa del Vino.
Accommodation: there are hotels in Santa Brígida.
Note: the walk is suited to both those approaching by bus or by car.

From the bus stop at the **Casa del Vino (1)** in **Santa Brígida** , follow the GC-15 towards the town centre and cross over a street to immediately turn off onto the semi-pedestrianised-zoned, Calle Real (sign: *Pa'l Pino*). Just at the outset of the street and to the right, the building for the "Water Association" (*Heredad de Aguas*), est. 1913, is easy to spot because of the "clock" on its gable. This does not show the normal time, but instead, established the length of time a certain amount of water was allowed to flow through the channels. Those who had water could cultivate, and thus, could accumulate money – in the days before tourism, agricultural commodities were the only source of wealth. Ever since the Conquista, in the 15th century, water has been under private ownership, meaning that it is traded like any other commodity – supply and demand establishes the price.

Passing charming houses 200m further on, turn left onto the Calle Muro – directly in front of the **church square**, which is set above the valley like a terrace, and opens up a lovely, far-

reaching view. After descending for 100m, follow the street hooking away sharply to the left that soon narrows into a concrete track, as well as the trail sign, *Ca'l Pino*. Soon, the track narrows even more to become a trail that leads along the floor of a *barranco*, where it reveals its ancient cobbles. The trail is flanked by bamboo cane, exuberant tree houseleek, and agave – purely pastoral! Not quite 600m on, we are standing on the floor of the **Barranco Santa Brígida (2)**, where the trail forks: to the left, leads to Teror along the Ca'l Pino

The island's wines are available at the starting point in the Casa del Vino.

(*Camino para El Pino*), a pilgrimage route, but instead, we bear diagonally right and follow the narrow *barranco* floor for a good kilometre more. The *barranco* is a botanical oasis; olive trees and juniper trees form a natural espalier and spurge is sprouting everywhere. From time to time, the sound of water becomes audible, issuing from a canal nearby. Another 600m further on, ignore a turn-off to the left and, not quite 200m more, where the trail broadens out to form a concrete platform, pass by a water metering station (right) and a water level gauge set into a wall (left). A good 250m further on, where the *barranco*, flanked by walls, narrows into a kind of canyon, the trail runs below a quaint, bridge-like construction spanning the gorge.

Shortly after, the Barranco de Alonso merges from the left, and a minute after that, you meet up with a fork: sharp left, a signed trail forks away to *Utiaca / Las Lagunetas / Degollada de Becerra*, but we continue heading straight on, then cross under a road bridge. 70m further on, below the hamlet of **El Arenal (3)**, our trail merges onto a concrete track where we veer to the right (to the left, on a second bridge, is the inscription *Caserío de El Arenal*). Soon, the concrete track becomes a dirt track as it descends through the broad **Barranco de la Angostura**. 500m further on, to the left of the track, is a house belonging to the **Heredad de Aguas**, the "Water Association"; a water trough is in front of it and, just after, a track turning off to the left and heading steeply towards the hamlet Las Meleguinas. This spot is very important to note because, 40m further on, leave the track behind by turning right onto a path that

219

The view from Llano de los Olivos of El Arenal.

crosses over the *barranco*, as it heads towards a wall, with the trail sign **"SL-06 Camino de los Olivos" (4)**. The cobblestone trail ascends along the right-hand flank of the *barranco* and soon steepens. A little later, ignore a turn-off to the left that is flanked by walls, then ascend in zigzags. Not quite 200m further on, bear right at a fork situated below a ruined wall, peppered with holes and, a few paces more, when the *camino* merges into an **intersecting trail**, the ascent comes to an end. Now turn right onto this trail which opens up a sweeping view over the Barranco de la Angostura and the grove of palm trees opposite. 100m further on, continue straight ahead, then pass to the right of a ruin and ascend to the plateau, **Llano de los Olivos (5)**. Here, we find ourselves standing on the south-western corner of a cleverly fenced-in sports ground where the trail forks: bear left and continue along the edge of the stadium, then turn diagonally right to ascend to the little **bus stop shelter (6)**, located in front of the entrance to the **Complejo Municipal de Deportes**, Santa Brígida's sports centre. Here, you could catch a bus and return to Las Palmas.

But we continue on to the main street, turn right onto it and follow the palm tree lined avenue for 600m to the large car on the left. Following the trail sign for *Casa del Vino,* turn left and, 100m on, meet up with the entrance to the park, **El Galeón**. This spacious oasis, situated at the edge of a grove of palm trees, is criss-crossed with trails that lead past artistic fountains and animal pens – this is a real highlight for the end of the walk (admission is free). After visiting the park, you could try some of the island's wines at the neighbouring Casa del Vino, accompanied by a *tapa* (closed Mon/Tues), before climbing up the final metres to the **bus stop** above the **Casa del Vino (1)**.

Indigenous Canary Islander stronghold near Telde

Just like the Roque Nublo and the Roque Bentayga (see Walks 1 and 29), Humiaga, too, was a "mountain sanctum" for the native islanders. Very well-camouflaged from without, it is easy, during this circular walk, to appreciate how marvellous the rocky fortress actually is! Not unlike the natives from those days, who guarded the stretch of coastline from Las Palmas to Gando, take in the entire eastern island and see far up into the central mountain range above.

Starting point: car park, 275m, at the outset of the track to the archaeological park, Cuatro Puertas. From Maspalomas take bus No. 36 to the Cruce Cuatro Puertas bus stop at the GC-100/GC/140 junction. From here, walk for about 10 mins on the road to reach the hamlet of Cuatro Puertas. From Telde or Agüimes take bus No. 35 to the Cuatro Puertas bus stop.
Height difference: 80m.
Grade: short and easy walk, sometimes without a distinct path.

From the **car park (1)**, ascend along the track. 240m on, pass a stone gate and one of the first information boards; a relief has been set into the wall showing a solar calendar, such as the native people may have used. At the **trail junction (2)**, turn right to begin the circular exploration route. Ascend over rock steps to reach the **Cuatro Puertas cave (3)**: four monumental portals (*cuatro puertas*) lead to a spacious cave measuring 17x7m, presumably used for religious rituals. Round depressions on the forecourt and in the

Looking like a gigantic face: the Cueva de los Pilares.

walls of the cave point to their use for libations, as does the gigantic U-shaped furrow cut into the rock of the cult site on the **summit plateau**. You reach this from the rear entrance to the cave by walking, without a distinct path, over the rock face slope. Afterwards, follow the instructions on the information board and head towards the coast, where a viewing platform appears on your right. At the platform, turn right and reach the **Cueva de los Papeles (4)** ("Cave of the Papers"). Beneath an overhanging rock, caves are found, cut into the rock face, and also boasting perfect portals and furrows chiseled into the bedrock. At the end of the panoramic plateau, reach a precipitous stretch of trail leading to the most fascinating part of the fortress complex, the **Cueva de los Pilares (5)**. From the semi-exposed "hall", just like looking through a giant window, enjoy a far-reaching view of the vast eastern plains – this is also an ideal spot for a picnic! Then, via the **Cueva de los Papeles (4)**, return to the enclosure fence, where our trail veers off to the left and the **trail junction (2)** marks the end of the circular walk. Via the track used during the approach, return to the **car park (1)**.

Cueva de
Cuatro Puertas (3)
Cuatro 316 m Cuatro
Puertas (1) Puertas (1)
275 m

1.2 km
0   0.50 h

Verdant miracle in the nature reserve "Gorge of the Kestrel"

Nowhere else on the island is this the case: here, the whole year-round, a stream is carrying water and, at two spots, creates cascades gushing over rock faces. The stream feeds olive trees, willows, holm oaks and bamboo cane, which in the narrow gorge, form an almost jungle-like vegetation. The trail constantly follows the stream which we must cross over, via rustic walkways, numerous times. High above the gorge, falcons and buzzards are circling.

Starting point: the car park and picnic area at the end of the GC-132, 450m. 8km east of Telde; no bus service. Approach from Telde via the GC-131 towards Lomo Magullo, then 6km further on, turn right towards Los Arenales (GC-132) and follow this road for another 2km until it ends.
Height difference: 250m in both ascent and descent.
Grade: the first 2.5km lead along a well-laid trail; only the final stretch is steeper and sometimes precipitous.

Note: at weekends, the initial stretch is very popular with the Canarios, but during the week, you will usually have the trail to yourself. After winter rains, rock pools form, which you can even use for bathing.
Alternative: after reaching the big waterfall, adventurous walkers could scramble further up into the *barranco* to explore even more waterfalls. This trail is, however, dangerous, with stretches of scrambling and the peril of slipping when it's wet!

A short break: en route in the Barranco de los Cernícalos.

The little waterfall at the edge of the trail in the Barranco de los Cernícalos.

Gran Cascada (6)
695 m
Sauzada (4)   Pequeña Cascada (3)
GC-132/Área   610 m   540 m   GC-132/Área
Recreativa (1)   Recreativa (1)
450 m   6.5 km

0   1.15 1.55 2.20 h

From the **car park and picnic area (1)**, ascend along the concrete track for a good 200m where, to the right of a meshed gate (trail board), the trail starts off into the gorge. The trail is flanked by dense bushes as it veers to the left at first and then to the right. A good 10 mins later, reach a **viewing platform (2)** where a **water channel** begins. A portal-like structure, the remains of a onetime well, marks the spot where we have to walk without a path, keeping close to the channel. The trail, however, immediately begins to appear again and, 100m on, leads for the first time over the watercourse – a procedure that will repeat itself a number of times. After a total of 1.3km, a lovely **little waterfall (3)** forms to the right of the trail – a fantastic photographic subject! Not quite another kilometre further on, cross through a **tunnel formed by willow trees (4**; *sauzada*). This is so dense that not a single ray of light is let through. 300m more, the ascent becomes steeper and somewhat complicated: the trail takes a sharp bend to the right with a **trail sign (5)**, then hooks to the left and climbs up high above the stream – temporarily without any shade. 3 mins later, we can take a breather on a **plateau**, a popular place for a rest break. Shortly afterwards, we can spot the entrance, closed with a mesh gate, of a **water tunnel** cut into the rock face. Afterwards, continue, sometimes step-like, sometimes along a very narrow outcropping of rock. After a couple of bends in the trail, we find ourselves standing in the "cathedral" – the Canarios have given this name to the towering rock face, vaulted by dense tree tops, where the **big waterfall (6)** tumbles down in two cascades – a fantastic spot!

After a good, long rest, return along the approach route: first, the precipitous alpine path, then over the plateau and, passing the **trail sign (5)**, bearing sharp to the left. The worst is behind us now: from this point on, descend easily, heading parallel to the stream and passing through the **willow tree tunnel (4)**. If you somehow missed the **little waterfall (3)** on the approach route, you could take another break there. If there was any recent rainfall, you could even take a refreshing dip! Afterwards, pass the **water channel (2)** and, at the end, take the concrete track to return to the **car park and picnic area (1)** at the starting point.

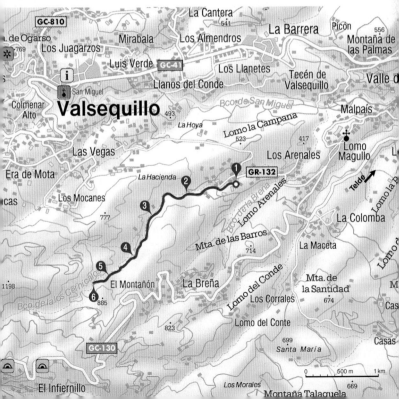

In the eastern mountains: spectacular gorges, craters and craggy peaks

The Barranco de Guayadeque, which stretches from the centre of the island to Agüimes in the east, is one of Gran Canaria's most interesting. In the narrow gorge, rare flora has managed to survive, and in the caves there, during archaeological excavation, pre-Hispanic mummies, pottery and inscriptions have been found. In the Museo de Guayadeque, visitors can gather information concerning the culture of the native islanders. Even today, the cave dwellings of the hamlet, Cuevas Bermejas, are still inhabited, including a chapel and cave bar. The walk leads to the Caldera de los Martales, a large volcanic crater with a diameter of 500m. The return route first leads over a mountain ridge and then along its sheer flank to descend into the valley.

Starting point: restaurant Tagoror, 983m, on the Montaña de las Tierras. Parking possible at the restaurant or along the street which leads up to the left before the restaurant.

Height difference: 820m in both ascent and descent.

Grade: a walk along an ancient, sometimes cobblestone *Camino Real* (way-marked as *S-37, S-42*) as well as tracks; strenuous, due to the height differences and the length.

Refreshment: cave restaurant Tagoror at the starting point, nearby the rest. La Vega.

Accommodation: in Agüimes / Ingenio.

Alternative: from the starting point, you can do a beautiful circular walk around the Montaña de las Tierras (1km/20 mins): with your back against the restaurant Tagoror, go left and immediately join a trail with safety railings. Walk past some cave dwellings to join the road where you either reach the restaurant Tagoror on your left or join the main walk.

Notes: 1) approach is only possible by car (8 or 10km from Agüimes or Ingenio). Alternative starting point for everyone staying at the centre of the island: Los Cascajales on the GC-130 km4.6.

2) between Waypoint 1 and 2, there are two places where the S-37 circumvents the track.

Winterly blossoms in the Barranco de Guayadeque.

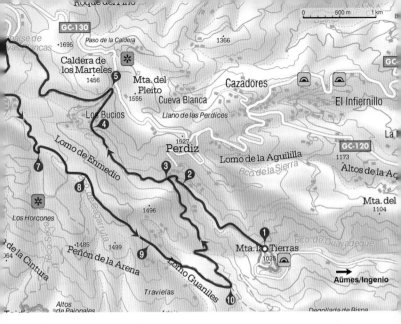

Starting point for the walk is the **Montaña de las Tierras (1)**, a "pointless" pyramidal summit in the middle of steep, *barranco* rock faces. In its natural plinth, a labyrinth-like system of caves have been dug, one of which today houses the **restaurant Tagoror** (native Canarian for "meeting place"). From the car park at the restaurant, pass through the arched gate and turn right to ascend along the narrow tarmac road which turns into a track after 270m – behind the La Vega restaurant. Leave the track immediately and follow the sign *S-37 Caldera de los Martales 4.5km* to the right. Walk high above the track, cross it and ascend below it before your trail joins it. In front of us are the rugged rock faces of the Barranco de Guayadeque, and behind us, the cubic-shaped mountain, Montaña de las Tierras.

After 30min from the starting point, the track crosses over the *barranco* before it joins a crucial **junction (2)** after 330m: 50m before reaching a house with a flat roof and fenced-in terrain, leave the track behind by turning left onto a trail (*S-37*) forking off which 170m on ascends to a fork marked by an olive tree and called the **Cruce del Olivo (3)**. Ignore the fork to the left (this will be our trail when we return after making a grand circuit) and turn right, instead. The trail climbs upwards and parallel to the *barranco* floor. A good 5 mins more, the trail changes over to the right-hand flank of the valley before it once again veers back to the left. In front of us are abandoned, terraced fields, which, in April and May, are often blanketed with yellow buttercups and tiny white daisies.

When we see a tumbledown house, 50m in front of us to the right, turn left to ascend along a trail that soon veers to run parallel again to the valley floor. In front of us, we can already see the dark, volcanic slopes, peppered with old pine trees, of the Caldera de los Marteles. The trail crosses over the valley floor while heading right, and ascends along an espalier of pine trees – volcanic scree has made walking difficult temporarily. Soon, a farmstead appears to the right: our trail meets up with a dirt track; turn left onto it, but leave it behind again, 70m further on: a sign pointing to the right and with the inscription "**Camino de la Caldera" (4)** leads us along a narrow path which, 2 mins later (fork), descends for a short time and then ascends again as it skirts around, at a good distance, the cluster of houses, Los Bucios, with its barking dogs. 500m on, the path merges onto a dirt track; turn right and ascend along it. A good 100m on, leave the track behind again by turning sharp left onto a broad trail, which leads along the southern side of the funnel-shaped crater, **Caldera de los Marteles (5)**; true, this is marked as a private trail, but it is open to walkers. At the outset, leading over volcanic terrain, but not quite 10 mins later, over solid ground, cross through an open pine wood and ignore the narrow paths, marked with cairns, forking off to the right and to the left.

In a clockwise direction, continue in a wide bend to skirt around a conical alpine hillock. As soon as we leave the pine wood, we can see in the distance the barrage of the (usually dried-up) lake, Cuevas Blancas, and shortly afterwards, you can take a backwards look to take in an interesting view of the crater, Los Marteles. The trail continues in a north-westerly direction, passes a *finca* on the right-hand side, and is flanked by cypress trees for a short stretch. The trail ends at a bend in the GC-130, which is known as the **Los Cascajales (6**; 1710m).

Shortly before meeting up with the road, turn left onto a track (sign: *S-42*) and ramble along this for the next two kilometres, passing through a gently rolling landscape, dotted with open pine woods, while following the signs for *Santa Lucía (S-42)* and ignoring every fork. 2.1km from the bend in the road,

Cruz del Socorro (7)
1681 m   Sepultura del Gigante (8)
Los Cascajales (6)   1557 m
Cruce del Olivo (3)   Mesa del Cuervo (9)
1250 m   1472 m   Cruce del Olivo (3)

Montaña de las Tierras/   Montaña de las Tierras/
Tagoror (1)   Tagoror (1)
983 m   17.4 km
                                           6.45 h
0   1.05   3.10   4.10   5.50   6.45 h

1500 m
1250 m
1000 m

you have to pay attention: a few metres before the third trail sign (to the left of the trail) with a wooden cross standing behind it, the **Cruz del Socorro (7)** which is difficult to see, leave the track behind: not along the trail flanked by stone walls to the left, but instead, along the narrow trail fork off diagonally left and descending. 25m on, this trail hooks to the left and, a minute later, merges into a track where we turn left to descend. 500m further on, ignore a track forking off to the right and, yet another 500m on, meet up with the saddle, **Sepultura del Gigante (8)**. To the left, enjoy a view of the reddish-coloured mountain, Sepultura del Gigante, and the upper reaches of the Barranco de Guayadeque.

Shortly before reaching Los Cascajales.

Keep along the track and, 250m further on, ignore a roadway forking off to the right. 2 mins later (100m to the right, at first meet an orange-coloured house), reach the **Mesa del Cuervo (9)**. Where the track forks off to the left towards a property blocked off by a chain, continue straight ahead along a trail flanked by stone walls (next to it, the country lane to the left can be used as an alternative). 570m further on, ignore a fork to the left marked by cairns and, 10 mins after that, reach a trail junction where two trails are descending. Either one is okay to take since they soon run parallel to each other and merge together again 60m further on at the trail junction, **Cruce de los Caminos (10**; almond tree); to the right, a trail heads for Temisas, and diagonally right, a trail to El Pinillo, straight to Agüimes.

We, however, turn left to skirt around a projecting rock, cross over the floor of a valley, and then head towards the Paso Bermejo, a "red-coloured pass" and the way to the Barranco de Guayadeque. The trail twists sharp to the left and opens a lovely view of the almost sheer rock faces of the gorge – also, you can spot the first houses on the *barranco* floor. 400m further on, bear to the right. The trail winds down in countless zigzags and, at the end, leads to the **Cruce del Olivo (3)**, the fork where our ascent began many hours before. Turn right, cross over the *barranco* floor and meet up with the **track (2)**, which leads somewhat precipitously, in about 40 mins, to the cave restaurants on the mountain, **Montaña de las Tierras (1)**.

Along the steep rock face of Guayadeque

A trip into the past: "Reddish Caves" (Cuevas Bermejas) is the name of the hamlet half-way along the barranco road. In point of fact, people are living here, just like their pre-Hispanic ancestors did, in cave dwellings. Even the village bar and the tiny chapel of San Bartolomé have been chiselled into the red-coloured rock face. Sheer rock faces tower above them – it's hard to believe that these can be surmounted! Yet, there is a way: via numerous zigzags, a trail winds up along a crevice in the rock while giving panoramic views. The best part awaits at the destination: over a sprawling high plateau, with golden, overgrown terraced fields, enjoy a view of the south-east coast, stretching from the Gando peninsula almost all the way to the island's southernmost tip.

Starting point: Cuevas Bermejas, 586m, GC-103, km5.5. You can park your car opposite the cave bar; there is no bus service.

Height difference: 250m.

Grade: steep, exhausting ascent and descent along an ancient *Camino Real*. This is always fortified at the brink of the abyss, nevertheless, it demands full concentration due to the irregular cobbled surface.

Refreshment: cave bar and restaurant Cuevas Bermejas, cave dwellings further

up in the valley of the Montaña de las Tierras.

Alternative: from the ridge, you could take the trail to Temisas, waymarked by the local government as *SL 2*, (or take the *SL 3/4* to Agüimes). The trail to Temisas leads via El Pinillo (a dead, monumental pine tree), from where you could also continue to the Cruce de los Caminos and then descend to the upper reaches of the Barranco de Guayadeque (see Walk 70). Via Montaña de las Tierras, return to your car at the starting point.

From the little church square in **Cuevas Bermejas (1)**, set off along a cobblestone trail, flanked by railings, to ascend the slope, passing flower-garlanded houses. 260m on, a **trail sign** (**2**, *SL 2 Temisas/SL 3 Pajonales/Agüimes*) points to the right, entering a steep crevice running up the rock face on the valley side. A sheep and goat pen is situated just past the trail sign, and to the right of the trail, a rock face pep-

View from the mountain ridge into the Barranco de Guayadeque.

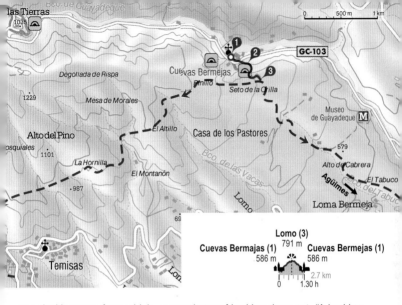

Lomo (3)
791 m
Cuevas Bermajas (1)   Cuevas Bermejas (1)
586 m   586 m

2.7 km
0   1.30 h

pered with caves, from which a cacophony of barking rings out. "A barking dog can't bite", says Diego, the owner of over 20 hunting dogs. Don't be put off by the barking – the dogs are all leashed.

High above, the mighty, almost sheer rock faces tower to the heavens, while the trail winds its way up along countless zigzags. *Valo* bushes with draping "thinning hair", gnarled Euphorbien, and little almond trees line the edge of the trail – in the spring, flowers in red, white, and violet appear. When the trail, about 25 mins later, levels out temporarily, you can catch your breath. Keeping on the level, this stretch leads at first along an overhanging rock, then passes a **cave**, sporting a trough and a little bench chiseled into the rock face (1.1km). From here, we can already spot a little, cross-like shape on the ridge, which we reach after a couple of steep bends: it's a trail sign on top of the **mountain ridge (3)** that points out how you can continue on: turn right with the *SL 2* towards Temisas, or left this part has often been chopped off – with the *SL 3* towards Agüimes (see Alternatives).

A broad, gently rolling rise sweeps away in front of us, overgrown in spurge vegetation. It is worthwhile to continue for 100m to the left to reach the rocky apex, where you can enjoy a splendid, sweeping view that stretches all the way to the coast.

The return follows the approach route: from the **mountain ridge (3)**, constantly descending in zigzags, pass by the barking dogs and the **trail sign (2)**, and back to the cave bar at **Cuevas Bermejas (1)**.

231

Crossing the entire island in two days

On Gran Canaria, there is also a Way of St. James (Camino de Santiago). In the name of Santiago el Mayor, the Reconquista, the expulsion of the Arabic Muslims from the Iberian Peninsula, was set into motion. Just as this ended (1492), new enemies were targeted: the heathen savages inhabiting the newly-discovered islands in the Atlantic. This explains why there are two pilgrimage churches on Gran Canaria dedicated to Santiago: one in San Bartolomé in the southern mountains and the other in Gáldar in the far north. In the Jubilee Year of St. James, every five to six years (next time 2026), many pilgrims

cross over half of the island along the Camino de Santiago under the sign of the St. James Scallop (see photo). The tourist office is marketing the Camino de Santiago as a complete traverse of the island from south to north, but the initial stage (S-54) is very unattractive and this is not included in this walk. The route suggested here favours the classical pilgrim's route starting from San Bartolomé.

Starting point: San Bartolomé de Tirajana, 887m. Bus stop/car park at the northern village limits; bus stop for line 18.

Destination: Santa María de Guía, 180m, or Gáldar, 43m. Bus stop for lines 103 and 105.

Total length: 35km, over the course of 2 days.

Height difference: about 1300m in ascent and 2000m in descent.

Grade: due to its length and the considerable height differences, this is a very strenuous trek, usually following along ancient *Caminos Reales*.

Accommodation: en route, you can spend the night in Cruz de Tejeda, but you can find cheaper places 10km farther south in Tejeda (see p. 28).

Note: at first, no accommodation available between Cruz de Tejeda and Guía, at the end of this walk, you will reach the Hotel Agaldar (www.hotelagaldar.com).

1st Stage: San Bartolomé – Cruz de Tejeda

15.2km / 6.00 hrs / about 1000m in ascent and 400m in descent.

The bus stop in **San Bartolomé (1)** is located a couple of paces above the church sporting the two sword-brandishing statues of Santiago. From here, follow the walk description according to that of Walk 37 (the return will be made in the reverse direction), following the street for 3 mins, heading away

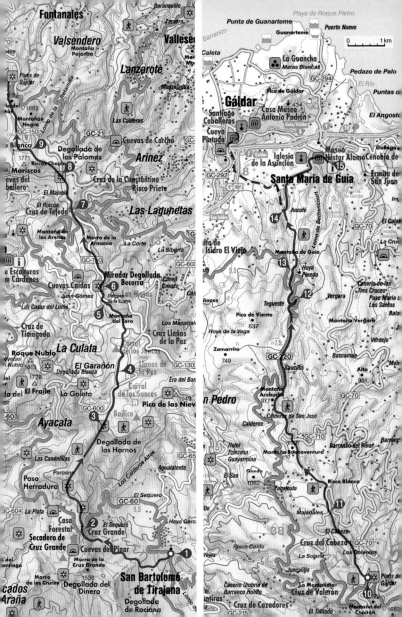

from the centre, and then veering left onto the steeply ascending GC-603. 5 mins later, turn right onto the Calle Juglar Fabian Torres to continue, but then leave it behind again another 200m further on by turning onto the *Camino Real (S-50) Cruz Grande – Cumbre*. This ascends persistently whilst opening up a splendid view of the Tirajana basin all the way to the crest of the pass, **Cruz Grande (2)** on the GC-60.

From here, walk along the tarmac for 50m towards San Bartolomé and then turn left onto the ascending trail (corresponds to Walk 7; signed: *S-50*). A little later, the trail hooks to the right and leads to a rest area with three crosses. At the neighbouring house (often with barking dogs!), the trail becomes a cobblestone *Camino Real*, ascending steeply. After a level section, a dramatic ascent begins: in boldly laid, seamlessly cobbled bends, the trail claws its way along the steep slope. Passing a little catchment basin, meet up with a rocky, high plateau. Cairns point out the way whilst heading towards a pine forest, where the path becomes more distinct. The next stretch of trail is uncomplicated: passing a wooden cross and the pass, **Degollada de los Hornos (3)**, descend another 1.3km to the GC-600 down below. Continue for 10 minutes, walking parallel to the road, and then turn left onto the trail, *S-50*, which leads to the recreational campsite, **El Garañón (4)**, and skirts around the fenced-in complex in a clockwise direction.

Following Walk 4 (the eastern section of the route), first cross through a pine forest, then traverse the slope, keeping on the level, until reaching the fork on the **Degollada de la Cumbre** (5; almost on the GC-150) – with a marvellous view of the mountain basin and the solitary, towering crag of Roque Nublo.

Here, keep to the left, now following Walk 25 (the return route), and immediately turn right again to reach, 300m further on, the *mirador* on the **Degollada de Becerra (6)**. Follow a trail that once again returns to the road for a short stretch before leaving it behind yet again. Passing a *finca*, continue along the rim of the Caldera, and then the trail ends at the bus stop on the **Cruz de Tejeda (7)**, where the first stage comes to an end.

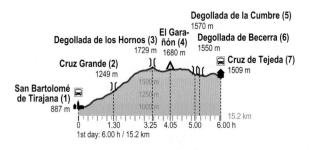

2nd Stage: Cruz de Tejeda – Santa María de Guía / Gáldar

19.8km / 7.30 hrs / about 300m in ascent and 1600m in descent.

On the next day, continue following Walk 9 to reach the **Mirador Degollada de las Palomas (8)**, 10 minutes after that, ignore the left-hand fork towards Artenara / Agaete and, instead, continue straight ahead along the track. Walk another 800m to meet up with a **fork** (**9**; lacking a directional sign), and turn right onto it, heading for Fontanales. This trail follows Walk 20 to reach the **Mirador Pinos de Gáldar (10)**. One would be happy to take a breather here, and longs for an inn to enjoy an interim overnight stay, but unfortunately, nothing is available, far and wide. Because of this, continue directly by following Walk 55 via **Majadales (11)**, **Tegueste (12)**, **Hoya de Pineda (13)** and **Anzofé (14)** to **Santa María de Guía (15)**.

En route along the Way of St. James: Beware: pilgrim crossing!

The church Santiago de Los Caballeros de Gáldar is located 2km away and is, sadly, not approachable via a walking trail, but instead, only along tarmac (the best choice is along the narrow road via Anzofé). Next to the church in Gáldar, there is a nice hotel.

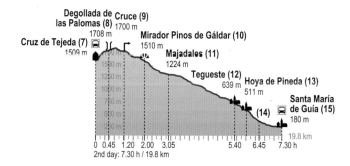

Index

A

Acusa Seca 64
Acusa Verde 65
Agaete 180
Agaete valley (Valle de Agaete)
  16, 171, 173
Altavista 72
Altos del Confital 204
Altos de Pajonales 142
Altos de Taidía 143
Andén del Toro 44
Arco de Atalaya (Santa
  Brígida) 215
Arteara 145
Artenara 16, 59, 62, 67
Ayacata 17, 40, 45
Ayagaures 151
Ayagaures reservoir (Presa de
  Ayagaures) 152

B

Bahía del Confital 202
Bandama 212, 214
Barranco de Azuaje 198, 199
Barranco de Guayadeque
  226, 230
Barranco de la Angostura
  219
Barranco de la Mina 92
Barranco de las Goteras 213
Barranco de la Virgen 191,
  196, 201
Barranco del Laurel 186
Barranco de los Cernícalos
  223
Barranco de los Palmitos 155
Barranco del Perchel 167
Barranco Madrelagua 90
Barranco Santa Brígida 219

C

Caldera de Bandama 208,
  210
Camino de Santiago 232
Cañada Aguas Sabinas 165
Casa de la Data 116, 119
Casa de Los Tilos 188, 189
Casa Forestal de Pajonales
  112, 115

Casa Forestal de Tirma
  69, 71
Casa Forestal Tamadaba 75,
  76, 78, 80
Casas de Bandama 208, 210
Casas del Lomo del Palmito
  156
Casas de Matos 198
Cercados de Araña 124
Chimirique 115
Chira reservoir (Embalse de
  Chira) 124
Cima Pedro González (Paso
  de los Palmitos) 155
Corral de los Juncos 43, 99
Corvo (Fontanales) 192, 194
Cruce del Olivo 227
Cruce Las Peñas 61, 84
Cruz de Acusa 62, 64
Cruz de Juan Pérez 43, 45
Cruz de la Huesita 116
Cruz del Cabezo 184
Cruz del Siglo 138
Cruz de María 69, 71, 72
Cruz de Mogán 162
Cruz de Tejeda 16, 56, 59,
  89, 92, 98, 102, 104, 234
Cruz de Timagada 107
Cruz Grande 17, 45, 50,
  129, 234
Cuatro Puertas, Yacimiento
  Arqueológico 221
Cueva del Zapatero 77
Cuevas Bermejas 230
Cuevas de Berbique 177
Cuevas del Caballero 56, 84

D

Degollada Blanca 35, 39
Degollada Cruz de Toril 61
Degollada de Aguas Sabinas
  166
Degollada de Becerra 94, 95,
  99, 234
Degollada de la Cumbre 44,
  97, 99, 234
Degollada de la Manzanilla
  128

Degollada de las Palomas
  36, 39, 57, 235
Degollada del Dinero 129
Degollada de los Gatos
  52, 55
Degollada de los Hornos 46,
  48, 51, 55, 234
Degollada de los Molinos
  131
Degollada de los Tres Pinos
  156
Degollada de Roque García
  63, 68
Degollada de Tauro 158
Degollada de Veneguera
  160
Degollada Piedras Blancas
  52, 54
Degollada Risco Faneque 77

E

El Arenal (Santa Brígida) 219
El Aserrador 114
El Espinillo 111
El Garañón, Campamento 43,
  45, 100, 234
El Hornillo 174
El Juncal 112, 115, 180
El Lomito 141
El Roque 111
El Sao 174
El Tablado 83
El Turmán (Agaete) 180
Embalse de Chira 124
Embalse de los Hornos 100
Embalse de Soria 122
Ermita del Carmen 213
Ermita Virgen de la Cuevita
  61

F

Fataga 130
Finca La Isa 102
Firgas 198, 201
Fontanales 16, 88, 186, 191

G

Gáldar 232
Gambuesa reservoir (Presa
  de Gambuesa) 152

H
Hoya de la Vieja 37
Hoya de Pineda 185
Hoyetas del Nublo 36, 39
I
Inagua, Reserva Natural 117
Ingenio 137
J
Jardín Canario 205
L
La Atalaya 212, 214
La Caleta 180, 182
La Cogolla 161
La Cruz Chica 89
La Culata 44, 100, 106
La Degollada 185
La Fortaleza 134
La Goleta 35, 40, 42, 48, 100
La Huerta Grande, Finca 40
Lajas del Jabón 73
La Laguna 196
Lanzarote (Valleseco) 90
La Ortiguilla 100
La Palmita, Finca 44
Las Arbejas 83
Las Calderetas 90
Las Goteras 213
Las Madres 201
La Solana 111
La Sorrueda 134, 136
Las Palmas 22, 202
Las Rosadas 91
Las Tederas 154
Llano de los Olivos 220
Llanos de la Pez 53
Llanos de Pargana 51
Lomo de la Rosa 90
Lomo del Marco 192
Lomo de los Almacenes 115
Lomo de los Galeotes 83, 87, 183
Los Berrazales 172
Los Hornos 43
Los Sitios de Abajo 132
Los Sitios de Arriba 132

Los Tilos, Reserva Natural 189
M
Majadales 184
Maspalomas 148
Mesa del Cuervo 229
Mirador de Ingenio 137
Mirador de la Sorrueda 132
Mirador de la Vuelta del Palomar 176
Mirador del Sargento 69, 71, 72
Mirador El Reventón 81
Mirador La Sorrueda 136
Mirador Pinos de Gáldar 82, 86, 183, 235
Mirador Presa de los Hornos 100
Mogán 160, 162
Molino de Fataga 131
Molino de los Araña 141
Molino Pequeño 131
Montaña de las Tierras 226
Montaña de las Vueltas 172
Montaña del Toro 43, 99
Montaña de Tauro 158
Montañón 48
Morro de la Armonía 94, 99
Morro de la Negra 113
Morro de las Vacas 128
Moya 186, 188
P
Pajonales, Reserva Natural 112
Palmitos Park 21
Pargana 47
Paso de los Palmitos (Cima Pedro González) 155
Pico de Bandera 78
Pico de las Nieves 50, 53
Pino de Casandra 121
Pinos de Gáldar 86
Playa Chica 167
Playa de Guayedra 178
Playa de Güi Güí 164, 166
Poema del Mar (aquarium) 21

Presa Cueva de las Niñas 116, 118
Presa de Ayagaures 152
Presa de Gambuesa 152
Presa de la Sorrueda 130, 134
Presa de los Pérez 174
Puerto de la Aldea 167
Punta de la Aldea 168
Punta Gorda 181
R
Risco Faneque 76
Roque Bentayga 108, 110
Roque Bermejo 177
Roque Nublo 35, 37
Ruta del Agua (Santa Brígida) 218
Ruta del Vino (Santa Brígida) 215
S
San Bartolomé de Tirajana 17, 127, 232
San Pedro 171, 173
Santa Brígida 218
Santa Lucía 130, 133, 135, 137, 138, 140, 142
Santa María de Guía 183, 185, 232, 235
Saucillo 184
Sepultura del Gigante 229
Siete Pinos 176
Soria 120, 122
Soria reservoir (Embalse de Soria) 122
Sorrueda reservoir (Presa de la Sorrueda) 130, 134
T
Tafira 205
Tamadaba 67, 74, 173
Tasartico 165
Tegueste 184
Tejeda 17, 102, 104, 106
Teror 89, 91, 194, 197
V
Valle de Agaete 173
Vega de Acusa 66

andén	walkway on a sheer rock face	fondo del valle	valley floor
atajo	short cut	hoya	depression, hollow
barranco	gorge	indicador de camino	trail sign
barranquillo	secondary gorge		
bifurcación	trail junction, fork	llano	plain
bosque	wood	lomo	ridge
caidero	steep section in a gorge	mesa	high plateau
caldera	volcanic crater, valley basin	mirador	viewpoint
		montaña	mountain
calle	street	morro	steep rock faces in a mountain range
camino de escalones	stepped trail	muro de presa	dam, barrage
camino real	Royal Trail	parada	bus stop
campamento	campsite	pared	steep rock face
cañada	narrow gorge, bottleneck	parador	state-owned hotel
		paso	passage
cartel informativo	information board	pico	peak
cascada	waterfall	pinar	pine wood
caserío	hamlet	pista forestal	forestry track
casa forestal	forestry house	presa	reservoir
coto de caza	hunting grounds	puente	bridge
cruce	crossing, junction		
cruz	cross	ramificación	branch in a trail
cueva	cave	risco	crag
cumbre	summit; special Gran Canaria: the central massiv	roque	crag
		rotonda	roundabout
degollada	col, saddle, pass	sendero	path, trail
desembocadura	trail merge		
		valle	valley
embalse	reservoir	zona recreativa	recreation area, picnic grounds
finca	farmhouse		

To compliment this guide, we recommend the
Road and Leisure map "Gran Canaria" (1:50,000) from
Freytag & Berndt

Front cover: The Canary larkspur is in full bloom in
the spring like here above San Mateo.

Photo on page 1: Ascent to the native Canarian
cult site at the foot of the Roque Bentayga, west of
Tejeda.

Photo on pp. 32/33: Acusa Seca: the view, over
abysmal precipices, reaches all the way to Tejeda.

131 photographs by Dr. Dieter Schulze and Dr. Izabella Gawin,
the photos on pages 17, 18, 137, 149: Patronato de Turismo de Gran
Canaria, photo on page 23: Free Motion Bike Center

Cartography:
66 walking maps to a scale of 1:50,000, three to a scale of 1:75,000,
two maps to a scale of 1:25,000 and 1:100,000 each
as well as overview maps to a scale of 1:325,000 and 1:550,000
© Freytag & Berndt, Vienna

Translation: Tom Krupp, Billi Bierling

The descriptions of all the walks given in this guide are conscientiously
made according to the best knowledge of the author.
The use of this guide is at one's own risk.
As far as it is legally permitted, no responsibility
will be accepted for possible accidents, damage or injuries of any kind.

4th edition 2022
© Bergverlag Rother GmbH, Munich

ISBN 978-3-7633-4816-9

MIX
Paper from
responsible sources
FSC® C021956

We heartily welcome any suggestion for amendment to this walking guide!
ROTHER BERGVERLAG · Munich
D-82041 Oberhaching · Keltenring 17 · tel. 0049 89 608669-0
Internet www.rother.de · E-Mail bergverlag@rother.de